Also by J. L. Schellenberg

Divine Hiddenness and Human Reason

Prolegomena to a Philosophy of Religion

The Wisdom to Doubt: A Justification of Religious Skepticism

The Will to Imagine

The Will to Imagine

A Justification of Skeptical Religion

J. L. SCHELLENBERG

Cornell University Press

ITHACA AND LONDON

First published 2009 by Cornell University Press

Printed in the United States of America

Library of Congress Cataloging-in-Publication Data

Schellenberg, J. L., 1959–
    The will to imagine : a justification of skeptical religion /
J. L. Schellenberg.
        p. cm.
    Includes bibliographical references and index.
    ISBN 978-0-8014-4780-8 (cloth : alk. paper)
    1. Religion—Philosophy.   2. Belief and doubt.   3. Skepticism.
I. Title.

    BL51.S4265   2009
    211'.7—dc22

                                            2009004247

Cornell University Press strives to use environmentally responsible suppliers and materials to the fullest extent possible in the
publishing of its books. Such materials include vegetable-based,
low-VOC inks and acid-free papers that are recycled, totally
chlorine-free, or partly composed of nonwood fibers. For further
information, visit our website at www.cornellpress.cornell.edu.

Cloth printing   10 9 8 7 6 5 4 3 2 1

In loving memory of my sister,
Lois Faith Wimble (1947–1997)

Contents

Preface

This book completes a phase of systematic thinking about religion and rationality developed within the conceptual and methodological framework of my *Prolegomena to a Philosophy of Religion* (hereafter *Prolegomena*) and carried to an interim conclusion by *The Wisdom to Doubt: A Justification of Religious Skepticism* (hereafter *Skepticism*). Together with its siblings it gives full shape and substance to the following idea: that the justification of religious skepticism does not mean the end of rational religion but is rather the condition of a new and more promising beginning. This idea is paradoxical, given the usual association of religion with specific beliefs. But the paradox is dissolved by an application of innovations from *Prolegomena* to the major considerations of *Skepticism*. The latter work forces us to notice all around us the shadows of our short evolutionary history. But having been alerted by the former work to a concept of nonbelieving faith appropriate to just such a place in time, and also to an important distinction between specific, ambitiously detailed religious claims and the more modestly general claim—the forgotten center of religion—lying behind them, we are able to put two and two together and arrive at a striking realization: that instead of *deepening* the problem of faith and reason, religious skepticism, rightly appropriated, permits us to *solve* it convincingly, moving us out of the bog of sectarian belief versus cynical unbelief in which we have been stuck and on to the next stage of religious evolution. Such, in outline, is the burden of this book.

But we need a little more flesh for those bones. *Skepticism* argued that we should all be complete religious skeptics, on the basis of considerations emphasizing the conjunction of human limitation and human *immaturity*, with the latter understood both evaluatively (we haven't done as well with the time we've already had as might have been hoped) and descriptively (we may yet have a very long way to go, developmentally speaking). That exemplar of human reason, science itself, testifies to the hundreds of millions of years that may remain for reason and also religion to be developed further.

Such points can be seen to underwrite a certain unexpected optimism with respect to the results of religious investigation, an optimism for the long term, nourished by the thought that detailed understandings of the Divine already devised may be but the first attempts at flight of a fledgling species. Of course, this might still seem to leave us looking toward the future, without any way of endorsing religion for the present. But in an evolutionary frame of mind, it is possible to see how religion and also the requirements of rational religion may be very different at different times. If, inspired by this thought, we ask whether a religious stance appropriate to our own rather *early* time might be found and start thinking about alternative religious attitudes, insight may dawn. In spite of our limitations and immaturity—and indeed because of them—a religious stance remains possible. This cannot, in the nature of the case, involve religious belief. But there is yet faith, which, as shown in *Prolegomena*, can be grounded in imagination instead of belief. Within the parameters of our limitations and immaturity, the distinctive importance of such a nonbelieving attitude suddenly snaps into focus; where before we might have found it irrelevant or second-rate (by comparison with religious belief), now, recognizing the force of the future, we find it urgently beckoning for our attention as the source of a solution to the problem of faith and reason.[1]

In the first part of this book, I show that especially because of our immaturity and the open future, the appropriate sort of faith must be twice skeptical: both nonbelieving and unwilling to commit itself to any sectarian content. It is not to be linked with any particular religious proposition about God or gods that may still have the mud of early evolution clinging to it but instead involves cognitively and conatively aligning oneself with the more general proposition clarified and for the first time named in *Prolegomena*, which all such religious propositions can be seen as gesturing toward: that what is deepest in reality (metaphysically ultimate) is also unsurpassably great (axiologically ultimate) and the source of an ultimate good (salvific). I call this claim *ultimism* to distinguish it from theism and

---

[1] For the benefit of the reader, the main results of *Prolegomena* (its central definitions and principles) are collected in outline form in appendixes at the end of this book. These may help to provide additional clarity from time to time, but bereft of context, some of the principles and definitions may seem puzzling. A fuller study of *Prolegomena* is recommended whenever this is the case. Having said that, the main information from previous volumes in the trilogy required for a proper comprehension of this concluding volume is provided in the Introduction.

other specific religious "isms." According to my argument, an imaginative faith focused on ultimism, if it can sustain an authentically religious form of life, is the only sort appropriate to human immaturity—an inquiring faith that among other things explores undeveloped ways of filling out the simple idea that shapes its commitments. And that such simple faith can sustain an authentically religious form of life is here shown in detail and for the first time.

This possibility may seem hard to imagine because we have got so used to detailed formulations and the demand for belief. But that religion's intellectual aspect has developed as it has in the actual world, with an emphasis on specific beliefs, is a purely contingent fact, and in thinking about other ways in which it might have developed we open windows to other, possibly better forms of religious practice in the present. Perhaps religion has, intellectually speaking, had a less than perfect start in the world—maybe immature humans have got ahead of themselves in all their talk about specific, detailed beliefs concerning ultimate things. I will be suggesting that this is indeed the case, and also that where attention is shifted from the specific to the *simple* and from religious belief to *faith*, we see the possibility of a better start, which reason can commend.[2]

That reason commends skeptical religion, and so strongly, is one of the most striking features of the intellectual vision here unfolded. (Adapting Kant, we may say that by denying belief we have made room for faith.) Against such skeptical faith, purified both in form and in content and taken up with proper sensitivity to the early stage of development in which we find ourselves, the counterarguments of reason are unavailing. And, even more interesting, when religious faith is construed this way—as a will, not to believe, as James famously said, but to *imagine*—arguments *for* faith abound, many of them variations on themes that have unsuccessfully been sounded on behalf of belief. As this book reveals, imaginative faith is not just to be tolerated but rationally to be encouraged, and considerations from every major area of our lives as well as from virtually every historical period of philosophizing about religion can be adapted to show this, when once the evolutionary impulse has been lit. As it turns out, a variety of evidential and nonevidential considerations from philosophy of religion as we have known it so far, though unable to justify the personalistic theistic belief so much at the center of concern for its main practitioners, can successfully be recast as arguments

---

[2] As we will see, there are valuable features of existing religious traditions that do not depend on specific religious beliefs, and their preservation or continuing influence is compatible with such a "new start." Skeptical religion need not entirely cut itself off from tradition or disregard tradition in inappropriate ways.

for ultimistic faith.³ Once misdirected, they can now be redirected and find their proper target.

Running like a thread through these results is the notion that the appropriate attitude toward religious claims is a skeptical or doubting or nonbelieving one and that common forms of religion, focused on detailed pictures of the Divine, are intellectually shortsighted, their belief premature. Thus our idea should be attractive to religion's critics. I invite those who have little use for religion-as-it-has-been, perhaps because of the excessive credulity, wishful thinking, dogmatic preaching, attempts at brainwashing, or lack of investigative zeal that can sometimes be found in it, to notice that I am on their side. But not only is skeptical reason fully appeased: because of the beliefless and nonsectarian form of religious faith that becomes visible when sectarian belief is deemphasized and proves to be rationally required, our idea also allows for the fondest hopes of those who have sought to reconcile reason and religion to be satisfied. And I invite those with antireligious inclinations to consider this side of things also—to "will to imagine" a different way of understanding the relations between reason and religion. What you will find here is a philosophical approach to religion very different in nature and results from any presently being prosecuted. It is an approach both radically deflationary and ambitiously developmental, one that exposes current religious and irreligious pretensions and reveals how far we have to go but also and at the same time justifies, for everyone, a strenuous and cognitively robust form of religious commitment—thus deciding the debate between faith and reason in a way that honors both and offering a new agenda to philosophy of religion.

Before turning to my acknowledgments, a personal note. This book does not in any normal sense recapitulate a "religious journey." (Of course it has learned from the religious journeys of others.) I am still getting used to the practical implications of my own ideas. It is as ideas that I have engaged them, even when they were ideas *about* practical implications. Of course ideas are not cold or dry for me. I am deeply committed to the life of the mind, to intellectual work. To me ideas are holy. And the pursuit of fundamental understanding and the pursuit of beauty are for me as one. There is a connection to religion here, for I have a tendency to be deeply moved by religious notions in a way that seems an extension of my tendency to be moved by Mozart or by an intellectual discovery. But I strongly hope it is on their merits that my arguments will be judged, within a frame

³ In *Skepticism* I defended various arguments for the *falsehood* of theism, though in a manner subservient to my larger skeptical purposes there. It may be worth noting that one need not accept atheism to endorse the arguments for skeptical religion defended here.

of reference that takes the love of truth and understanding as paramount. If my arguments are successful, I will be *one* of those who needs to significantly further participation in an explicitly religious form of life.

My sincerest thanks go to John Ackerman, Paul Draper, Dan Howard-Snyder, Steve Maitzen, Terry Penelhum, Bill Wainwright, and Don Wiebe for their help with this book. Lad Sessions and Robert Audi I would (and hereby do) single out for their especially extensive and helpful comments. Instructive responses to the book's ideas came from students in philosophy of religion at Mount Saint Vincent University and Dalhousie University and from members of audiences at the University of Calgary, Dalhousie University, the University of Western Ontario, and the University of Toronto and at meetings of the Society for Philosophy of Religion. I am grateful for all this input, as also for financial support received at crucial stages from Mount Saint Vincent University and from the Social Sciences and Humanities Research Council of Canada.

Richard Swinburne defended the idea of faith without full-fledged belief in his *Faith and Reason,* and although I disputed that idea when I was his student at Oxford, a version of it is now the centerpiece of my own solution to the problem of faith and reason. I'm pretty certain he has his doubts about some aspects of my notion of skeptical religion, but if the latter turns out to be sustainable, then in this as in so many other matters philosophical, we will be indebted to Richard for pointing the way.

My sons, Matthew and Justin, are to be congratulated for both recognizing the upsides and putting up with the downsides of having an absent-minded philosopher for a father. I hope they will see themselves reflected in what I say about value in this book. To my wife, Regina Coupar, inspired and inspiring companion in the exploration of trackless wildernesses, unfailing supporter of all my writing, belongs a love and a gratitude beyond words.

This book is dedicated to the living memory of my "big sister," Lois, who gave me a special gift by setting me on a path of reading and writing and imagining long before school—and even more by respecting what I read and wrote and imagined. Though I and her other students are now sadly bereft of her presence, I continue along the path. I hope she would be happy with where it is taking me.

The Will to Imagine

Introduction

The new vistas to which I am seeking to draw our attention were rendered in broad strokes in the preface. Here I wish to clarify a few technical and conceptual details that readers unfamiliar with my *Prolegomena* or *Skepticism* will want to know about in order fully to understand how my vision is worked out in the chapters that follow. I also wish to expose more clearly the structure of the working-out. Although the present volume's central contentions and the main support it provides for them should be readily comprehended even by someone unfamiliar with the earlier ones, the three books share a distinctive framework that colors all aspects of my presentation here and is not completely self-explanatory. So let me begin by saying something about that.

The central or basic religious proposition, which—according to a technical definition of "religion" defended as appropriate for philosophical consumption in *Prolegomena*—a proposition must entail in order to be religious, is the claim that there is a metaphysically and axiologically ultimate reality (one representing both the deepest fact about the nature of things and the greatest possible value), in relation to which an ultimate good can be attained. This claim, as indicated in the preface, I call *ultimism*. The content of ultimism, as thus expressed, may seem somewhat loose and abstract, and it may be tempting to make it more precise through philosophical analysis. But it is important that we don't impose too much analysis, so as to allow for a suitably wide range of actual forms of religiousness within my definition and a suitably wide range of possible new elaborations for the imaginations of early humans like ourselves to feed on.

Now, although ultimism *is* typically elaborated or, as I shall usually put it, *qualified,* decked out in specific religious garb, it may instead be in its

1

naked beauty that we behold it and integrate it into our religious practice. This is argued in Part I of the present book, where I also argue that
a practice thus focused on generic or simple ultimism is the *only* form of
religious faith that can be justified for twenty-first-century skeptics[1] (that it
is the form of faith that is justified, *if any is*), defending this claim against
a variety of objections.[2]

The skeptical state I shall be assuming to be rationally required on the
basis of earlier work in *Skepticism* involves both *categorical* skepticism and
capacity skepticism. Categorical religious skeptics are in a state of doubt
or nonbelief with respect to the proposition "There is truth in religion,"
which is logically equivalent to the disjunction of religious claims or the
proposition "At least one religious claim is true," and thus also to ultimism (if ultimism is true then at least one religious claim is true, and con-
versely). Since, as seen in *Skepticism*, sufficient and overall good evidence
of truth is available for neither ultimism nor its denial, and non-epistemic
factors do nothing to alter the situation in favor of believing one of these
propositions, it follows that we should be categorical religious skeptics.
If we do not immediately find ourselves in a state of doubt or nonbelief
(passive skepticism) with respect to ultimism by listening to rational arguments, then we should deliberately pursue it (active skepticism) through
appropriate private and public behavior: avoiding endorsements on either side of the issue, better acquainting ourselves with evidence to which
we find ourselves resistant, and so on.

What about capacity skepticism? Capacity skepticism is skepticism about
whether we (still) early humans have the cognitive and other properties
required to be able to access basic truths about the existence of an ultimate reality, or about the details of the nature any such reality must possess. Capacity skepticism comes in two forms, *qualified* and *unqualified:* the
former is skepticism regarding the claim that *as presently constituted* we are

---

[1] I use the phrase "twenty-first-century skeptics" fairly often in this book. Let me point
out here, in connection with its first use, that the connotation of "twenty-first century" I
have in mind is not what one might usually find, bound up with a sense of human *advancement,* but rather the opposite. In light of how much time the future of intelligence on our
planet may encompass, we must say that ours is *only* the twenty-first century in a timespan
that may include not just 21 centuries more but 10, 50, 100…times that number of centuries more.

[2] In *Prolegomena*, chap. 3, I adopted a definition of "religious proposition" according
to which a proposition is a religious proposition only if it is independently capable of
informing a religious practice. If anyone were inclined to think that simple ultimism is
not independently capable of informing a religious practice, they would therefore, by my
standards, be required to deny that it is a religious proposition! My investigations in Part I
will, among other things, lay this idea to rest and confirm that simple ultimism is indeed a
religious proposition in the full sense of that phrase.

capable of discerning the truths in question; the latter is skepticism about whether humans will *ever* possess this capacity. These points are important, since they reveal one way of defending categorical religious skepticism—a way I have employed in the earlier work, by reference to the sublimity of an ultimate reality in conjunction with all that the past has prevented us from seeing and all we must suppose the future may hold in store (the result is what I call *complete* religious skepticism). This way of arguing can be quite effective, since to hold or to endorse any belief of the relevant sort about an ultimate salvific reality we would obviously need to take ourselves to possess the capacity in question, and thus doubt with respect to the capacity claim must rationally lead to an absence of any such believing tendencies, and to an endorsement of categorical skepticism instead.

If we accepted a very common assumption about religion, which sees it as tied up with belief of religious claims, these conclusions from *Skepticism* about the justification of religious skepticism would certainly suggest that a nonreligious response to ultimism is rationally preferable to any religious one. Surely if complete religious skepticism is rationally required, the nonreligious side of things has the upper hand! But having learned from *Prolegomena* that—and how—the aforementioned assumption is false, we can only be moved by the power of skepticism to take another step and ask about the rational status of religious *faith*, for faith we now see to be compatible with skepticism.

But before addressing the rational status of faith, we need to become better acquainted with my unorthodox understanding of faith itself. By the "faith response" I mean a *complete* response to ultimism combining what I call propositional and operational faith. Propositional faith is faith *that*—faith directed to a proposition. To fill this out a little: propositional faith involves voluntary assent to a proposition, undertaken in circumstances where one views the state of affairs it reports as good and desirable but in which one lacks belief of the proposition. In thus assenting to a proposition, one adheres to a certain policy: a policy of mentally going along with its content in relevant contexts (as opposed to questioning or criticizing or ignoring it, or simply keeping it at arm's length)—of imagining the world to oneself as including the relevant state of affairs and mentally endorsing this representation (in thought "taking its side," aligning oneself with it, deciding in favor of it, selecting it to guide one). Such an attitude is different from propositional belief, which is a disposition to experience states of mind in which thinking of the relevant state of affairs involves thinking of the world—states of mind in which one is involuntarily and passively being *represented to* rather than actively *representing to oneself*. Also unlike belief, the attitude of propositional faith does not typically issue in verbal affirmation of the proposition as true. (Such verbal affirmation contextually implies that we believe and is generally recognized as doing so; hence the person of faith may be expected to avoid it as misleading.)[3]

But all of this is only propositional faith. Propositional religious faith is important to my argument and indeed fundamental, and especially in Part I it will frequently be our focus. However, there is also what I call *operational* religious faith, which is realized when someone acts on propositional religious belief in pursuit of a religious way, or else on propositional religious faith (in doing so, she exhibits faith *in* a putative ultimate and salvific reality). Though, as just indicated, propositional belief can be the cognitive core of operational religious faith, the important point here is that when the cognitive core is instead beliefless propositional faith, we see a quite distinct, full-blooded response, which I am calling the *faith response* to ultimism—a response that ought to be considered alongside believing, disbelieving, and purely skeptical responses. Someone who adopts such faith after becoming a religious skeptic does not lose her skepticism; thus not just any skepticism will represent a distinguishable response to ultimism. The skepticism that does represent such a distinguishable response I call *pure* skepticism. A purely skeptical response to ultimism is a response involving passive and/or active categorical religious skepticism but without the admixture of faith.

Let me say a little more now about the relation between faith and active skepticism about ultimism. It is only when one is in a state of doubt about ultimism (passive skepticism) that one has the option of deciding to have faith. (As we saw before, such faith does not remove one's doubt—one still believes neither ultimism nor its denial, which is what I mean by "doubt about ultimism"—but simply adds another layer to one's total psychological and volitional state.) If, on the other hand, one is only on one's way from religious belief to doubt, perhaps using active skepticism to get oneself all the way there, one is not yet in a position to exercise the faith option. One cannot "avoid endorsements on either side of the issue"

---

[3] Recently, as I discovered after writing *Prolegomena*, cognitive psychologists and philosophers of mind have been giving renewed attention to the neglected topic of imagination, defending, in particular, the existence of a "distinct cognitive attitude" (DCA) created by propositional imagination, "a kind of content-bearing state, tokens of which play a functional role distinct from that of the most familiar propositional attitudes (beliefs, desires, intentions, etc.) and distinct also from perception and hallucination" (Timothy Schroeder and Carl Matheson, "Imagination and Emotion," in *The Architecture of the Imagination: New Essays on Pretense, Possibility, and Fiction*, ed. Shaun Nichols [Oxford: Clarendon Press, 2006], pp. 19, 23). When viewed within this context, my work can be seen as extending discussion of the DCA in a reassessment of the concept of faith.

and "better acquaint oneself with the evidence to which one finds oneself resistant" while stepping out in faith, holding the state of affairs ultimism represents before one's mind and voluntarily giving one's assent to it. So religious faith is incompatible with *active* skepticism directed toward ultimism.[4]

Is this a problem? I suggest it is not. All it shows is that only those who have fully negotiated the transition from religious belief to doubt are in a position to exercise the faith option. Those who—though at some level recognizing the force of skeptical arguments—have not done so (if any such there be) have not yet managed to become skeptics in the *full* sense of the word, and so we should not expect the faith response to be available to them. Their agenda, the work they need to do, is different from that which is here suggested as appropriate for the doubter.

But a related set of issues now arises. How different, really, is the faith I have been talking about from the believing state I have gone to so much trouble to criticize, given the assent involved in the former (the assent that made us think of it as incompatible with active religious skepticism)? And how important can it be to move from the latter to the former, given their similarities?

Here one needs first to notice that the converts to a faith response I envisage include not just former believers but also former disbelievers and pure skeptics. The question whether the transition to faith is much of a transition, or an important transition, arises only in respect of former believers. Even here—and this is a second point one should note—the transition may, all things considered, be expected to involve quite a significant shift, since the faith I will be defending is a nonsectarian faith focused on ultimism and most believers are sectarian believers, focused on one or another qualified version of ultimism.

But would there be much of a shift for those former believers (if any) who were already focused on something like simple ultimism before, believing that there is a religious reality, to be sure, but unwilling to say much more about it than that? What would be the point of losing such belief only to present to oneself the same proposition in faith?

My third observation is that even here we have what must be regarded as a significant difference, if it be granted that religious skepticism is *justified*. If we assume that it is justified, as given my previous work I am doing, then we see that it would be *rationally inappropriate* to believe that ultimism

---

[4] It *is* compatible with active skepticism directed toward the *denial* of ultimism. Former disbelievers who still find the denial of ultimism attractive may need active skepticism to keep themselves from slipping back into disbelief, in which state a faith stance would be much more difficult to sustain.

is true, involuntarily experiencing the world ultimistically. To do so, one would have to think that the total evidence for ultimism is in favor of its truth, and it is a mistake to do so—a mistake that any careful investigator will seek to avoid once it is recognized as such. And the faith stance is in fact phenomenologically quite different from belief of ultimism (as the description above of faith, with its emphasis on a *voluntary* assent, confirms), despite being expressible by the same proposition. Furthermore, unlike belief, it is quite capable of being justified. The metaphor of putting a new foundation under a house is inviting here: the new foundation that faith provides for the religious life does many of the same jobs—for example, providing psychological support—as belief may once have done (and in this respect it is *good* that the two attitudes are similar!), but, as the discussion of this book will confirm, in a number of important respects it does them in a more admirable and approvable manner, helping us to move forward in the journey of religious evolution.

Let us turn now to concepts involved in talking about the *rational status* of religious faith. Having been enabled by our recognition of the distinction between simple and qualified ultimism to determine, in Part I, that faith with respect to simple ultimism is possible and that it is the form of faith that is justified, if any is (that it is the only faith option that a religious skeptic could bring to the bar of reason with the hope of a favorable verdict), we subsequently turn to the question whether such faith *is* justified. Here there are different questions one might ask. First, is faith with respect to simple ultimism *negatively* justified? That is to say, is it the case that no response to ultimism—whether a believing, disbelieving, or purely skeptical response—is better than such faith? How, if at all, may challenges to the idea that this is so be repelled? But we can also ask whether skeptical faith is *positively* justified—is the faith response the *best* response one can make to ultimism and thus rationally required? How can arguments in support of such a view be developed?

Now, as we will see, certain aspects of the negative justification issue have already been dealt with in my earlier work, especially in *Skepticism*. The challenges that remain to be considered here, applying comparative principles of negative justification worked out in *Prolegomena*, arise primarily from two suggestions: that the imperative to have skeptical faith conflicts with other important (and overriding) obligations, and that certain attitudes other than such faith (e.g., hope) are more appropriate than faith itself to such aims as—in connection with the issue of positive justification—I will be arguing skeptical faith is best able to satisfy. As can be seen from the end of the previous sentence, no neat division between the question of negative justification and the question of positive justification is possible: we are best able to give a final answer to the former by dealing convincingly with the central issue raised by the latter. In Part II I clarify the issues concerning negative and positive justification involved here, setting the stage for the rest of the book, and also show how easily, when faith is imagination-based instead of belief-based, we may answer the arguments against faith that most immediately suggest themselves—arguments claiming that skeptical faith is not so much as negatively justified because it must involve a betrayal of the demands of reason.

Then in Parts III and IV I systematically discuss six "big names" from the history of philosophy of religion—Anselm, Leibniz, Paley, Pascal, Kant, and James—showing how much more effectively they can be marshaled in defense of skeptical religion than in defense of theistic belief. The arguments of these figures are mostly famous for being failures. What I expect our thoughtful skeptic considering the faith option to see is that when the concerns and insights of their authors are adapted to the new context of skeptical religion, spectacular failures can be turned into spectacular successes. Specifically, in these chapters we are able to turn up a multitude of aims that can be used, in conjunction with principles set out in *Prolegomena,* to show that skeptical religion is both negatively and positively justified.

In Part V this conclusion is made unmistakably clear, and here also I develop several additional ways of arguing for the positive justification of faith—"modes" of skeptical religion—appealing to all the various areas of our lives. The upshot? Skeptical religion is at our stage of evolution not only tolerated by reason but welcomed with open arms.

By showing us how undeveloped we are both spiritually and intellectually (this was one of the messages of *Skepticism*), at the same time revealing a religious alternative to the attitude of belief and making us more discriminating about its possible objects (these were intended contributions of *Prolegomena*), reason therefore opens up an investigative space in which it can be shown that religious faith is rationally required: the modes of skeptical religion, as it turns out, are as powerful as the modes of religious skepticism. Though we are far from competent in many respects, we can see that the cause of religion has been advanced, and we can also see interesting new directions that religion and rational inquiry concerning religion might take in the future. Or we *will* see when all is said and done in this book.

Before we get to the latter's detailed investigations, let me add two more clarifying points or sets of points. The first concerns my occasional use of the language of evolution. "Evolution," "evolutionary," and similar terms are here to be taken in the broadest possible senses. We will need to remember that there are various possible mechanisms of evolutionary change in religion, including but not restricted to those of biological evolution, whether natural or contrived. Furthermore, I do not assume that the results of evolutionary change (of whatever sort) must necessarily mark *improvements*. Certainly what natural selection counts as "good" depends entirely on the needs of creatures in the environments into which they are thrust, and it is far from obvious that these must, in our future, include such things as a sharpening of human theoretical ability. A deepened capacity for particle physics or philosophy of religion probably wouldn't increase the fitness of humans stuck on a planet decimated by asteroids and facing another ice age. Having said that, and exercising where appropriate the wisdom to doubt, we can see that evolutionary improvements of various kinds are *epistemically possible*. (And when I speak in this book of something being epistemically possible, I mean that it is neither known nor justifiedly believed to be false.)

Second, I want to highlight a point from *Prolegomena* which will help to bring more clearly into focus just what I will be saying when, as a result of my investigations here, I claim that religious faith is justified. The point is this: I am primarily concerned with faith as a *type*, not as a *token* (or tokens). Sometimes it is a certain *way* of having faith that we have in mind when we speak of faith, and to use that term correctly we need not presuppose that faith is realized in anyone (even if its appropriateness to this or that mental or social context is discussed). When we speak thus, we are speaking of faith as a type. But in another sense what we may have in mind is *his* or *her* faith, and in speaking of (e.g., evaluating) faith thus understood, we speak about certain states of the individual person who possesses it. This is faith as a token. Now when we consider the justification of a faith type, what we are looking for is a kind of *worthiness* that abstract discussion of what is preferable and should be embraced, or else inferior and should be avoided, can help us discern; whereas when we evaluate faith tokens, the relevant desideratum is what we may call *responsibility*: the proper fulfillment of all relevant duties and the exercise of virtue in the formation and maintenance of faith by the individual in question. In claiming that religious faith is justified, I am therefore claiming that a certain faith type is worthy of being instantiated (ultimately, more worthy than all alternatives—the best response). It is compatible with my conclusion that some or many individuals who make other responses are quite undeserving of a charge of irresponsibility in respect of their responses. To put it another way, many individuals may be justified in holding religious or irreligious beliefs or in being purely skeptical about religion even if religious and irreligious beliefs and pure religious skepticism (the relevant belief and skepticism *types* now) are not justified for them or for anyone else, because of the justification of religious faith.[5] (Of course,

---

[5] This focus on types is influenced by my understanding of the tasks of philosophers of religion, set out in *Prolegomena*. As I say there (p. 179), "philosophers, in developing their

as suggested above, there is a point of meeting between type and token evaluations in that it follows from my type evaluation, if it is sound, that any individual *who reasons aright* will not be able to avoid the arguments for faith without irresponsibility.)

With all these conceptual and terminological points having been clarified, we are in a position to state quite clearly and precisely what I will be arguing for in this book: I will be arguing that it is a faith response to simple ultimism (incorporating both propositional and operational elements) that is justified for twenty-first-century religious skeptics, if any type of faith response at all is justified (Part I), and also that this faith response *is* justified, and is justified in the strongest possible sense (Parts II–V). Not only is no response better for our time, but this is the response that, all things considered, we *should* make, in the sense that it is the best response we can make to religion, more worthy than any alternative, and thus positively justified for us all. Let us now proceed to the detailed arguments for this complex claim.

---

abstract evaluations of possible responses to religious claims and debating their merits, are pioneers and scouts looking for a terrain in which to live; they are seeking to provide an aid and a guide for the concrete choices and pursuits of individuals. To alter the metaphor, they are in the business of assessing and ranking candidates so that we can make a more informed vote."

PART I

PURIFYING FAITH
Why the Best Religion Is the Most Skeptical

IF MY ARGUMENTS in *Prolegomena* are sound, then the possibility of faith, which might seem to have been taken away by the results of *Skepticism*, has never been absent. Thousands of pages of apologetics have been premised on the view that no one can be religious, or procure the benefits of religion, without the attitude of religious belief. But this view is false. Faith and skepticism are perfectly compatible.

Now some who were religious in a traditional way before encountering skepticism may find in this fact a quick way home: the path from the dark valley through which they have traveled they will see as a path circling back to the starting point. That is to say, the religious inquirer reduced to nonbelief by our arguments in *Skepticism* may now seek to return to the traditional, sectarian claims she was there persuaded to lay down, simply substituting a faith response for one grounded in belief. In the first part of this book, however, I argue against such a *re*turning or turning back. Skeptical considerations concerning our immaturity not unrelated to those making religious and irreligious belief rationally impossible in the first place also conspire to prevent such a move (these are developed in terms of certain rational aims of openness, authenticity, and stability in Chapter 1). And when we straightforwardly and openly address the facts of our situation, exploring the radical nonsectarianism that seems rationally mandated instead of shrinking from it on the assumption that it must be corrosive of religious attitudes and dispositions, we will find ourselves attracted to a quite different and unexplored understanding of religious commitment (this understanding is fleshed out in Chapters 2 and 3). All things considered, then, the *best* religion—the only form of religion that could possibly be justified for twenty-first-century skeptics—is completely simple and nonsectarian, skeptical not just in form but also in content.

Ultimism and the Aims of Human Immaturity

1. A Diachronic Conception of Religion

One of the main ways *Skepticism* opens up space for religion, as noted in the preface, is in what it has to say about our future, which may be ridiculously longer than the human past. Estimates vary, but it is about 50,000 years since the Earth first saw beings anatomically and behaviorally like us, capable of practicing some form of religion. Now contrast that with the fact, so routinely overlooked or neglected, that although the Sun will eventually scorch our planet, Earth may remain habitable for as long as another *billion* years more.[1] The moral of the story is that we (and/or other intelligent species of the future) may yet have an extremely long way to go—this is epistemically possible.

What emerges from this idea—and here we move beyond *Skepticism* though proceeding on the foundation it has laid—is that we need more fully to apply what I call a *diachronic* conception of religion, according to which religion is a propensity having many possible incarnations, a feature of human life (and perhaps other forms of life to come) that can in important ways grow and change and evolve throughout the life of species and of the planet. Most philosophical discussion of religion these days appears to be carried out under the influence of what I call a *synchronic* conception, by which I mean a view that identifies religion with attitudes and/or practices of religious humans living at the present time, in the early twenty-first

---

[1] As recently confirmed by K. P. Schröder and Robert Connon Smith, "Distant Future of the Sun and Earth Revisited," *Monthly Notices of the Royal Astronomical Society* 386 (2008), 155–163.

century (together, perhaps, with whatever from our past is presupposed thereby). This is a severely and inappropriately restricted view. For even if all existing religion were seriously flawed and all existing religious claims false, one would intuitively want to say, in the light of a broader evolutionary awareness, that these facts provide no good reason to give up on religion—thus revealing the presence and operation of the diachronic conception. Because the intellectual results of the exercise of the religious impulse may over much future time become greatly improved, we ought not in this context tie religion to its existing instantiations. We should, indeed, get used to thinking about the possibility that religion may flourish even if its presently existing instantiations are eventually well covered over by the sands of history.

But to this a critic may be inclined to respond: "You have yet to show how the story you're telling is compatible with rational religion *in the present*. I'm ready to accept that the future includes new religious possibilities that we ought not ignore. And I can also see the point of a diachronic conception of religion. But what do these realizations provide one now, other than a basis for a kind of evolutionary religious skepticism, and for wishing one had been born 100,000 or 1,000,000 years later to see how things pan out? How can we ourselves, today, approach any unequivocally positive perspective on religion?"

The skepticism to which the critic refers is indeed justified; it is defended at length in *Skepticism*. But precisely because this is a skepticism dynamically turned toward the future, we can provide a crucial distinction to answer the critic's distinction between future possibilities and rational religion right now. This crucial distinction is a distinction between what rational religion might be expected to look like at *later* times in an evolutionary process and what it might be expected to look like at *earlier* times. The point is that we must recognize how rational religion may look *very different* at an earlier time, such as ours, than at later ones (100,000 or 1,000,000 years in the future). When considering whether the problem of faith and reason can be solved, therefore, we need to think about what form of religion, if any, is fitted to *our* place in time.

This point cannot be overemphasized. And now we need to go all the way back to *Prolegomena* to apply it: for even if any kind of detailed religious belief and religious practice grounded therein is arguably premature at present—appropriate, if ever, only after much more time has elapsed—perhaps some form of beliefless religious *faith* will still be appropriate today. And perhaps among the evolutionary shifts that will belong to human religion given its diachronic nature is precisely the one we can ourselves instigate by noticing this distinction and acting on it.

This possibility of a shift from belief to faith was one of the hoped-for contributions of *Prolegomena*. But only in the light of *Skepticism* and the diachronic thinking based on it do we truly come to appreciate its potential value. For now, even if religious belief is unjustified and skepticism must be the order of the day, there is no reason to think that we have arrived at the end of religion. Religion can be born again.[2]

2. *Faith and Ultimism*

The shift from belief to faith is important. But another is equally so, and also to be grounded in *Prolegomena*. This is a shift from theism or any other detailed "ism" to ultimism as the *object* of faith. It is only with the conceptual distinction between theism and ultimism that such a shift and its ramifications for immature beings like us can even be contemplated. This distinction was a long time coming. Religion has been so caught up in attempts to say more exactly, in fuller detail, what the Ultimate is like (God, Brahman, the eternal Buddha-Nature...), and reflection on religion has been so caught up in assigning names to the corresponding claims (theism, monistic Hinduism, Buddhism...), that the central claim of all, the intellectual heart, the core of religion, has until now been largely overlooked—not receiving so much as a name! Having brought it into focus, however, and having given it a name, we can also consider its religious contribution. I want to argue that the latter is significant indeed.

Let's start here by considering more closely the relation between ultimism and other religious claims. In this context it is helpful to refer to ultimism itself as *simple* ultimism and to the other claims as *qualified versions* of ultimism. The former is simply the claim that there is (metaphysically and axiologically) an ultimate reality in relation to which an ultimate good can be attained; the latter are all those claims—often large conjunctive claims—that entail simple ultimism but add religious content to what it says about ultimates, filling that out in some way (thus they entail simple ultimism whereas simple ultimism can only be said to entail their disjunction). Perhaps something more specific and detailed is said about the nature of the ultimate reality, or else about the nature of the good realizable in relation to it. Typically, of course, content will be added about *both* of

---

[2] Some of the material in this section is developed more fully in my paper, "The Evolutionary Answer to the Problem of Faith and Reason," which is to appear in Jonathan L. Kvanvig, ed., *Oxford Studies in Philosophy of Religion*, vol. 2 (Oxford: Oxford University Press, 2009).

these things. Think, for example, of orthodox Christian doctrine concerning the existence of a personal and triune God who created the world and also lived and died in it as a man in order to facilitate, for humans, the life of the Kingdom of God, or the Hindu idea that through awareness of reality as one and spiritual, our souls, eternal but bound by the law of karma to the world of matter, may be released from the cycle of rebirth and realize identity with the One Reality, Brahman. (The more spare claim that there exists a personal God who will bring at any rate some of us to salvation—i.e., traditional theism—also counts as a qualified version of ultimism, by my definition.) When I sometimes refer to such claims as "sectarian," it is because through their additional content they typically generate incompatibilities and divisions between themselves and many other actual and possible interpretations of ultimate things.

All such propositions, being religious propositions, are possible objects of propositional religious faith. And each of them, entailing simple ultimism as it does, represents a possible "faith response to ultimism" in the broadest sense of that phrase. (After the discussion of this part of the book is concluded, that phrase will be given a more restricted interpretation, which focuses on simple ultimism alone, but here at the beginning there are more possibilities to consider.) Our question in this first part of the book can be stated as follows: Should any of these propositions be seen as having more of a claim on our attention than others? When thinking about what to bring to the bar of reason for scrutiny, can we already see that it will have to be a form of faith whose propositional component is directed to some one of these objects rather than others—that there is some one form of propositional religious faith such that, if any form of propositional faith is justified (i.e., negatively or positively justified), it is that one?

Now it may seem that *which* propositional faith to seek to justify (what object of faith to select for examination) is a minor matter—just stake out the terrain that interests you, someone may say, and focus on that, leaving open the possibility that many other objects of faith are also appropriate. May not many forms of ultimistic faith be justified? Might not many *different* objects of faith each be involved in a rational religious commitment? But I suggest that, because of what can be learned from *Skepticism*, especially about the open future and human immaturity, it is possible to narrow the field of candidate objects of faith to one—to simple ultimism alone. It seems to me that there is good reason to break out of the circle of particular religious claims and consider instead the general claim they all presuppose, which they must by definition presuppose to be religious. (Persons dissatisfied with one set of particular claims have often simply exchanged it for another, going from one set of details to different details, instead of leaving details behind altogether, as I am recommending—think of the various attempted "reformations" of Christian doctrine all the way down to our own day.) A commitment to this general claim, the forgotten center, can ground an interesting and genuine form of religion in its own right. Leaving the dilemmas and dead ends of traditionalism and sectarianism behind, we simply break into a new religious possibility, a possibility that comes into view only with the clarification of simple ultimism and the distinction between that proposition and qualified versions thereof. One who has faith of this sort, while recognizing that religious belief is unjustified, voluntarily assents to simple ultimism alone (propositional faith) and acts on her assent (operational faith), seeking to do what it is appropriate to do given the truth of that claim.

But why suppose that this simple (or, as we might more provocatively say, purified) faith has the distinction of being the form of religious faith that is justified for twenty-first-century religious skeptics, *if any is?* There are several reasons. But all can be developed in terms of one of the principles arrived at in *Prolegomena* (see Appendix B) in the context of a discussion of circumstances in which faith is unjustified (note that in this principle "faith" refers to a combination of propositional and operational faith):

> P12. If, in certain circumstances *C* in which one might have faith, some aim (independent of the aim apparently calling for faith) that should all things considered be pursued by anyone in *C* can only or best be pursued by not having faith, then faith is in *C* unjustified.

According to the first reason for focusing on simple ultimism, an aim that should all things considered be pursued by twenty-first-century religious skeptics who adopt a religious faith response is the aim of maintaining as much openness to actual and possible religious claims as may feasibly be combined with a clear and substantial religiousness (call this the "openness aim"). And this point, in conjunction with P12 and some other highly plausible propositions (or propositions that can be made plausible), yields the desired conclusion that only simple religious faith can be justified, as we will soon see. But before getting to that, let me explain and defend the openness aim.

3. *The Openness Aim Explained*

The first questions likely to arise in connection with the openness aim ask what I mean when I say "as may feasibly be combined with a clear and substantial religiousness" and why I have introduced this constraint. Let's start with "religiousness." What I mean here is simply religion in the sense of that word developed in *Prolegomena*, where it was argued that religion should, for philosophical purposes, be understood as involving a commitment fundamental among one's commitments to cultivate dispositions appropriate to the state of affairs represented by ultimism, which either in belief or in faith one takes to obtain: religious persons, perhaps without deploying this terminology, and usually in connection with some qualified version of ultimism, make central to their lives the project of conforming how they live to the standards suggested by there being an ultimate reality in relation to which an ultimate good can be attained. This may sometimes be a struggle, and the dispositions involved may be stronger or weaker, but so long as the commitment in question is the most deeply influential among one's commitments and regarded as such, it counts as a religious commitment.

As can be detected in these points, religiousness, as I understand it, is really just operational religious faith under another name: it centrally involves a commitment to do certain actions (though notice that these involve the cultivation of various dispositions, including emotional ones) which one sees as appropriate given the truth of the claim or set of claims that provides one's focus, be it believed or voluntarily taken on board in propositional faith—perhaps actions not at all appropriate otherwise.

What about "clear" religiousness? Well, this is just religiousness with a definite shape: delimited and articulable, not fuzzy and indeterminate. And "substantial" religiousness? Here I have in mind that a form of life could evince clear religiousness and nonetheless be somewhat thin and undemanding, not lending itself to much development, not involving a wide range of dispositions that need to be cultivated or many actions that should be done—not something that can truly fill a life, seriously engaging the attention of an intelligent and dedicated person for a significant proportion of his or her time. Substantial religiousness is religiousness to which such descriptions do not apply.

That brings us to "as may feasibly be combined with." Notice first that I do not say "as is *compatible* with": I mean more than would be realized were some skeptic in some possible world to, for a time, bring off the combination of religiousness and the relevant degree of openness; I mean that it should be practicable in the long term for skeptics in the actual world— that any of *us* is able to combine those two things by trying hard enough and can live out such a life without disruptions or sacrifices that a skeptic seeking faith rightly would not wish to make. All of this is still somewhat vague, but it is clear enough for present purposes and will become clearer as, in the next two chapters, we consider challenges to the clarity, substantiality, and feasibility of the form of "religion plus openness" which I shall be urging skeptics to regard as their only rational option.

So why build such a constraint into the openness aim—why is the imperative one of openness *to the extent* that may feasibly be combined with a substantial religiousness? One answer to this question must be given in terms of argumentative strategy. Simple ultimism alone, which I wish to defend as the proper object of propositional religious faith, would commonly—precisely because of its limited content, because of a certain "emptiness" from which it may seem to suffer—be regarded as somewhat *less* than capable of grounding a form of religion that is clear and substantial as well as feasible. Precisely because of this apparent fact, it would also often be dismissed by those seeking a suitable object of faith, even if its minimal content were shown to be in a certain intellectual respect attractive. My emphasis on simple ultimism will therefore be most persuasively defended by reference to the openness aim if I build into my statement of that aim a reference to clarity, substantiality, and feasibility. (If that emphasis *is* persuasively defended by reference to this aim, then the cited complaint will be preempted.)

Of course there is a prior and more general point here: my emphasis on simple ultimism can persuasively be defended by reference to the openness aim only if the suggestion that twenty-first-century skeptics should have that aim is itself persuasive. What is required at this stage is a plausible imperative that even those with religious inclinations can accept. And if I suggested that religious skeptics considering faith should be *so* open to religious propositions of various kinds that no clear and substantial religiousness could feasibly be adopted, I would obviously have something that is more than a little controversial, which someone with religious inclinations would rightly find unacceptable.

"All right," our questioner may now say, "so you've got an imperative that avoids that sort of *im*plausibility. You have yet to indicate what makes it overall plausible. Indeed, you have yet to tell us what the 'openness' you've been talking about really amounts to."

Let me start my response by dealing with the latter issue. What I mean by openness to religious propositions involves possessing a certain multiform disposition in relation to them, including such qualities as intellectual vigilance (keeping the propositions in mind and working to remain aware of evidence pertaining to their truth or falsity), evenhandedness (giving to each a similar degree of respect and consideration), and readiness or willingness to accept (being emotionally and intellectually prepared to discover truth in any one of them). One who possesses such a disposition will—by implication—lack certain other dispositions in relation to the propositions in question: dispositions such as scornfulness, or fear, or condescension, or a desire for them to be false, or simply—for whatever reason—a tendency not to think about them.

But one could possess such a disposition and still exercise it only in relation to a few religious claims. What I have in mind when I use this word "openness" is something more magnanimous than that, something that can be increased along both of two dimensions: both the strength of the openness disposition and the number of significant—that is, nontrivial—versions of ultimism in relation to which it is exercised.[3] So let us say that the greater the strength of one's openness disposition and the larger the number of religious propositions in relation to which it is exercised, the more open to religious propositions one is.

So why should our twenty-first-century religious skeptic seek as much in the way of such openness as is compatible with a genuine and substantial religiousness? One obvious reason is that such openness is connected to certain recognized virtues, which humans in general should cultivate: intellectual alertness, flexibility, magnanimity, fairness, respect, humility—these are good and all-too-rare qualities that we should take every opportunity to cultivate if we are seeking to make advancements in the process of human evolution, and accepting the openness aim involves seizing just such an opportunity. There is also the point that the skeptic we are considering would not *be* a skeptic were it not for openness already displayed in connection with the skeptical propositions involved in her present position. She has learned that she must always be ready to see things in a completely new way. So why would she give up this attitude now? But, it may be said, perhaps the skeptic will, through a similar openness, come to see that there is good reason to adopt religious faith. This may be accepted. Indeed, I will be arguing for just that conclusion. And perhaps having faith will in some way circumscribe the skeptic's openness. But surely we should not expect that the skeptic who finds herself in such circumstances will yield any more openness than is required by real religiousness—and recognizing this brings us precisely to the openness aim as I have formulated it.

However, there is still a lacuna to be filled in here. Whenever one has good reason to believe a proposition to be true, one no longer has any reason (nor can it be the manifestation of a virtue) to express in relation to its alternatives openness as defined above. (One would, of course, still want a less demanding "openness," involving something like the third item mentioned above: readiness and willingness to regard one of the alternatives as true should it come into a better light.) Indeed, if one is truly a lover and seeker of truth and understanding, one will want to *make use* of propositions one considers well supported in pursuing *those* goals. And if

---

[3] I leave the reference to significance tacit hereafter.

one does so, one clearly gives certain propositions priority over others and leaves behind a stance of complete evenhandedness and impartiality.

The way to deal with this should by now be obvious. What we need to make explicit and indeed to focus on in this defense of the openness aim is the fact that our religious skeptic is indeed a religious skeptic! The true force of the case for openness is only apparent when we are mindful of our generally skeptical orientation and the points about the great disparity between past and future and a diachronic conception of religion outlined earlier. Any faith that is justified, we must assume, will be a faith appropriate for skeptics. And skeptics are not believers. Furthermore, given what can be learned by studying the most powerful arguments for religious skepticism, whose content must shape one's orientation thereafter, there is strong pressure in the direction of just such openness as I have described. Skeptical arguments show that we may well be at a very early stage of human intellectual and spiritual development, with a great deal needing to be learned about the full range of religious possibilities. Many detailed conceptions of the Divine, both actual and possible, may remain to be more fully understood and evaluated. Proper spiritual and intellectual sensitivity will lead anyone aware of these things to avoid closing off a potentially huge range of such possibilities.

Allow me to develop this point. Take any religious proposition. Three possible attitudes toward it can immediately be distinguished: (1) One thinks the claim is true and so believes it. (2) One does not think this, but thinks it the likeliest among religious options—thinks that, while perhaps not more probable than its denial, it is more probable than competing religious claims, which (as one supposes) together with one's own claim form a limited and definable set, some member of which is true if any religious claim is. (3) One does not think this either, but thinks the claim to be one among a limited and definable *though not at present adjudicable* set of competing religious claims, one of which is true if any religious claim is.

A religious skeptic should be moved by her skepticism past any and all of these attitudes. Clearly, skeptical arguments of the sort I have presented in *Skepticism,* if successful, will remove *belief* of traditional claims, and so move us past (1). I suggest they should move us past (2) as well: awareness of religious diversity, combined with a not very well developed understanding, in most parts of the world, of many religious options in other parts, suffices to render even the more modest stance of (2) unjustified at this stage of human development. And thus we arrive (at least) at (3). Now the stance of (3), as can be seen, still presupposes that the set of competing options which ought to influence our judgments is limited and definable. A person holding this view will think that a lot of careful investigation lies ahead of her; she will also think she knows where to look, and at least roughly what the relevant claims are—they are the claims of extant religious traditions! But this confidence, I suggest, will be taken away by appropriate reflection on the arguments for capacity skepticism I have developed. The truth is that we are not in a position to fix the range of relevant religious options: our ignorance is such that any traditional claim must be seen as quite possibly belonging to an indefinitely large set of actual and possible competing religious claims, which is at present, and may for some time remain,[4] *both nondefinable and nonadjudicable.* Let us call this skeptical attitude, attitude (4).

Now suppose that someone looking for a suitable object of faith finds herself with attitude (4). Is it not evident that she should seek the object of faith that permits her to show as much religious openness as possible?

To this it may be replied that (as indicated above) the openness aim has the force I need it to have in this context only if it is an aim that the twenty-first-century skeptic has *all things considered* good reason to accept. And perhaps this is not the case, at least for some skeptics. In particular, for those who are former believers, the openness aim can have only prima facie force—force that is overridden by the fact that they will already have deep and meaningful experience of a particular religious tradition. In a situation of this sort, where we have a former believer driven to skepticism who now notices the possibility of faith, it is quite appropriate for the skeptic to stick with what served her well in the past instead of leaving that behind and exploring unproven options, even if the latter are compatible with some form of religiousness.[5]

How should we respond to this? Well, we might begin by asking why the former believer's experience of her tradition was "deep and mean-ingful," and why it "served her well." Surely the answer must be given at least in part in terms of the fact that she *did believe* it told the truth about an ultimate reality! If she is now, in faith, to re-adopt the specific claims she formerly believed and approximate that experience, she must assent to them and act on them, thus bringing their content back to the fore-front of her consciousness and activity, and, as part of this, setting aside all questions about the possibility of truth in competing claims, many of which she now as a skeptic realizes are or may be epistemically on a par with, or even epistemically preferable to, her own (though she hasn't yet carried out the specific investigations required to see), and many of which her capacity skepticism will suggest may not yet have been discovered.

---

[4] Perhaps it will *always* be so, but our ignorance concerning matters religious is such that we don't even know that we won't ever know more—we are ignorant also about the extent of our ignorance.

[5] This seems to be the attitude supported, for example, by William Alston's discussion of related matters in his *Perceiving God* (Ithaca: Cornell University Press, 1991), chap. 7.

She must allow part A of her investigation, as we might say, to foreclose parts B through Z. And there seems to be something seriously wrong with such a result. Surely our newly minted skeptic will herself feel that there is something wrong with it. A true conversion to skepticism of the sort for which I have argued will involve for any former believer a complete shift in orientation. And from her new vantage point, what she will find is that the result in question looks like nothing so much as a path to intellectual and spiritual stultification—a way of bringing to a grinding halt any process of religious development that might be under way for her. It seems to part ways with the deepest love of understanding and any desire to contribute vitally to our arrival, not just as individuals but as a race, at the truth about religion—a project that may well require skepticism for a long time yet, and a spirit not of isolationism but of cooperation with other inquirers, of many times and diverse perspectives. These points, in conjunction with our previous points above, provide more than enough reason to suppose that, *if and insofar as more openness than this is still capable of being combined with a clear and substantial religiousness,* our chastened and enlivened former believer/skeptic will and should seek such openness.

4. The Implications of Openness

Suppose, then, that the openness aim is one that our skeptic has all things considered good reason to adopt. How exactly do we get from here to the conclusion that a perfectly simple religious faith is justified, if any is?

As follows. Begin with a statement of the openness imperative itself:

(1) An aim that should all things considered be pursued by twenty-first-century religious skeptics who adopt a faith response is the aim of maintaining as much openness to actual and possible religious claims as may feasibly be combined with a clear and substantial religiousness.

Then add the following premise:

(2) The larger the number of actual and possible religious claims with which the object of one's religious faith is compatible, the better one can pursue the openness aim, provided a clear and substantial religiousness remains feasible.

This premise seems obviously true, given that (a) the larger the number of religious propositions in relation to which one's openness disposition is exercised, the more open to religious propositions one is, and that

(b) if the proposition with respect to which one has faith is incompatible with some other proposition, one can hardly show a great deal of openness of the relevant sort in relation to the latter. Faith is certainly a more "eyes open" attitude than belief, but it still involves making an intellectual commitment that requires setting alternatives aside and thus paying less attention to them—which is to say, no longer being fully open to them. Having seen this, we should also note the obviousness of the following proposition:

> (3) Simple ultimism is compatible with a larger number of actual and possible religious claims than any qualified version thereof.

It follows from the conjunction of (2) and (3) that

> (4) Provided simple ultimism feasibly grounds a clear and substantial religiousness, the openness aim can best be pursued if the skeptic makes simple ultimism (and no qualified ultimism) the object of her religious faith.

And, of course, I plan to argue that

> (5) Simple ultimism *does* feasibly ground a clear and substantial religiousness.

Hence, we can conclude, from (4) and (5), that

> (6) The openness aim can best be pursued if the skeptic makes simple ultimism (and no qualified ultimism) the object of her religious faith.

But from (1) and (6) it follows that

> (7) An aim that should all things considered be pursued by twenty-first-century religious skeptics who adopt a faith response can best be pursued if the skeptic makes simple ultimism (and no qualified ultimism) the object of her religious faith.

Now it is a straightforward application of principle P12 stated above (justified in *Prolegomena*) to say that

> (8) If some aim that should all things considered be pursued by twenty-first-century religious skeptics who adopt a faith response

can best be pursued by making simple ultimism (and no qualified ultimism) the object of her religious faith, then, if the object of a skeptic's faith is some qualified ultimism, her faith response is unjustified.

And the conjunction of (7) and (8) yields

> (9) If the object of a skeptic's faith is some qualified ultimism, then her faith response is unjustified.

Now by contraposition on (9) we obtain

> (10) If the skeptic's faith response is justified, then the object of her faith is not some qualified ultimism.

And, clearly,

> (11) If the object of the skeptic's faith is not some qualified ultimism, then it is simple ultimism alone.

But from (10) and (11)—by hypothetical syllogism—we arrive at

> (12) If the skeptic's faith response is justified, then the object of her faith is simple ultimism alone,

which is what was to be shown.

5. *Other Rational Aims of the Immature*

Thus the openness aim on its own is quite sufficient to establish that ultimistic faith is justified, if any is. But there are at least two other aims that can be used to support the same conclusion. I call them the "authenticity aim" and the "stability aim." These two appeal more directly to religious considerations than did our openness aim, but it will become evident that any twenty-first-century skeptic considering her options in the shadows cast by our short evolutionary history will reasonably be influenced by them. Here we can proceed in a slightly less roundabout way than before, beginning in each case with a version of premises (1), (4), and (6) above, after which the argument runs just as before.

But first let me say what I mean by authenticity and stability in this context; why they are desiderata; and why our twenty-first-century skeptic should go as far, in protecting them, as may feasibly be combined with an emphasis on clear and substantial religiousness.

By authenticity I mean that the propositions grounding one's religious form of life *really entail ultimism,* and not just in the trivial way represented by tacking on to some claim about God or gods "and this reality is ultimate and salvific." By stability I mean that they *not be vulnerable to being superseded* as one's understanding grows, either by other religious propositions or by some entirely nonreligious view of the world. Earlier in this chapter I assumed that qualified versions of ultimism entail simple ultimism in a pretty straightforward and nontrivial manner. But now we need to complicate that assumption. It would be easy for immature creatures like us, at a relatively early stage of evolution, to have before our minds something that we *regard* as a notion thus entailing ultimism but that is in fact an impostor, some lesser notion by which we have been distracted. Religion, as we can see just by reflecting on ultimism, invites us to strain our intellect and imagination to the utmost in considering its central axiological idea, and to extend this notion boundlessly in every conceivable direction, in order thus to reach the idea of something infinitely rich and deep. At least upon taking this idea reflectively into account, our skeptic will want to settle for nothing less: she wants authentic religion, if any at all; she will aim to avoid the danger of inauthenticity. While she might not reasonably sacrifice a rich and deep and clearly focused form of life for assurance of authenticity, it seems evident that she should aim to do as much to protect it as can feasibly be *combined* with an emphasis on such things.

Similarly, our skeptic will rationally find most desirable a propositional base that is not liable to being swiftly replaced as her understanding, still so undeveloped, continues to grow. Religion provides a form of *life,* and many of its practical benefits might be lost if it proves unstable. One way in which it might prove unstable is related to the point about authenticity: the skeptic might discover the *in*authenticity of her focus and feel the need to replace her focus with ideas more likely to be authentically religious. But there are other ways. It might be discovered, for example, that the religious view underlying her form of life is false. Again, while the skeptic should not be expected to go so far in protecting stability that she loses the other desiderata of clear and substantial religiousness, she should certainly be expected to go as far, when selecting a focus for religion, as can feasibly be combined with an emphasis on such things.

So we have a basis for two more versions of premise (1) above, which may be stated as follows:

(1*) An aim that should all things considered be pursued by twenty-first-century religious skeptics who adopt a faith response is the aim of providing for religious *authenticity* as full a protection as may feasibly be combined with a clear and substantial religiousness.

(1**) An aim that should all things considered be pursued by twenty-first-century religious skeptics who adopt a faith response is the aim of providing for religious *stability* as full a protection as may feasibly be combined with a clear and substantial religiousness.

And the next step, of course, is to show that in each case we can add the relevant (4)-type premise emphasizing simple ultimism:

(4*) Provided simple ultimism feasibly grounds a clear and substantial religiousness, the authenticity aim can best be pursued if the skeptic makes simple ultimism (and no qualified ultimism) the object of her religious faith.

(4**) Provided simple ultimism feasibly grounds a clear and substantial religiousness, the stability aim can best be pursued if the skeptic makes simple ultimism (and no qualified ultimism) the object of her religious faith.

It shouldn't be hard to see how this latter move, in its two instantiations, can be defended. Start with the authenticity aim. Advocates of the various qualified versions of ultimism that we see in the world—Christian, Hindu, Buddhist, and so on—certainly *think* they are talking about something ultimate and salvific. And, of course, if we add this assumption to their descriptions of purportedly religious phenomena, we will trivially generate the relevant entailment. But do the descriptions themselves entail ultimism? What if, given our evolutionary limitations, the tie here is less than secure? From an evolutionary perspective we are in a position to notice that much of what humans have come up with so far may represent only poor attempts to fill out that ultimistic vision. Common religious conceptions such as the personalist conception, the idea of God, might not produce something worthy of the label "ultimate." Maybe, in talking about such things as a personal God, we are still talking about something that would in fact be limited. (Isn't any personal idea in a certain sense unidimensional?) If so, how are we talking about something capable of being both metaphysically and axiologically ultimate? The various more common, specific, and detailed religious claims with whose names we are familiar are *trying* to describe something ultimate, and it is in virtue of this fact (taken together with the fact that their assumption of success is always at least tacitly present) that they can be called religious at all, but they may fail.

Looking such considerations in the face, and aware of our distinction between qualified versions of ultimism and simple ultimism, the twenty-first-century skeptic will certainly be led to look upon the latter with more favor. By keeping the claim of simple ultimism firmly at the center of our frame of reference, eschewing all qualified versions thereof, we have something whose content marks the real object of religion. We can then be sure that we really are thinking about *religion* (as opposed to some impostor by which we've been distracted), and more confident of this than in any other circumstances. Thus (4*) seems clearly true.

What about (4**)? Well, other religious ideas can always be superseded by more authentic discoveries. Perhaps, for example, it will be obvious millions of years hence that the idea of the Ultimate as a person-like being was an idea that arose relatively early in human evolution but then was set aside as its inauthenticity became more and more evident. But the idea of the *Ultimate* by definition cannot suffer a similar fate. Our interpretations of it may change, but the idea itself cannot be religiously superseded. Also, other religious ideas may be proved false—if my arguments in Part III of *Skepticism* are correct, then this has occurred for the personalist conception already—but it will at least be harder to reach such a conclusion in respect of simple ultimism, because of its greater generality. With less content comes less vulnerability. Indeed, no religious proposition is more likely to remain undisturbed by apparent proofs of falsity long into the future than simple ultimism. Thus, all things considered, if our aim is to achieve a stable religious point of reference, we can do no better than to select simple ultimism as the center of our vision. And if so, then (4**) too is clearly true.

From here the path of argument is familiar. First introduce from above the assumption (5)—that simple ultimism *does* feasibly ground a clear and substantial religiousness; (5) taken together with (4*) entails

> (6*) The authenticity aim can best be pursued if the skeptic makes simple ultimism (and no qualified ultimism) the object of her religious faith.

And (5) taken together with (4**) entails the parallel

> (6**) The stability aim can best be pursued if the skeptic makes simple ultimism (and no qualified ultimism) the object of her religious faith.

But (6*) taken together with (1*) leads us back to (7); and so does (6**) taken together with (1**). And from there the reasoning unfolds just as before, leading us twice more to

(12) If the skeptic's faith response is justified, then the object of her faith is simple ultimism alone,

which was the goal of our reasoning.

6. *Conclusion*

Every premise and inference of the reasoning in the previous sections can be seen to be justified—with the exception of premise (5), which tells us that simple ultimism can feasibly ground a clear and substantial religiousness. Everything now hangs on that proposition. If it is false or doubtful, the project of this part of the book falls apart. But, equally, if, as I intend to show in the next two chapters, there *is* an attractive alternative way of being religious here—a nontraditional form of religion that combines the relevant desiderata—then our conclusion, given everything else we have seen (three times over!), must surely be that traditionalism and elaborated ultimisms have all to be decisively left behind by any twenty-first-century skeptic investigating her faith options. So let us explore in greater detail what such a faith *without* detail would look like.

Faith without Details, or How to Practice Skeptical Religion

Since it is religious skepticism that pushes us in the direction of the simple brand of faith I will be defending, and because such faith is by definition adopted by one who is in doubt about religious claims, it is appropriate to refer to it as *skeptical* faith and to refer to the religion it instantiates as *skeptical* religion (the descriptor "ultimistic" will also be used from time to time: the contrast readers may note with "theistic" is intentional). Now skeptical religion, as I have already suggested, would be considered by many to be something less than capable of satisfying the clarity/substantiality/feasibility constraint I have built into the openness, authenticity, and stability aims. I begin the discussion of this chapter by considering some ways in which one might seek to give more substance to such a charge.

1. The Emptiness Objection

Where the idea of a faith response to simple ultimism is concerned, a critic might suggest that we immediately have at least three issues: (1) How *does* one have faith with respect to a proposition as general and vague and virtually empty as simple ultimism? In particular, how is there anything here to "hold before one's mind"? If this very fundamental question cannot be answered, then skeptical faith is quite unfeasible. (2) Because of the aforementioned emptiness, how is there enough content for us to answer questions about *which* actions are appropriate to the truth of simple ultimism? How, it may be asked, are we to know what our operational faith—faith *in* the reality referred to by this claim—should include if the properties of that reality are unspecified? How can we articulate what is involved in trusting it to "save" us unless we know what to do in order to be saved, and how can we know this unless we posit more specific properties?[1] Here the focus is on clarity, though subsequent discussion will turn up some feasibility concerns as well. (3) Even if the previous issues are resolvable, how can simple ultimism suggest *enough* distinctive and diverse actions to give any significance or substance, any richness or fullness, to a life of faith? Here the matters of clarity and feasibility move to the sidelines, and the searchlight is intended (primarily) to reveal insubstantiality.

All of these issues stem from an alleged "emptiness" in simple ultimism. So let me address that. As a matter of fact, by saying that the reality in question is *ultimate* (both metaphysically and axiologically) and *salvific,* we do posit some relevant properties. We certainly have nothing as lacking in content as John Hick's "Real," which, influenced by Kant, Hick describes as in itself completely unknowable and indescribable.[2] Hick has been much criticized for this feature of his "religious hypothesis," which is otherwise admirable in many ways, but it is important to recognize that—although Hick sometimes uses such labels as "the Ultimate" in place of "the Real"—my notion of simple ultimism does not share this feature. In saying that a reality is metaphysically ultimate, we say that its existence is explanatorily the most basic fact, that it is deepest, most fundamental in the nature of things; in saying that it is axiologically ultimate, we say that it has unsurpassably great value. And it is the *combination* of these two elements taken together with the content specified by "salvific"—the idea that the value of the Ultimate *can be communicated to us;* that by relating ourselves appropriately to the Ultimate, our own deepest good can be realized—which produces something distinctively religious, according to the definition of "religion" we are utilizing. There is certainly some abstractness here, which is needed to accommodate the huge diversity of actual and possible significant interpretations of ultimism (if I offered some "precisifying" philosophical analysis, I would simply be generating one such interpretation, contrary to my stated wish to have a suitable framework proposition for religion that does not foreclose the future). But in seeing that we have something distinctively religious here, something that can clearly be distinguished from what a materialist might say, who nevertheless thinks there exists something metaphysically ultimate, and from what a certain sort of cosmic pessimist might say, who thinks there is something axiologically ultimate but holds that it must forever be out of reach,

---

[1] My way of putting this second issue owes something to correspondence with Michael Martin.

[2] See John Hick, *An Interpretation of Religion* (London: Macmillan, 1989).

since completely out of our league—in seeing all this, I suggest, we see the significant content that remains even in simple ultimism.

To add to the argument, let me now point out that simple ultimism has some pretty obvious entailments. Since having propositional faith here, mentally going along with this ultimistic proposition, means also in faith going along with all the propositions one takes it to entail,[3] such entailments provide more evidence of the significant content available to ultimistic faith. ("Simple ultimism alone," as indicated in the previous chapter, means "simple ultimism exclusive of qualified ultimisms," not "simple ultimism exclusive of all other propositions including its entailments.") So what are these entailments? Well, for example, if simple ultimism is true, then there is a reality transcendent of the natural world. If it is true, then a certain popular sort of philosophical naturalism (which claims that there is no such transcendent reality) is false. If ultimism is true, then it is a dimension of reality transcending nature that is most fundamental and important. If it is true, then the core of reality is on the side of the good, and indeed in some sense *is* the good. If it is true, then—even though we might have a hard time seeing exactly how—the universe or our environment in the largest sense is, as William James would have said, friendly, that is, not indifferent to our deepest needs. If ultimism is true, furthermore, then it is through associating ourselves with the reality of which it speaks that we can best make contact with true value. If it is true, then the sort of inquiry that, if successful, will bring us to the deepest understanding of the world is religious in nature. And there are further entailments that we will be noticing in due course.

There is also the fact that certain propositions are entailed by simple ultimism taken together with obvious truths. For example, since, given the fact of deeply damaged earthly lives or earthly lives cut short, the promise represented by the term "salvific" could hardly otherwise be fulfilled, we can derive the claim that there will be some sort of afterlife for at least some of us.

But the last sort of move in particular may inspire only a new version of the "emptiness" objection focused on my claims concerning value and their alleged implications: with due regard to our finite limitations, which I have emphasized, should we not be led to wonder whether those claims

---

[3] As indicated in *Prolegomena*, p. 134 n. 5. More precisely, we should say "in faith going along with all observed entailments that one has no independent good reason to believe" (I thank Joel Pust for pointing out the need for some such qualification). In this context, however, it may be expected that the relevant entailments will normally be entailments about which one will be in doubt if one is in doubt about ultimism and thus entailments themselves calling for faith.

can be given much content or justification? How can we assume that the axiological concepts and beliefs we possess tell the final truth about value (to which "final truth" ultimism clearly refers)—that our actual, present standards of evaluation conform to the *correct* standards? Might not the final truth about value be quite beyond us, at any rate as we are presently constituted? And if so, how can talk of "ultimate value" or "deepest good" or of the universe being "friendly" tell us very much? (For example, how can we then be sure—even given apparently dismal facts about some human lives—that if simple ultimism is true there will be an afterlife for some of us?) If, moreover, it is its value-related elements that are supposed to distinguish simple ultimism as a religious claim and provide a basis for distinctively religious faith and religious action, then how, given these points, has such a basis really been provided?

In response, I would suggest that although there *is* a certain respect in which the final truth about value should be viewed as quite possibly beyond us if my skeptical arguments are correct, in other—important—respects this is not so. It is true that if such is the case, we should regard many of our thoughts about what *has* value or about *how* value is realized in things as limited and quite possibly imperfect in their apprehension of the truth. But even so, certain general facts determined by the concept of value and by certain necessary truths associated therewith (unavoidably regarded as such) may legitimately be relied upon and viewed as fundamental.[4]

Let me develop these points a little further. Call *x* whatever it is that makes for the deepest, most valuable life, and suppose you think you know the appropriate filling for *x* and also think that you possess it or are coming to possess it, being led thereby to a positive state of mind (as opposed to agitation and despair). Now suppose you learn that you might be mistaken about the appropriate filling for *x*. Even so, you cannot be mistaken in thinking that whatever *is* the correct filling for *x* is *worthy* of a positive state of mind (as opposed to agitation and despair) on the part of anyone who possesses it or is coming to possess it: just an understanding of the concept of value will give you *this* much. And so we already have significant content, distinguishable from other possibilities, quite capable

---

[4] My argument here is in line with the argument of *Skepticism*, chap. 8, where I defend the use, for the sake of inquiry, of certain unavoidable belief-forming practices, including the practice of forming beliefs about such apparently necessary truths. It is interesting to note how fundamental to the activity of philosophy is this dependence on seemingly self-evident and necessary value claims: just in *formulating* intellectual goals or *engaging* in inquiry of any sort, one must judge that certain things—for example, arriving at truth or understanding—are *good* and have *value;* and such judgments will typically not be based on anything beyond themselves. Hence it seems clear that rejection of a general value skepticism in connection with the present inquiry is justified.

of contributing to a distinctive world-picture and distinctive motivations (more on this below) for one who has faith that simple ultimism is true.[5]

As for necessary truths: it is unavoidable and quite appropriate for us to believe that certain relevant value claims have this status—take, for example, the claim that complete justice would enhance the human condition or that an infant whose life is permanently terminated before she has experienced anything untouched by intense suffering has not attained the deepest good possible for a human life (just try believing that there is a possible world in which the introduction of justice makes no contribution to value or in which an infant of the sort I mentioned has achieved as much fulfillment as a more extended life might have held). Such claims we can hold as true and as necessarily true even without knowing in detail what salvation or wholeness or liberation is all about. And the application of our second example to my claim above about an afterlife is obvious.[6]

It may also be observed, in connection with the previous points and in further response to the present objection, that the religious person who is properly skeptical and properly aware of her limitations will exhibit a continual intellectual and moral straining and striving—a continual effort, in faith that such exists, to realize more adequately and fully what truly *is* valuable and to leave imperfect approximations behind as soon as they are discovered to be such. (One might usefully think in this connection about the common religious emphasis on growth and development in the religious life.) And this shows how distinctive actions in connection with the notion of ultimate value may be dictated even in circumstances of an appropriate skepticism about value. Indeed, it shows that the possibility

[5] Compare a situation in which a parent leaving on a trip tells her child that she will bring him "something nice." The child may have no clue what this will be, or even what the relevant range of options includes, and yet, if he takes his parent's word for it, be affected in much the same way as if he did know.

[6] Most of us, at least upon reflection, do indeed find certain value-related propositions of the sort relied upon here intuitively compelling and just as seemingly certain and necessary as anything in mathematics or logic. Interestingly, this includes moral philosophers who, while sometimes abjuring any purely intuitionist moral theory, very commonly speak of bringing "reflective equilibrium" to our "considered moral beliefs"—where the latter are normally viewed as intuitively grounded and in Brad Hooker's term "independently credible," that is, not in need of support from any evidence beyond themselves. (See his *Ideal Code, Real World* [Oxford: Clarendon Press, 2000], p. 13.) Hooker has an impressive list of moral philosophers who come out on the side of such a view. For a particularly sophisticated and subtle contemporary defense of our reliance on seeming self-evidence in ethics, see Robert Audi, *The Good in the Right* (Princeton, N.J.: Princeton University Press, 2004). As Audi (p. 2) and others have shown, even noncognitivists in ethics, theorists who hold that moral utterances express not beliefs that are literally true or false but rather feelings or commitments, may need to take certain attitudes as basic and non-inferentially grounded starting points for moral discussion.

of certain such actions arises precisely *because* of such skepticism, which is perhaps as full a refutation of the present objection as one could want.

I suggest, therefore, that the objection fails and that simple ultimism is far from empty. Already from the content-related items we have mentioned one can begin to discern how the three issues mentioned above are to be dealt with. That is, one can begin to sense the feasibility of assenting to this proposition (traditional, sectarian religious claims are no doubt much more familiar to us than the simple ultimism they presuppose, and their evident content may seduce us into thinking it impossible to get a grip on anything *less* content-full, but such is not the case). And one can begin to define the patterns of behavior that are appropriate given the truth of simple ultimism, and those that are not, and to see that the former make for a rich and substantial religious life. But, having so far only made some room for these points, let me now attend to them more explicitly and fully.

2. The Feasibility of Skeptical Propositional Faith

What exactly is brought to mind for one who has faith that simple ultimism is true, and just how does one adopt such faith? Relevant here is the proposition that there is a metaphysically and axiologically ultimate reality, in relation to which an ultimate good can be attained, and also such incompletely evidenced entailments of this proposition as are known to one. Someone who comes to have faith with respect to simple ultimism finds herself without evidence sufficient to cause belief of these propositions (recognizing that they may be false or perhaps even in some hidden way incoherent), but positively evaluating the states of affairs they report, she nonetheless tenaciously pictures or imagines the world to herself as a world in which they are true and committedly gives her assent to what is thus held before the mind (mentally taking it as her cognitive base, meanwhile pushing alternatives aside and leaving the issue of its accuracy behind)—where "tenaciously" and "committedly" are meant to emphasize that one does these things regularly, seeking over time to turn the mental actions involved into stable dispositions.

The picturing I am describing here of course need not involve literally visualizing the universe arranged or rearranged in some manner (though it might): one can think of such propositional contents, bringing them to the forefront of one's mind, holding them there in a mode of entertaining, and do so recurrently, without the distinctive phenomenology of visualization. And given the discussion of the previous several paragraphs, it is not hard to see what sorts of things one who engages in such behavior is thinking *of:* one is thinking of there being something combining highest reality and value; of there being a fundamental pattern of meaningfulness in things (even if it will never more than dimly be discerned); of things genuinely making sense; and—even when nature's grip is most cold—of something deeper, always deeper, that is indeed deep*est* and also best and is winning or else will win out in the end, permitting the realization of the best that humans could seek for themselves and for the world (even if it is not something they have yet learned to seek). Of course such thoughts, thus explicitly formulated, need not continually be running through the mind of one who has faith that simple ultimism is true. Perhaps there is some "tag" standing for the whole conjunction of ideas, such as "All shall be well," or some symbol, such as—choosing one possible example at random—the Greek letter omega, which the individual teaches herself to bring to mind at regular intervals and especially when relevant matters arise; or perhaps our person of faith recurrently imagines the universe flooded with light, sweeping darkness away. There are indeed many ways in which, and through which, one might rightly be said to be thinking of the content of the propositions concerned.

Now our discussion of feasibility has in this case been focused on whether there is any propositional content here for our minds to get a grip on—whether we can have *this* sort of faith just by trying to. There is no need to consider whether making the effort involved in having faith would cause us to incur undesirable sacrifices and so be unfeasible in that distinguishable sense, since in assuming that the skeptic wants *some* sort of faith, we are assuming it to be acceptable that, in one way or another (with respect to one proposition or another), such an effort be made. No doubt this effort may sometimes prove to be demanding, a wrestling with angels: anyone disturbed by this should remember how propositional faith and operational faith can be mutually reinforcing, and remember also that faith is supposed to be a virtue! But for the reason given, this fact does not have any special relevance here.

It seems evident, therefore, that the first issue posed to us at the beginning of this chapter admits of swift resolution.

3. *The Clarity of Skeptical Operational Faith*

Now for the second of the three issues raised by the emptiness objection— whether (and how) such simple propositional faith can suggest and support a well-defined religious form of life. How might one, by engaging in practical reasoning on the basis of simple ultimism and behaving accordingly, contribute to the formation of a clear religiousness?

In many ways. Some of these have already been suggested, in connection, for example, with what we saw was the need for skeptics to seek continually to improve their understanding of the sort of value that might rightly be called "ultimate." I begin here by developing this theme of investigation a little further, in an attempt to show how religious inquiry can be turned into *religious* inquiry—into one component of a distinctively skeptical form of religious practice.

So how might the enterprise of cultivating dispositions appropriate to the truth of ultimism come to include such inquiry for one who has the skeptic's purposes and picture of things, and what will be the nature of this inquiry? Well, if ultimism is true, then, as we saw earlier, it is through more deeply associating ourselves with the reality of which it speaks that we can best make contact with true value, and in that case it is appropriate—given the purpose to further the human good or at least her own good that she may be expected to possess—for the skeptic to seek that deeper relation. But it will obviously be conducive to (even if not indisputably necessary for) seeking it successfully to have some understanding of the nature of the Ultimate and also of the value it represents and—relatedly—of how this value is connected to our good. (Certainly the critic from the beginning of this chapter who was enamored of the emptiness objection should be happy to agree with me here.) Since we don't *start out* with a full understanding of such things, and indeed are quite ignorant in this respect, it follows that one way of acting on faith that ultimism is true will involve engaging in an inquiry intended to *fill out* our understanding of them. It further follows, precisely because of the ignorance of the inquiring skeptic, that she must expect that any experience at all may lead to insights of the greatest importance. She should be open to finding value in unexpected places and also to having her principles of value expanded or altered in unexpected ways. Thus the most sensitive and discriminating attentiveness to each passing experience and the most wide-ranging study is evidently worth pursuing. And all of this, since it can be traced back to pursuit of a good associated with ultimism, must be regarded as authentically religious.

Can we say anything more specific about the nature and objects of this attentiveness and study? Let's start with attentiveness. When considering its objects we have to allow as relevant every stitch and fold in the fabric of our lives: the needs, capacities, and experiences associated with thinking, feeling, eating, drinking, sleeping, lovemaking, relating to others, walking in the woods, driving a vehicle, working with tools, coping with pain, and a thousand other "everyday" occurrences. For the practitioner of ultimistic religion, all of these things must be taken to have a deeper source and a potentially deeper significance than one would normally entertain in the absence of a religious sensibility. Since in having ultimistic faith I am going with the idea that an ultimate good in which I may participate is latent in reality, and it is unclear just where or how it is to be found (or even just what, in its details, it may involve), I had better learn to be more fully and appropriately alert in all my moments (including those I share with others or spend in listening to others' experiences), stretching my capacity for fine-grained appreciation of what is going on both in me and around me, open to and welcoming of changes and the surprising insights and opportunities they may bring instead of solidifying the patterns of the past and imposing my expectations on the world. This will make it more likely that I can contribute to a distillation of the information involved in becoming aware of the relevant facts about value, should they exist, as I am imagining that they do.

Now I have distinguished between "attentiveness" and "study," and though in the end this distinction may prove somewhat artificial, it will be useful for us to follow it out here when thinking about the nature of the attitude sought by the religious skeptic in connection with all such experience and activity as I have mentioned. It is natural to think of this as a meditative attitude, combining elements contemplative and (broadly speaking) reverential, constituting a disposition to be fully and respectfully present to such experiences and activities when they are undergone or engaged in, and reflective about them afterward—a "being fully present" and "reflectiveness" that is nourished and made more acute by seeking in periods of silence and concentration, or else in perception-enhancing activities (e.g., art making), the alignment and unification and receptiveness of one's powers and propensities that may be required for experientially based knowledge of ultimate things. Our skeptic will practice and apply the best techniques of meditation and contemplation known to her, and be interested in learning whatever she can about how to improve her attentiveness in these ways. And in doing so she will be exercising her distinctive religiousness.

But won't all of this attention to attentiveness make the religious skeptic we have described somewhat monochromatic in her interests? Won't it, moreover, make her contexts of activity and interaction rather *solemn*, and prevent her from acquiescing in flights of fancy, flashes of wit and humor, informal chatting—all things that add richness and interest to daily life? To this criticism (a reminder of the need for feasibility) we might respond with William James's observation that religion is above all *serious*,[7] and with the associated point that if it is *religion* we are seeking, a certain degree of solemnity and of what to others may appear as undue single-mindedness

---

[7] William James, *The Varieties of Religious Experience* (New York: Penguin Books, 1982), p. 38.

is not just to be tolerated but required. However, a better reply will point out that one can hardly be "fully present" to the whole range of human experience and expect the Divine in unexpected places without entering into such unsolemn forms of experience and interaction with the world as have been mentioned in just the manner that the critic—perhaps unduly influenced by *conventional* religion—supposes to be incompatible with a contemplative and reverential attitude. If such things really do add to the interest and richness of life, should we not expect our attentive religious skeptic to glory in them as much as in anything else, and to be ready to find news about ultimate things precisely in their non-solemnity? And to see that an undesirable single-mindedness or all-consuming obsession with being properly attentive is not to be feared, we need only more explicitly distinguish, as separately occurring, (i) the having of these experiences and the doing of these actions from (ii) the rumination over their significance and also (iii) the meditation or contemplation practices undertaken to enhance the sensitivity and penetration of (i) and (ii). The religious person I am imagining need not be giving conscious attention to attentiveness in the *very moment* of eating or working or laughing or whatever; indeed, if she were, she would not be freeing herself to enter into such moments fully.

With this criticism of attentiveness having been dealt with, we may turn our attention from attentiveness to "study"—and here I have in mind the various practices grounded in reading and observing, thinking and discussing which that word is normally used to designate, any intentional activity designed to expand our (propositional) knowledge and deepen our understanding concerning some subject. But study of what? What sorts of study count as acting on one's faith that ultimism is true? Well, certainly a religiously toned study concerned with any of the things already mentioned would count (which is why the distinction between study and attentiveness may break down in the end). Indeed, a very wide range of subjects present themselves to the skeptic in her ignorance as needing to be studied. Some sense of how wide can be derived from what I say in Chapter 4 of *Skepticism* about areas where we might, in the relatively near future, hope to find new and useful evidence relevant to the truth of ultimism—for example, in communication between (and concerning) religion and religion, religion and science, religion and art, and religion and philosophy. Our skeptically religious inquirer might, with her own unique purposes, and depending on the nature of her investigative abilities and opportunities, in some way address topics in any or all of these areas, as well as others not here mentioned.

Now such study may not immediately yield detailed results of the sort claimed by traditional believers, which the inquirer can incorporate into her life (such as knowledge that there is a personal God who intends all these things to be taken literally as gifts and to inspire a response of worship); but *precisely because* it is exercised within a context of relative indeterminacy recognized as such, the information base relevant to human spiritual investigation may be expected to be considerably enriched by it (given that details concerning the Ultimate are not assumed, many possible interpretations may be generated)—a result required if any development in this area of human understanding is to occur. The religious inquirer, if a skeptic in our sense, will see her studies as contributing to this end of human religious development. Her findings and those of all who join her may well be preliminary, and will be seen, at least initially, as epistemic possibilities to be set alongside other epistemic possibilities; but in arriving at them, she is acting on her aim to fill out our understanding of ultimate things—a form of behavior that, as we have seen, is quite clearly appropriate to the truth of ultimism, since it is one that may facilitate a deeper relation with the Divine.

So much for the religious practice of inquiry. It represents an important dimension of skeptical religiousness. But there are others too. Consider, for example, how our lives can sometimes seem fragmented, resisting significant unity; we may lose focus and despair of fundamental order and meaning. But as we saw earlier, it is written into ultimism and its entailments that there is a fundamental pattern of meaning and order in things. The religious person is therefore called to use this as a point of emotional stability, ordering her life in accordance with what she sees when she imagines ultimism true, navigating through apparent chaos with its encouragement on her mind.

Here too ignorance and limitation may be helpful; the complexities of reality are such that there can be a huge disjunction of ways in which what appear as infinitely knotted problems are capable of dissolving into new and meaningful perspectives that add layers of depth to one's life. In faith one must constantly teach oneself to be more open to such things, to look for them and take advantage of them when they appear, in imagination crediting them to the truth of ultimism.

There are also some further entailments of ultimism, entailments additional to those mentioned earlier, in which a similar practical relevance is evident. If ultimism is true, then chronic worry and anxiety—as well as a preoccupation with such forms of gratification as are easily available in the present—must betray shortsightedness. And if it is true, then what might otherwise appear as unduly risk-taking behavior on behalf of the good in fact more fully aligns us with the deepest nature of reality. It follows that we act on our faith that ultimism is true if in light of the latter's content we seek to *diminish* our worry and anxiety and our preoccupation with self-gratification in the present, and to *appropriate* the religious value of (what would be called) risk-taking behavior on behalf of the good when the opportunity to do so arises. The point is that faith with respect to ultimism must serve to put into a very different perspective from ones I might otherwise assume all my ordinary activities and concerns. All my worries and wants are now placed into the much larger context it offers and relativized thereby. And given such faith I have much less reason than I otherwise would to grasp at limited goods of the moment—as if they appear just by chance and must swiftly be seized before all opportunity to participate in goodness is gone—instead of putting myself on the line for the sake of possibly deeper and more enduring goods.

Some practical examples: How important, if I am a person of ultimistic faith, is my frustrated desire to have a new instead of a used vehicle or computer? How fearful (i.e., worthy of fear) are the illnesses that beset me? After all, I am having faith that much deeper and richer and more interesting things are afoot in the world than the possibility of driving around in a new car, and indeed, "driving around" might largely be instrumentally valuable in relation to those deeper things; thus I should seek to be content with the used car or computer I can afford, so long as it is serviceable. And I am having faith that ultimately all will be well; so I should seek to train myself to resist the disconcerting—and distracting—thoughts to which illness can give rise. Moreover, I might, on the basis of what it seems I am learning from the forms of inquiry we have just discussed, and from apparent necessary truths about value, respond affirmatively and resolutely to any opportunity to be of use in difficult parts of the world—for example, an invitation to participate in peace-making activities on the borders of Israel and Palestine—instead of allowing myself to be deterred by fear or other self-serving rationalizations grounded in short-term concerns. Or I might respond in the same way to a job offer that will have me moving out of my comfort zone—for example, I might move from my cozy home in North America's urban East to the relative unknown of the West, in order to pursue teaching that I think will broaden the influence of my ideas about fruitful ways of harnessing nuclear energy, or about the diminishment of religious violence, or even about the proper interpretation, in changed circumstances, of the American Constitution. Or I might submit, with similar resolution, to medical experimentation in the final stages of a terminal illness that promises to bring me much pain but may contribute to the healing of many in the future.

In any of these ways and many others like them I may seek to bring my life more fully into alignment with the content of ultimism, which in faith I am taking to correspond to reality. What they involve can of course be difficult at times, but even faith's difficulties only give new meaning (and plausibility) to the idea of faith as virtuous or meritorious. In any case, the point being defended here—that a faith response to ultimism can be put into action—is powerfully assisted by what we have seen.

But against some of these points objections may be raised. How, for example, can one cultivate emotions of the sort that go with, say, an increase in serenity without cultivating the beliefs such emotions presuppose? Emotions—as is generally accepted in the philosophical community these days—entail beliefs. To experience serenity in the face of an illness, for example, I must believe that all things considered, I will be okay. But a skeptic, of course, has got to get along *without* such belief. Hence her religiousness cannot involve the cultivation of the associated emotion and so cannot be shown to have clear content by reference to such behavior.

Here I think we need a more nuanced picture. *Imagining* such a proposition to be true and mentally assenting to what is imagined, especially in the absence of a belief that it is false and in the presence of a *positive evaluation* of the state of affairs involved (which evaluative belief can be every bit as real and strong for the person of faith as it is for the religious believer), may by itself produce the cognitive core needed for the relevant emotion. There is good reason to think that where this is in place, and cultivated over time, one may elicit the feeling state that is also required and experience some degree of such emotion—in this case, of serenity. (Recent studies bear this out.)[8] Another point is that in my description above of the impact of faith on the skeptic's emotional life I referred only to the *diminishment* of *negative or unwanted* emotion (in this case, anxiety), not to the *production* of *positive* emotion. And there are many ways in which one might successfully pursue the former—including ones involving the process just described—even if the latter is out of reach.

A further objection to the clarity of skeptical operational faith advances the following questions: Should faith that ultimism is true be thought to make risk-taking behavior of the sort I have described appropriate, rather than *complacency*? After all, everything is going to come out okay in the end, isn't it? Why should I put myself on the line for something the Ultimate will take care of?

But this objection forgets that ultimistic religion is taken up within a framework including attention to intuitively obvious moral principles, which bid us to involve *ourselves* in resisting evil, and which, in conjunction

---

[8] See Timothy Schroeder and Carl Matheson, "Imagination and Emotion," in *The Architecture of the Imagination: New Essays on Pretense, Possibility, and Fiction*, ed. Shaun Nichols (Oxford: Clarendon Press, 2006). Outside their chapter, in the same volume, see esp. pp. 8, 11, 96, 99. See also Robert Nozick, *The Examined Life: Philosophical Meditations* (New York: Simon & Schuster, 1989), p. 88.

with faith that ultimism is true, must ready us to imagine that something can be done about the horrors around us, if we put our shoulders to the wheel. (Here, as elsewhere, it is useful to compare what is appropriate in the way of behavior given the truth of ultimism with what would be appropriate otherwise. If ultimism were false, and were assumed false, we would have much less reason to think that the relevant causal relations are such that the world will be responsive to our efforts to heal its ills.) Moreover, the criticism presupposes a rather thin understanding of the religious role and value of risk-taking behavior on behalf of the good. The point of the latter is not just to "get things done," though that will naturally appeal to one who adopts religion with moral sensitivity. It also represents a way of seeking to deepen one's connectedness to any salvific reality there may be, of seeking to align one's own powers and propensities with those one imagines to be operative, at the deepest level, in the nature of things. How better to seek to deepen one's relation to a mysterious reality axiologically ultimate and also salvific than to deepen in oneself an engagement with the furtherance of good precisely in those places where it seems most stubbornly hidden or absent?

But the criticism we have been considering can be developed further. Suppose I am right in suggesting that "risk-taking behavior on behalf of the good" is indicated. What is to prevent the risk-taking behavior a religious person selects from being something rather less benign and more troubling than those I have mentioned in my examples? Might it not instead involve something like, oh, say, flying airplanes into towers? The general point here is that if we lack, in the basic ultimistic proposition, detailed content ruling some actions out and others in, perhaps only a partisan (in this case, liberal) bias will lead us to suppose that the actions that ought to be taken, given an imperative of risk-taking behavior, can clearly be delimited.

Let me respond first to the "general point," as it is asking for far more than is required for the clarity I am defending in this section. In fact, it is guilty of a kind of level confusion: it confuses the clear (and delimiting) point that *risk-taking behavior on behalf of the good* is called for with a clear specification of *which actions should be taken in instantiating such behavior.* In recognizing the relevance of the former, we already contribute to a well-defined skeptical religiousness; we do not need the latter for this purpose. For confirmation of this claim, notice how we will take some Jewish or Buddhist or Christian form of religion to have a clear and distinct shape even while allowing for disagreement among practitioners of that form of religion (for example) with respect to how exactly one should observe Shabbat or meditate on the *anatta* doctrine or witness to others about the saving power of Christ.

Now for the specific example—of terrorist acts on behalf of what is thought to be the good. I would suggest that such harmful terrorist acts (and other actions relevantly like them), done in the name of religion, arise in part from reflection on a much narrower range of investigative data, and from much narrower loyalties, than our practitioner of nonsectarian religion could ever countenance. (In a sense, and ironically, it is precisely because our skeptic is disposed to allow less detail into her cognitive commitments that the sort of risk-taking behavior we might expect from her is not of this sort.) Also operative, one suspects, is a confident religious belief—belief sufficiently confident to override the normal influence of common moral principles—and thus an attitude incompatible with propositional *faith*.[9] All things considered, then, this second development of the criticism is no more successful than the first.

4. *The Substantiality of Skeptical Operational Faith*

What we have seen so far illustrates how practical reasoning might proceed for a skeptic who in faith takes ultimism and its implications as a point of departure, and suggests a clear shape for the religious life resulting therefrom. What is coming into focus is a life that reflects an extension and significant enlargement of the concerns of any sensitive and conscientious moral agent: a life that involves more than would otherwise naturally be forthcoming in the way of a cultivation of optimism about, and meditative attentiveness to, the details of the world and how they may find their place within a surpassingly positive whole, and also continual attempts to bring all of one's activities and dispositions into line with this optimistic vision. But there are still more ways of deepening and extending what has been said. And in seeing these, we will be able to put beyond all doubt that simple ultimism suggests not only some clearly defined content for the life of faith, but also enough distinctive and diverse content to give

---

[9] In connection with my emphasis on faith as opposed to belief there may now arise the further objection that in "acting on" ultimism—seeking to do what is appropriate to do if it is true—one must surely cultivate belief that it is true. If ultimism is true, then obviously it is appropriate to believe it! This apparent problem can be dealt with by noticing, once again, that the more exact description of what we are about here is "acting on *propositional faith* that ultimism is true," and in this expression the continuation of propositional faith (as opposed to belief) is of course presupposed. What the person of operational faith should do is whatever seems appropriate to the truth of ultimism *and consistent with the attitude by means of which she embraces it.* One might also notice that the *most* exact or fullest description I have offered (see *Prolegomena*, p. 124) adds the qualification "given...the rest of *S*'s worldview," which worldview, for the person of faith, includes the proposition that evidence sufficient for belief is unavailable.

a very significant shape and substance—a robustness and richness and fullness—to such a life. (Ultimism, though it may in a sense be thin, is very far from being bland.)

Let's begin here by stepping back and placing some of what we have already said into a slightly different perspective. This will, at once, allow us to display the substance and richness we have already noticed to better effect, and provide a basis for the layers I wish to add to our picture of skeptical religiousness. And so consider how what we have at this point really represents *three mutually reinforcing dimensions or directions* within the skeptic's religious life—which we might distinguish as "downward" (into the depths of an understanding of ultimate things), "inward" (into the self, with the aim of reshaping its fundamental dispositions), and "outward" (into the world and an engagement with its needs).[10] All three of these can contribute to a transformation of the individual and of the world in ways that may partially manifest or in some manner prefigure the "salvation" or "wholeness" or "fulfillment" that ultimism bids us accept as the world's inheritance. And especially the last two are quite naturally linked to the notion of "ego-transcendence" (which is, to borrow from John Hick, a movement from self-centeredness to reality-centeredness; to borrow from Jesus, losing the self and so finding it) in terms of which the most profound religion, propelled by what the mystics say and a sense of humility before the Ultimate, has always sought to express itself. Surely all of this is not just clearly but also (in the relevant sense) *substantially* religious.

But a life for which ultimism provides the framework is, in many ways, a demanding life. Movement in those three directions and the associated transformation toward ego-transcendence does indeed bring us from propositional to operational faith, but anyone planning to undertake this form of travel is well advised to find and make use of whatever means of support may be available. And so we arrive at the idea of *two distinct levels* in the skeptic's religious life: we have the actions and dispositions that would immediately reflect the content of one's faith in ways already mentioned (these might be called first-order or lower-order religious practice), and then, also, the actions and dispositions that make actions and dispositions at the former level easier, more natural, or stronger (second-order or higher-order religious practice). Development at this second level is obviously also appropriate, given our knowledge of ourselves, if ultimism is true, and represents another goal that the skeptic acting on ultimism will pursue. In pursuing it, she does whatever seems most likely to help her

---

[10] Perhaps, depending on ability, temperament, and opportunity, the skeptic will focus more on one of these three directions than the others, but we should expect that some attention will be given to all three.

avoid or counteract what would militate against doing the things already mentioned—to avoid laziness, inattentiveness, superficiality and narrowness of vision, for example. Through noticing this aspect of skeptical religiousness, by the way, and through noticing the resources and forms of support that are available to the skeptic here, we can see in another way how an earlier suggested complaint about the *feasibility* of skeptical religion—that is, about our capacity to carry it out—is preempted.

No doubt there are various instruments of such higher-order development. Some—for example, private contemplation and meditation—I have already alluded to. But one of the most important (in part because it can incorporate the others), and one that has the further great advantage of providing a context in which everything we have said about the skeptic's religious life can be integrated and unified, is that of *religious community*. What I have in mind is a social group to which our religious skeptic belongs, whose members are all committed to the same general religious goals and also to assisting one another along the religious path. Participation in such a community can provide a structure for one's religious life, and enable one to sustain one's motivation for it and to pursue it in a disciplined fashion. From others in the community one may learn much of value, which may subsequently be incorporated into that life. And, of course, if the reality of spiritual transformation involves growth beyond ego-centeredness, as our own previous reflections already support, we have something that will most commonly and appropriately be expressed in relations with others.

Thus our person of nonsectarian faith might be expected to seek a community[11] of like-minded individuals, to make its purposes her own and act accordingly, allowing her dispositions to be shaped by the regular carrying out of religious commitments in company with these others. She may, as part of this, attach herself to a religious mentor, someone she considers to be farther along on the path she herself is traveling. And progressively becoming more fully freed from the blindness of ego-centeredness and coming to see and feel others' needs as clearly and deeply as their own, the members of such a religious community might be expected to support one another's survival and flourishing in a variety of ways and to engage *together* in much risk-taking behavior on behalf of the good of the sort earlier described.

[11] Or "communities," in the plural—it may be that she draws for support and discipline and relational growth and joint projects on individuals and groups from *various* parts of her life, deriving from the conjunction of all of these what others may find in a single community.

A moment ago I suggested that such being-with and being-for others in community has instrumental value in relation to the higher-order development of individuals. But one should not be misled by this to infer that instrumental value is the *only* value religious community can have for those who commit themselves to skeptical religion, or that skeptical religion is, at bottom, a purely individualistic endeavor. Indeed, neither of these propositions is true. This point can be secured simply by noticing that individuals can hardly realize the instrumental value in question— can hardly allow themselves to be shaped by or deeply and genuinely committed to life with others—unless they approach community with at least some *non*-instrumental motives, caring about it and its members for their own sakes. (There is a distinction here between justification and motivation which utilitarians since Sidgwick have been inclined to emphasize.) More important, however, is the fact—already mentioned a time or two— that "acting on ultimism" is not something done in a vacuum but instead necessarily mobilizes other parts of one's worldview, which for a properly sensitive skeptic will include propositions about the intrinsic value of other people and certain sorts of relationships with others in community, as well as about the desirability of a certain balance between self-relatedness and other-relatedness. Indeed, the presence in the skeptic's worldview of such propositions ought to be ensured by progress at the first-order or lower-order level of skeptical religion: from any of the paths of inquiry, self-awareness, and service, and certainly from their union, she will in time be brought face to face with them. It should be evident, therefore, that in what I have said about community we see not just some momentarily convenient but dispensable, or fundamentally utilitarian, coming together of individuals (say, in a reading/discussion group), but rather a deep emphasis on community-mindedness that is integral to skeptical religion.

This emphasis on community and the actions undertaken therein, understood as contributing to *both* of the aforementioned two levels in the skeptic's religious life, will be augmented in the next chapter's discussion of interaction with extant traditions and thus receive more support there. (What I've said about religious community so far is quite compatible with its being comprised simply of skeptics, who seek together to carry out the general commitments described in this chapter, developing new traditions of inquiry, discipline, and service without seeking any formal ties to religion as we have known it.) But already we can see, I suggest, that, together with all that has come before on the three dimensions of first-order religious practice, the emphasis on second-order religious practice convincingly shows how even *simple* ultimism suggests enough distinctive and diverse actions to make for a rich and full and substantial religious life.

5. *Some Further Objections*

In concluding this chapter, I want to answer three objections representing considerations that might prevent some of the foregoing from being convincing (even if only because one or other of its unfamiliar ideas—or else the notion that we need to be open to the unfamiliar here—has not yet sunk in).

(1) "It's all well and good to talk about having faith that the deepest reality is also the best and is winning or else will win out in the end, permitting the realization of the best that humans could seek for themselves and for the world. One might expect a religious person to believe this or at least have faith that it is true. But how could there be such a reality—how, in your terms, could there be a reality both axiologically ultimate and salvific—unless something like personal theism were true, unless, that is, the Ultimate is a *conscious being* who *intends* to bring the relevant good state of affairs about and has the *power* to do so? In other words, upon looking closely at the content of ultimism, it appears to entail theism (or something relevantly like it). But then, certainly, for anyone who recognizes this, choosing a purely simple instead of a qualified form of ultimism as the object of propositional faith will be impossible and so unfeasible."[12]

I answer that even if we were required to postulate consciousness and intention in the Ultimate to make sense of an ultimate good obtainable in relation to it, there would still be a simple/qualified split because of the many different ways in which such consciousness can be understood, ranging all the way from the usual theistic, panentheistic, and polytheistic options to scenarios not yet worked out but epistemically possible in which one finds consciousness and intention all right, but only as a small part of a much larger reality—perhaps one of which we are presently incapable of forming so much as an inkling. (In other words, the criticism's "or something relevantly like theism" hides a large disjunction.) But, significantly, it is far from clear that consciousness and intention *are* logically required here. Why should it not be an undesigned fact about reality that the good, properly understood, wins out and that there are ways for us to participate in this? Many philosophers are already willing to accept other such facts (for example, that contingent things exist), so why should it be supposed logically impossible that the scenario at issue here obtains as one? Notice

---

[12] I am grateful to Stephen Maitzen for the stimulation provided by his pressing this objection in correspondence.

that plenty of good things are realized without conscious design—those who find naturalism an epistemic possibility would have to say that *every-thing* good and not created by us might fall into that category. So to make sense of the notion at issue, perhaps we need do no more than to imaginatively extend this fact sufficiently far, supposing that in some undesigned manner unknown to us, all shall be well, and all manner of things shall be well.

Perhaps the reply will be that a designed good would be *better,* and that any reality in relation to which only an undesigned good can be attained, a reality without consciousness and intention, would have to be less than axiologically ultimate—contrary to what is claimed by ultimism. But this notion appears to reflect no more than one-sided familiarity with—and perhaps attachment to—our own experiences of consciousness and intentional creation and/or god-oriented religious ideas. To properly defend her claim at this point, the critic would need to provide a detailed specification (and comparative evaluation) of all the possibly relevant ideas, both extant religious ideas and ones thus far undeveloped, and of course no one has even attempted this. Nor should we expect success in such an attempt, certainly not at the present stage of human evolution. Of course that is not to say that the critic's claim is *false*—perhaps it will turn out to be correct. And it is important to see that our practitioner of skeptical religion need not deny this. All she need do is point out that there are many epistemic possibilities here—including some of those cited by the critic—and that in this intellectual climate no one can justifiedly claim to see that ultimism entails theism or anything like it.

(2) "Even if objection (1) is unsuccessful, it does appear that nothing *as* simple—as abstract, bare, and featureless—as you are proposing can be expected to be very appealing to the prudent skeptic. That is, even if ultimistic religion is *possible* for her, it is going to appear far too *demanding* (and in that sense unfeasible)—and so should not be expected to catch on any time soon. As Rodney Stark has it, 'people care about Gods because, if they exist, they are potential exchange partners possessed of immense resources.' And again: 'If there are no supernatural beings, then there are no miracles...prayer is pointless, the Commandments are but ancient wisdom, and death is the end. In which case the rational person would have nothing to do with church. Or, more accurately, a rational person would have nothing to do with a church *like that.*'[13] In light of these facts, why

---

[13] The passages from Rodney Stark are quoted with approval by Daniel Dennett in his *Breaking the Spell: Religion as a Natural Phenomenon* (New York: Viking, 2006), p. 191 and p. 197, respectively.

should we expect a skeptic to sacrifice the attractions of sectarian faith for what you are offering?"

But here again we see the unquestioned influence of things familiar—in this case the slant is not just theistic but Christian (notice Stark's reference to "church"). Have we spent enough time thinking about how, for example, death might fail to be the end without a suitably powerful personal being ensuring that such is the case? And shouldn't we avoid the assumption that religion is by its very nature self-interested (notice the reference to "exchange partners" and the suggestion of means-ends rationality) and that what the religious are interested in obtaining for themselves is inevitably such as they can with any hope of success pursue only by supposing that a God or gods will provide it for them in response to some well-defined action of their own? This is religion for infants. And although it is not to be denied that there are plenty of religious infants around, we may surely hope that our skeptic, chastened and enlivened by her skepticism, and influenced by moral principles that take her far beyond self-interest, will not be numbered among them. Though one of her aims, if she takes up religious practice, will indeed be an "ultimate good," we have seen how natural it must be for her to associate that good with the development of selflessness and the sharing of value with others.

(3) "Even if there are some errors in the reasoning undergirding objection (2), it is still hard to see why anyone should find skeptical or ultimistic religion very appealing. There is very little to, as it were, grease the wheels and move one to carry on. Suppose we imagine a community of skeptics interested in religion who have banded together. Still there is nothing very focused for them to get a grip on in their ritual or contemplation, and of course you don't even let them believe the little they do have! So why should anyone find what you have proposed to be anything more than a thin, watery, unpalatable broth by comparison with the rich stew of (what you are calling) sectarian religion, focused on a God or gods?"

Well, if I wanted to play with those metaphors, I could say that it is all too easy to choke on thick stew, and that a thin broth goes down nicely. (A thin broth can also be pungent!) There will be more on this in the next chapter, but here it suffices to point out, in a more summary fashion, that the religious world already includes individuals and communities reticent to put much detail into their doctrine, who flourish nonetheless. Think only of some Zen Buddhists—or even of the Unitarian Universalist Association. Though religious persons fond of personalistic, theistic detail have been heard to joke that "it's pretty hard to pray to a 'ground of being,'" not everyone finds the notion of a ground of being or other, similarly abstract notions religiously uninteresting or unstimulating, and of course not everyone thinks religion entails prayer. Here it is important that we try a little harder to exercise the will to imagine (in the sense in which that means being open to new religious possibilities).

To fill out what I have said about staying thin, let me briefly add a few points. I have mentioned a time or two that simple ultimism is equivalent to the disjunction of all more detailed religious propositions, both actual and possible. Now this disjunction may be rather large indeed. And it seems to me that recognition of the potential hugeness of the disjunction—of the richness of the range of possibilities here—may fulfill a psychological role in the life of the person of nonsectarian faith somewhat analogous to that fulfilled in the traditional believer by attachment to one of its disjuncts. Thinking of this richness without knowing what would be preserved by the correct conception and what set aside—which of course describes the state of mind of the meditating skeptic, in one of its modes—is one way of being freed to enter more fully into what "ultimate" really means. One should never underestimate the religious power of mystery.

There is also the point that a skeptic who adopts religion of the sort described in this chapter may very well be the recipient of what would be called "religious experiences," and that such experiences may fulfill a motivational function ("greasing the wheels") even where they do not produce belief. It is commonly assumed that one who has a religious experience—a powerful sense of the numinous, perhaps—must be left with a cognitive residue of ultimistic belief, and that only thus can her experience provide motivation to carry on, religiously. But this does not seem to be the case. A skeptic influenced by arguments against the belief-justifying power of religious experience of the sort I presented in Chapter 8 of *Skepticism* might have religious experiences, without preserving for very long or at all any tendency to believe religiously that comes with them. Yet she might be affected by her experiences, and in ways that make it easier for her to *imagine* the world religiously and also to act accordingly, which is to say that the experiences might have a motivational effect directly, without the intermediary of belief. Where the skeptic is a one-time believer, it is also possible that the experiences she has in the context of her new, more simple form of religion will be *new experiences*—less sectarian experiences, perhaps, or ones suggesting new possibilities needing to be investigated and urging and enabling her to continue with the investigation.[14]

---

[14] And even among our nonreligious experiences—or experiences not explicitly religious in nature—there may be many that are similarly motivating. As Charles Taylor has recently argued, for all of us, "in some activity or condition, lies a fullness, a richness; that

Such points, contemplated within the larger context of this chapter's discussion, may already be sufficient to lay our latest feasibility objection to rest along with the previous ones. But before we can be sure they are in their graves, we will need to consider at some length another important way of raising the feasibility concern.

---

is, in that place (activity or condition), life is fuller, richer, deeper, more worthwhile, more admirable, more what it should be....Perhaps this sense of fullness is something we just catch glimpses of from afar off....We are deeply moved, but also puzzled and shaken. We struggle to articulate what we've been through. If we succeed in formulating it, however partially, we feel a release, as though the power of the experience was increased by having been focused, articulated, and hence let fully be." (*A Secular Age* [Cambridge, Mass.: Harvard University Press, 2007], pp. 5–6.)

Simple Faith and the Complexities of Tradition

There are various reasons for wondering how skeptical religion, as I have described it in the previous chapter, must or can be related to traditional religion. Perhaps, as suggested once or twice already, we wonder whether the relationship might add something to the *substance* of skeptical religiousness. But a logically prior question is whether there can be any significant positive relationship here at all. And this gives rise to a new feasibility problem for skeptical religion. In this chapter, after articulating the problem in a bit more detail, we will discover various ways of bridging the gap between skeptical and traditional religion and erasing the concerns that have been raised. And, in the process, we will also find extra evidence for the substantiality of skeptical religion plentifully displayed.

1. *Is Skeptical Religion Unrealistic?*

It may seem, on the basis of previous chapters and the broad skeptical background to this discussion, that ultimistic religion must be carried out in isolation from traditional forms of religion such as Christianity, Islam, or Buddhism—that we're really talking about the development of completely *new* religious structures and communities. After all, I have suggested that "traditionalism must decisively be left behind," and that religion needs to be "born again." How *could* our twenty-first-century skeptic have much to do with religious people from such traditions as those mentioned, if she rejects the claims on which their religious practices are based? She thinks we are *only* in the twenty-first century, that literally hundreds and thousands of centuries of religious development may lie ahead of us. Thus she can hardly be expected to take traditional religion seriously.

But in that case, so it may be said, skeptical religion is far too radical, and indeed quite unrealistic. How can we expect a form of life that so divorces itself from the past to catch on, or to long sustain the interest of those who initially find it attractive? How can it put down roots sufficient to sustain itself, within a life or within the world? If there were no religious traditions already, ultimistic religion might represent a fine way to start, but of course there are, and many twenty-first-century skeptics will show the signs of their influence. *In this context* there is need of some way to *link* any continuing religiousness with existing religious traditions. But on my proposal such serious interaction is impossible. Therefore, my proposal is quite impractical and unfeasible.

A number of separate issues are raised by this objection. First, we must consider whether an "interactionist" or "engagement" option is most naturally suited to the large majority of us. It seems that, because of the great diversity among types of individuals, this is probably not the case: many human beings, indeed, may find the possibility of moving out into unexplored areas—of being intellectual and spiritual pioneers—quite appealing. The criticism may best apply to those skeptics who once were religious in a more traditional mode; perhaps for them some form of *re*integration with one or other of the traditions will indeed appear desirable. But not all converts to religious skepticism will be former believers. Some will have been disbelievers before. And why should *they* want a connection with traditional, sectarian religion? They may, indeed, be perfectly content with a community of skeptics of the sort described in the previous chapter.

But a more fundamental issue invites òur attention: Has the gap—the opposition—between skeptical and traditional forms of religion not been exaggerated? Some skeptics may indeed want to "go it alone," but a more mature and measured faith response to ultimism may lead elsewhere. Since ordinary, sectarian religious practices have sustained the religious impulse so far in the history of the world, we might indeed in some way be cutting ourselves off from the root if we didn't seek to learn something from them. And perhaps the enlightened among skeptics seeking faith will see this and so find the alternative to interaction unacceptable. It might also be argued that interaction with sectarian traditions simply provides additional avenues of religious activity for the practitioner of skeptical religion, that it represents only more facets of what I have called the different "directions" of her religiousness. The skeptic can (and should wish to) act on her simple faith by seeking closer relations with the sectarian traditions, humbly expecting to learn something about the Ultimate in *these* unexpected ways—at the very least finding this form of "religion to religion" contact helpful in the task of getting clearer about what is *possible* where the more detailed nature of the Ultimate is concerned.

So, on reflection, the alleged gap must shrink. By noting the possible importance of interaction or positive engagement with the traditions, we have already found a way of showing that our simple religionist, whatever her initial inclinations, is in no way required to deny it. Rejecting traditionalism does not entail turning a deaf ear to the traditions. It is very important to recognize here that by traditionalism I have meant adherence to traditional, sectarian *claims*. Since what is potentially of religious value in the traditions often does not depend on the truth of sectarian religious claims, one can reject the idea of adherence to such claims without losing out on that value. And rejecting the idea of sectarian adherence does not entail rejecting sectarian claims—at least in the sense in which to reject a claim means holding it to be false. The skeptic may only be in doubt about many such claims.[1]

On reflection we can also see that much of the beauty in religious scriptures (for example, stirring expressions of human frailty and religious longing) and much of the wisdom of religious teachers (for example, much of what is included in the Four Noble Truths and Eight-Fold Path of the Buddha) retain their power to motivate and illuminate even for one who, rejecting sectarianism, assents only to simple ultimism. And though most "traditional" religious claims are also "sectarian," it must be said that the traditions, properly viewed, will also be seen to include propositional formulations that are much less inclined to ascribe specific properties to the Divine. (Think of what would be said by the Islamic mystics known as Sufis as compared with the detailed beliefs of Islamic fundamentalism.) If, then, our individual wishing to take a nonsectarian approach to religion is looking at *these* aspects of the traditions, she will find much less to disagree with.

What all of this already suggests is that there may be common ground and areas of overlap linking the sort of nonsectarian faith I have been describing with at least some of what is to be found in the traditions. We need now to consider more carefully to what extent this is so, and what it implies concerning possible and practical forms of interaction or integration. I proceed by offering examples of possible interaction, sufficiently filled out to ensure that we can judge the extent to which they are realistic. And I begin by describing some possible forms of interaction (indeed, integration) between skeptical religion and Christianity—not just because it is likely that most of my readers are Christian or most deeply influenced by Christian traditions but also because, of sectarian forms of religion,

---

[1] Though if she accepts my arguments against traditional theism (see Part III of *Skepticism*), she *will* reject, hold to be false, such sectarian claims as entail traditional theism.

those that are Christian still tend to be among those in which a doctrinal and, as we might say, doxastic emphasis are most likely to be found. Here, then, we are likely to find as sharp a challenge as any to my attempt to close the gap between the skeptical and the traditional, the simple and the complex.

2. An Example: Skeptics and Christians

Suppose we have a skeptic—call her Sophie—who was once a believing Christian and, having become aware of all that I have discussed concerning both skepticism and faith, is inclined to adopt once more a religious form of life, centered on simple ultimism. And suppose that she is considering how this might be developed and structured. Naturally she will wonder whether there is any connection with the Christian tradition and her old community that is compatible with her now completely nonsectarian faith. Notice that her first problem will be one even persons of *sectarian* faith must face, insofar as their faith is beliefless: the problem of finding acceptance in the Christian community for her state of nonbelief, when the attitude associated with Christian commitment is generally one of belief. So in this respect she is no worse off than her sectarian colleagues. How might this problem of form (faith instead of belief) and her additional problem of content (her faith being directed to ultimism only, and not to any sectarian Christian propositions—e.g., that Jesus was literally God Incarnate) be resolved through renewed participation in her former community?

It may be helpful to consider more than one ecclesiastical possibility here, beginning with (what would be called) a fairly liberal one. If this *is* a proper description of Sophie's former community, then it may seem that she would not really experience any problems at all. Liberal Christians, on the usual understanding of this phrase, tend to be more willing to tolerate religious differences, either just leaving them alone in an attitude of friendly coexistence or actively seeking to learn from them. Sophie's description of her faith is therefore more likely to intrigue them than to put them off. There is, however, still the question of whether she could really be *religiously* integrated into the community once more, since she does not believe or have faith that the Ultimate is in any sense personal (which most liberal Christians tend still to believe, however vaguely), and since her faith does not obviously have any connection with the Christ images at the center of even liberal Christian beliefs and practices. Will she not be alienated by this, feeling pressure to return to what she has left behind and, if not able to do so, sensing that she really does not belong? Well, perhaps she will—it may be that Sophie is better off carrying out her faith commitment in another context. But there are also ways, which may well be realized, in which religious reintegration could occur.

Perhaps, for example, Sophie, sitting in her old pew or in conversation with old friends, is able to reinterpret the sectarian religious language of her community, thinking of it symbolically or metaphorically instead of literally. (As we will see in a moment, not *all* of the language of her community—much less all of the language Sophie uses in articulating what is central to her simple faith—will need to be interpreted in an exclusively nonliteral mode.) And so when there is a reference to God caring for us, perhaps she mentally "translates" this into the observation that things so often turn out better than it seems they will, and that more and more she is noticing windows of opportunity for problem-solving just by more actively and attentively looking for them with an attitude of expectation. And perhaps in imagination, and with a renewed assent, she represents the world to herself as one in which all of this has a transcendent source, and in which ultimately all shall be well. Further, when there is a reference to the death or resurrection of Christ, while perhaps also being reminded of and reinvigorated by the example of Jesus of Nazareth, who was not deterred by suffering from fulfilling his mission, as he understood it, she thinks of the ego-centered life of material pursuits which she is determining to leave behind, and the vision by which she is guided of value transcending any earthly thing and perhaps any present conception, in whose light the world has taken on a new and even richer appearance.

Such a process of metaphorization can provide *many* possible and religiously meaningful directions for thought and experience, utilizing any traditional doctrine as a point of departure; and so there is an important sense in which what the skeptic is developing for herself here is a "thicker" and more substantial religiousness, rather than the "thinner" and watered-down religiousness with which metaphorization is often associated by those who believe the claims involved to be literally true. The skeptic will not believe the relevant doctrines, literally construed. She may even believe such claims literally *false* if she sees that they depend on an attempt to fill out the ultimistic claim—for example, a personalist, theistic attempt—that she regards as unsuccessful. For this reason I would not say that Sophie can go so far as to call herself a Christian; she is now an advocate of skeptical religion. But that need not prevent the claims in question from performing a religiously useful function within the overall economy of her religiousness.[2]

---

[2] Perhaps it will seem that there must be a sort of duplicity involved in the practice based on metaphorization. Won't the skeptic appear to others, and also—at some level—to

As it happens, some liberal Christians—though they are more radical than the rest—are already inclined to accept and to promulgate metaphorized versions of the detailed sectarian claims of their tradition, so there may in the end be very little to separate Sophie from at least some members of her community in this example. Perhaps we may expect her to see this, and to be inclined to help others consider this step (and to help those who are already taking it to see that it does not entail a nonliteral understanding of all religious claims, including the simple claim that there is an ultimate and salvific reality). If this is the case, and if everyone involved is able also to see that taking this step does not remove but rather intensifies the need for deep intellectual exploration of ultimate things, Sophie may well find a place within her former community which religiously nourishes both herself and them, despite her lack of specifically Christian belief or faith.

What, now, if Sophie's former community is less liberal—perhaps fairly orthodox and evangelical? Is there any hope of religious reintegration in such circumstances? It is of course important to emphasize once more that Sophie may not wish for any such thing. But her former life in such a community, which she has found helpful and meaningful, and whose ethos she still finds a natural point of departure, emotionally, for attempts at a deepened spiritual life, may lead her to want to consider the possibility and make the effort.[3] Is there any chance that it will be successful?

---

herself, to be endorsing the literal content of these claims? But why shouldn't the skeptic be perfectly explicit about what she is doing, treating it as part of her own practice to be continually spiraling around to new interpretations and incorporations of things past, as well as new patterns of relationship with others, in this way making growth and development and more nuanced and complex but still peaceful relations with others explicit themes of her religious life? Moreover, if—perhaps to some extent through her own influence—it becomes more generally known in religious communities that there are these different ways of relating to creeds, hymns, etc., no one will be in a position immediately to assume of *anyone* that he or she is treating them literally and so to be misled if that is not the case.

[3] Here we once more bump into the issue, raised in the previous chapter, about the relation between emotion and belief. If, for example, when singing a hymn she learned as a child, Sophie experiences certain familiar emotions, isn't she also—at least for that period of time—in the grip of old beliefs that as a skeptic she is supposed to have shed? We can support a negative reply in stages: (1) First we must notice that the skeptic may be responding to the more general *implications* of what she is singing instead of to what she is singing per se (for example, to "I have a spiritual mission or vocation that is urgent and important and in harmony with the fundamental structure of things" instead of to "I have heard You calling in the night"), awareness of which has always at least implicitly been involved in the production of her emotion. (2) Next we should remember that, as we have found recent scientific studies to confirm, *imagining* these propositions to be true and mentally assenting to them can provide a cognitive core strong enough to support the feeling states characteristic of religious emotion. (3) Third (and here again I refer the reader to earlier discussion), we ought to recognize that it is not up to this "cognitive core" alone to generate the

I don't see why such an effort must *inevitably* be unsuccessful—though here the obstacles are more formidable. To evangelical Christians, both the specifically Christian content of religious claims and their literal interpretation, as well as the attitude of belief, may be expected to be more important. And so while her former community may well respond to Sophie in love and with an attempt at understanding, they are fairly likely to think that their love requires them to seek to persuade her to accept a more traditional form of religiousness; and the tension between her stance and theirs is likely to be more noticeable and troublesome.

Having said that, if Sophie has some grit and ingenuity, interesting and unexpected results may still occur. Evangelicals will like what they hear when she points out to them that she does not understand *all* religious claims metaphorically—that there is a hard bedrock of propositional content, literally construed, in her faith, one that they too accept. And this first recognition may lead naturally to a second: that many of the implications or entailments of their quite different propositional bases are the same. (It is important to notice that not all implications of sectarian claims are themselves sectarian.) The contents of an evangelical "statement of faith" will, for example, entail that there is an ultimate and salvific reality and also, as part of this, that the natural or physical world is not all there is; that what "more" there is should be construed as related to our own deepest needs and aspirations in a positive way; that there is an afterlife; that spiritual gain is to be preferred to material pursuits, where these conflict; and that humility in the face of the transcending ultimate reality is an important and religiously essential attitude. All of these things Sophie also accepts, in faith. And the actions and dispositions appropriate to the truth of these propositions will therefore be ones both Sophie and her evangelical friends emphasize.

We have, then, a couple of factors possibly leading to greater unity between Sophie and members of her community. But her evangelical friends may, further, come to admire her determination to adopt a religious form of life even in the absence of the confidence that sustains their own, and perhaps—though here one waxes optimistic—even be led to reinterpret or reject some of the claims of their tradition which do not sit well with such admiration and which they may regard as relatively inessential, for

---

feeling state: it has the help of a positive evaluation of the proposition involved, which for the person of faith may be every bit as real and strong as it is for the believer. (4) Finally, we must acknowledge that for the skeptic who finds herself with "old emotions," things are not actually quite the same: the feeling state is familiar and similar, but it is also somewhat bittersweet in a way it was not before precisely because the beliefs she once held are gone, and because her faith-centered cognitive state has to coexist with the recognition that her faith is a risk.

example, the old claim that all nonbelief is due to sin. And, of course, this might lead in many directions, with discussions about what really is essential to Christianity, and about the importance and implications of intellectual humility, cropping up everywhere. All in all, a more critical and investigative spirit might begin to emerge in such a community, and while Sophie may still be regarded by many of its members as something of an anomaly, that she will not be able to practice her religion meaningfully together with them is far from obvious.

On the basis of such considerations, I would be inclined to conclude that Sophie's nonsectarian faith need not prevent her from interacting with members of the Christian tradition, and even her former community, in a way that is religiously meaningful for her. Of course this does not mean that she can properly call herself a Christian. But the structure of her old religious life may, despite the considerable changes in her religious attitude and outlook, also provide a structure for her new one.[4] And it seems likely that a similar story can be told where the tradition in question is Judaism or Islam or Hinduism or Buddhism...instead of Christianity. Indeed, given that these traditions (perhaps with the exception of Islam) tend to be less doctrinally and doxastically oriented than Christianity, in them interaction and integration should be easier to realize. Now, of course, not everyone who arrives at the nonsectarian faith I have described will wish to integrate their religiousness with some existing religious tradition in this way, and there is nothing that requires them to do so. All I have here been concerned to show is that this is an option available which one may realistically pursue, contrary to the claim of the objection we are considering.

3. *The One-to-Many Option*

In the previous section I discussed some examples of what might be called *one-to-one* interaction between skeptical and traditional forms of

---

[4] It may be wondered whether, given the close connections I have imagined between Sophie and her sectarian community, we should not expect her to fall back into her old religious life, and to *lose* her new religious attitudes and outlook. Perhaps this will always be a possibility she has to ward against. But if—as seems feasible—she seeks out other skeptics, ensuring that her community is not *restricted* to sectarian-minded individuals, and if she engages in *active* skepticism as needed, reminding herself of the arguments that brought her to a more simple faith in the first place, there is no reason to suppose that the threat of such a reversion is any more serious or any less capable of being woven into her religiousness than that of any other reversions (e.g., to ego-centered behavior) she must continually be on her guard against in order to live out her religion successfully. (There will be more on these issues in Chapter 5.)

religiousness—and, in particular, one-to-one interaction in an integrationist mode. In such cases the skeptic's interaction with nonskeptical religion is, in the main, restricted to a single tradition. It is time to notice a very different form of possible interaction, what I call *one-to-many* interaction. This form of interaction too should be sought by those attracted to one-to-one interaction, as a way of augmenting or extending the latter; and it represents an alternative to one-to-one interaction for those skeptics who consider engagement with the traditions important but are not seeking integration or reintegration with any one of them. In developing this option, we will come to notice that there is an important sense in which—ironically—the practitioner of skeptical religion is *more* able to benefit from the particularities of the traditions than traditional adherents thereof, who, seduced by their belief, feel no need to get to know very many (if any) of the religious particularities falling outside their own religious category. It is even possible, as we will find, for one-to-many interaction to be practiced in what it would be natural to call an integrationist mode.

Let us now consider these possibilities, and why someone might wish to pursue them, more closely. A basic point to be made in this connection concerns the ignorance about much religious life in the actual world, both past and present, from which most of us suffer. Our skeptic is likely to recognize that in her preskeptical incarnation (whether her form of life then was religious or not) she got by on very little information about large tracts of religious phenomena; and she should also recognize that one of the reasons, though only one, for the present justification of religious skepticism is precisely this ignorance, shared with many others and productive of a situation in which many actual and possible versions of ultimism remain quite inadequately discussed. Recognizing all this, and given the features of her own religiousness that were sketched in the previous chapter, she has a very good reason to get to know the traditions better.

Each of the three "directions" of skeptical religiousness I have distinguished contributes to producing this reason. Interaction with the traditions may be expected to yield information pertinent to the inquiry, and resources to enhance the meditative attentiveness (not to mention continual opportunities to practice the latter), which belong to the "downward" direction. Interaction with the traditions may also be expected to be a source of helpful advice and inspiration in connection with the goal of reshaping the anxious and grasping dispositions of the self, the pursuit of which belongs to the "inward" direction. Further, it must generate ever new contexts and perhaps also partners for the constructive social action, the risk-taking behavior on behalf of the good, that belongs to the "outward" direction of skeptical religiousness. By *interaction* here—as the last point especially suggests—I have in mind more than just reading about the religious life of the world or in other ways restricting oneself to forms of contact that permit a large degree of personal detachment. I mean also getting to know religious people from various traditions and in other ways personally involving oneself in the latter. Only in this way can one really come face to face with the details of the world's religious life, as anyone who shares the skeptic's concerns (particularly her investigative and contemplative concerns) will wish to do.

This sort of one-to-many interaction with the religious traditions of the world is something that *any* practitioner of skeptical or ultimistic religion has good reason to seek, regardless of whether she wishes to maintain a special connection with one of the traditions. Indeed, it represents only another way of acting on one's faith that simple ultimism is true. It follows that we already have a complete solution to the problem that is my central concern in this chapter. The skeptical religionist who lives out her faith will have *more* positive interaction with the particularities of extant religious traditions than traditionalists themselves, rather than less, as the objection must claim. Thus any feasibility concern that may seem to be raised by such an objection is erased.

However, before leaving this chapter I want to examine one more possible form of one-to-many interaction—one that, as earlier suggested, we might indeed wish to term "integrationist" on account of the degree of intimacy between skeptics and members of various traditions that it exhibits. Actually, this "one more possible form" breaks down into at least two distinct possibilities. (1) The first involves an interesting extension of the one-to-one interaction discussed in the previous section. Here the skeptic's Christian community, say, represents but *one level* of a multilevel community, a community that shares certain very general goals (which the skeptics it includes may be leading all to see are bound up with a shared commitment to ultimism), goals that bring its various levels—Christian, Jewish, Hindu, and so on—together regularly for inquiry, contemplation, and social action. Perhaps the larger community even shares property, such as the space where, individually or jointly, its constituent groups meet. (2) The second possibility is a religious community of skeptics—but of skeptics who have come together from various traditions, to which they were originally wed in the sectarian, believing mode. Such individuals would bring the resources of their traditions with them, contributing what was distinctive and useful in them to the pursuit of goals held in common. In a scenario of this kind there might sometimes be, at the practical level, a weaving together of certain elements from diverse traditions, but notice that this does not amount to the sort of *credal* syncretism that would rightly be thought objectionable. Our skeptic, though certainly engaged in exploring diverse sectarian religious claims from extant traditions, is not committed to any attempt to blend or piece them together for the purpose of generating a new object of faith, not just because—on account of incompatibilities between them—success in such an attempt would be logically impossible, but also because the result of success would still just be another qualified ultimism tempting us to terminate religious investigation in its early stages.

Now it may seem that in such reflections all connections to the real world have been severed: that I am here indulging in nothing more than free-wheeling futuristic speculation and wishful thinking. But this assessment betrays less than full familiarity with what the world is starting to see in the way of interreligious discussion and cooperation. For one example, I would mention the journalist Winifred Gallagher's explorations of pluralistic and "neoagnostic" religious trends in her book *Working on God,* whose first chapter includes a description of how a Jewish synagogue in New York City is sharing space with a Methodist church, and how the two communities have forged a mutually respectful interfaith partnership.[5] Other examples may be found in *Encountering God: A Spiritual Journey from Bozeman to Banaras,* by Diana L. Eck, a religious studies scholar and director of the Pluralism Project at Harvard University. Eck writes:

> In developing a sense of *we* that is wider than the *we* of culture, religion, or clan, it will be important to have an image of what kind of human relatedness we wish to bring into being. People of each religious tradition have dreams of what the world should ideally be and how we should all be related to one another even though we are not all the same. Glimpsing one another's dreams is an important step in beginning to reimagine the *we.* Do we imagine ourselves to be separate but equal communities, concerned primarily with guarding one another's rights in a purely civic construction of relatedness? Do we imagine ourselves to be related as parts of an extended family, or as many families of faith? . . . Imaging a wider *we* does not mean leaving our separate communities behind, but finding increasingly generative ways of living together as a community of communities. To do this, we all must imagine together who *we* are.[6]

In such contexts, possibilities of the sort I have just sketched can hardly be considered unrealistic. Rather, they show that even in some such apparently unfeasible integrationist mode as I have briefly described, the "will to imagine" of skeptical religiousness represents a quite natural response

---

[5] Winifred Gallagher, *Working on God* (New York: Random House, 1999), pp. 21–31.

[6] Diana L. Eck, *Encountering God: A Spiritual Journey from Bozeman to Banaras* (Boston: Beacon Press, 2003), pp. 227–228.

to—and, in some cases, a natural extension of—recent developments in the actual world. Indeed, given the obvious connections to the discussion of "higher-order" religiousness and particularly of community in the previous chapter, we have now won the right to say this: not only can the *feasibility* objection we have been considering be answered, but we can also use the materials developed in doing so to reinforce points earlier made about the potential richness and fullness (in other words, the *substantiality*) of the skeptic's religious life.

Perhaps it will seem to some that in thus resolving the issues of feasibility and substantiality, I have strayed dangerously close to objectionable features of so-called new age religion. It may seem that in closing the gap between skeptical and traditional forms of religiousness I have simply promoted the opposite error of *confusing* or inappropriately *blending* these various forms of life. This sort of reaction is to some extent addressed in my comments above about credal syncretism, but here let me address it explicitly, so as to be sure that I have preempted any prejudiced conflating of what I am up to with what is intellectually objectionable in the so-called new age religion.

It's not hard to make the right distinction here, if one has eyes to see. For one thing, new age religion, insofar as it is intellectually objectionable, features, as already suggested, a careless syncretism or mixing of detailed religious *propositional contents* from various traditions: a little bit of Buddhist thinking from over there thoughtlessly combined with some native American thinking from over here, and so on. This is what its oft-mentioned "fuzziness" consists in. But simple ultimism excludes *all* such details. And while the faith grounded in it may come to be practiced with the help of ideas from one tradition or another, these will be ideas *about* practice or else doctrinal notions appropriated in a metaphorical mode. Ultimistic faith is faith *after* skepticism; it is indeed interested in creating something new, but it is not in the sense just mentioned "new age."

Objectionable new age religion also features a strong and virtually immoveable *belief* that the spiritual realm is real. This too—obviously—is absent from a faith response to ultimism, which presupposes skepticism. New age belief, moreover, tends to arise and flourish within a perspective naively ignorant of science, and often flies in the face of established scientific results. Ultimistic faith, on the other hand, grows in part from respect for the results of science; its skepticism is an *evolutionary* skepticism and it boasts no specific results of the sort that could possibly come in conflict with established science.

Finally, it is often complained that new age religion is rootless and superficial (this is related to the "fuzziness" point), forgoing the riches of long tradition for swiftly shifting infatuations of the moment. Here there might seem more of a connection with ultimistic faith, since the latter too appears relatively unconcerned about the past. But what the ultimistic perspective proposes for us, though new, is a demanding commitment instead of some glittery infatuation. And it is deeply rooted in a serious evolutionary stance, which can absorb the fullest, most fine-grained understanding of the history of religion (and indeed is in part based thereon). Moreover, it can, as we have seen, drink deeply at the fountains of past religiousness without becoming intoxicated at any one of them.

So let us be clear that ultimistic faith is not new age religion. There is no spiritual interest here that grows from confusion and religious illiteracy and could just as well or better be quenched by getting fully acquainted with the heart of some tradition such as Christianity. Rather, there is an attempt to think new thoughts about religion against the background of a shift from past to future within a skepticism that places *all* existing religious approaches in doubt—so-called new age as much as traditional.

4. *Results of Our Discussion*

Simple ultimism is set at a good distance from us, conceptually speaking: not so close and defined in its features as to foreclose all investigation and make us forget our place in time, but not so distant as to be incapable of touching us. It is as general a claim as one could adopt in faith without leaving religion altogether, general enough, indeed, to permit investigation of every other religious claim—every disjunct from that big disjunction. But even so we can get excited by what it represents (although conventional religion is often less interesting than naturalism, the *central idea* of religion is able to transcend this and any other non-ultimistic vision infinitely). We can even identify some of our "religious" experiences as possibly giving us some early form of contact with what ultimism represents, instead of falling into premature identification of their object with one of the standard conceptions of existing religion. And now we have also seen that simple ultimism has enough content to provide the basis for a clear, feasible, and substantial religious form of life. We thus have the best of both worlds: a framework for ongoing religious investigation of the whole panoply of more detailed religious claims, both actual and possible, to none of which one is committed, and also an object of religious intellectual and emotional and practical commitment, *ultimism itself*—the disjunction instead of any of its disjuncts.

So things look good for ultimism. Although until recently unrecognized and nameless, this claim now turns out to be the only one with any chance of being appropriately engaged in a religious frame of mind as we seek to emerge from immaturity. For as we saw in Chapter 1, if simple ulti-mism grounds a sufficiently attractive (i.e., a clear, substantial, and fea-sible) nonsectarian alternative to any sectarian faith response, then, for all the reasons bound up with the imperatives there mentioned, tradition-alism or sectarianism—that is, adherence to traditional, sectarian claims that qualify ultimism in some way—must decisively be left behind by any twenty-first-century skeptic seeking an object of faith. In this and the previ-ous chapter we have found plenty of reason to conclude that simple ulti-mism does indeed ground such an alternative. The inference—and with it the final conclusion of Part I—is obvious. If, recognizing the possibility of faith without belief, one wishes to pursue a religious path, one should also choose a faith without details.

PART II

Testing Faith

Is the Best Religion Good Enough
(to Satisfy Reason's Demands)?

SO FAR IN the book I have been concerned to establish that it is a simple or ultimistic or skeptical faith response that is justified for us early humans, *if any is*. This religious option must be regarded by the twenty-first-century religious skeptic as the only one worth pursuing. And, of course, getting clear about these things has permitted us to get a lot clearer also about exactly what this neglected faith response would involve, were it to be implemented. Having thus identified the target of our discussion, we must now move to consider arguments aimed at knocking it over and also arguments designed to prop it up. If the former arguments succeed, then such faith—and ipso facto *all* religious faith—is rationally unjustified and we should remain pure skeptics. Then even the best religion is not good enough to meet reason's demands. If the latter arguments succeed, then every one of us should be aiming at this sort of faith in a very different way—making it, as it were, the central target of our lives.

In this second part of the book, we want to learn more about the structure of such evaluative discussion—a structure dictated largely by my discussion of justification and of principles of negative and positive justification in *Prolegomena*—and also to deal with the most vigorous *challenge* to faith, an attempt to shoot it down which, if successful, would show that faith is not so much as negatively justified (henceforth "faith" and "faith response" just *mean* "simple or ultimistic or skeptical faith response"). We will find, in Chapter 5, that arguments in support of this challenge can be shown to fail when interpreted—as here they must be—as aimed at our sure- and swift-footed skeptical religion, newly divested of traditional baggage. But to help us interpret these results, within the context of the book as a whole, I first set out in Chapter 4 the overall structure of faith justification and our task in respect of it more fully and clearly.

The Structure of Faith Justification

1. *Principles of Negative Justification*

Since the business of evaluating responses to ultimism—as indicated in the Introduction—is at bottom a comparative venture, any challenges to faith are at least implicitly claiming that some other response to ultimism is preferable to the faith response. And in showing that no such challenge succeeds, we are showing that the faith response is at least as good a response as any other and so it is not the case that it should not be made—which is to say that it is negatively justified.

My discussion of these matters derives its structure from four basic principles worked out in *Prolegomena*. These principles specify certain conditions. In *Prolegomena* I called them the More Appropriate Action, the Unwarranted Evaluation, the Probable Falsehood, and the Greater Good conditions, respectively. Each condition is sufficient to remove faith's negative justification. And at least one *must* obtain if faith is unjustified (that is, if it fails to be so much as negatively justified). Hence, naturally enough, the relevant challenges will be ones claiming that one or other of these conditions obtains in the case of ultimistic faith. Here are the principles (for the context, see Appendix B):

P9. If, in certain circumstances C in which one might have faith, some other disposition or action is more appropriate to the aim apparently sanctioning faith, then faith is in C unjustified.

P10. If, in certain circumstances C in which one might have faith, it would not be good for the proposition involved to be true, then faith is in C unjustified.

P11. If, in certain circumstances C in which one might have faith, belief in the falsity of the proposition involved is epistemically justified, then faith is in C unjustified.

P12. If, in certain circumstances C in which one might have faith, some aim (independent of the aim apparently calling for faith) that should all things considered be pursued by anyone in C can only or best be pursued by not having faith, then faith is in C unjustified.

If any one of the conditions specified by these principles obtained, there would be a better alternative response, and so the faith response would fail to be as much as negatively justified. If, for example, a favorable evaluation of the state of affairs referred to by ultimism were unwarranted, some alternative to a faith response would have to be superior, and similarly if reason showed that the proposition involved—ultimism—was very probably false (in which case a disbelieving response would trump the others) or that there was a greater good requiring or benefiting from the absence of faith.

Now I have put these last points hypothetically, and in a couple of cases what we have is *only* hypothetical, since work I have already done shows that the condition in question does not obtain. Think first of P11, which, applied to our situation, refers to a condition that would obtain if ultimism were properly regarded as probably false and thus properly disbelieved. The investigations of *Skepticism* reveal that this is not the case (neither religious belief nor disbelief, but rather some form of religious skepticism, is justified) and therefore reveal that P11 cannot be used to show that faith is unjustified. By the same token, of course, they show that the alternative any challenger must seek to defend, by appealing to one or other of the remaining principles, is that of pure skepticism (if neither belief *nor* disbelief is justified where ultimism is concerned, then some form of skepticism is justified; and if that is not a skeptical faith, it can only be pure skepticism).

So what *of* the remaining principles? Well, it is quite easy to show that the Unwarranted Evaluation condition of P10 is no more applicable than the Probable Falsehood condition of P11 just mentioned. Indeed, it would be most deeply incoherent to suggest that it would not be good for ultimism to be true. For if we share existence with an *ultimate* reality, then, by definition, a degree of intrinsic value is realized than which there could not be a greater. And, of course, an ultimate human good would be good! Thus it is abundantly clear that P10 cannot be brought to bear here. This leaves us with P9 and P12, and with the awareness that one of the conditions represented by these two must hold if a faith response is unjustified (i.e., not negatively justified). Let's examine them in turn, beginning with P12.

P12, as will be recalled, has already put in an appearance in this book, in Part I, Chapter 1. There it was called upon to help us set aside as unjustified all forms of faith more content-full than simple ultimistic faith. Here in Part II it will be utilized by the challenger in an attempt to show that simple ultimistic faith should also be rejected. Specifically (and this is the central topic of the next chapter), our challenger will argue that a very great good indeed is ruled out by faith: namely, being true to reason. In flouting the verdict of reason and undermining its proper influence on us, so she says, the person of faith makes it impossible for such a good to be realized in her life. This is a challenge that we must expect will be very popular and vigorously championed in some quarters, so it is important that we address it carefully and thoroughly.

What we will find when we do so is that no argument presented in its defense succeeds. But is that enough to dispose of a P12-type challenge to the negative justification of faith? The challenge we have been talking about—phrased in terms of faith's betrayal of reason—represents, so it may be said, but one form that a P12 challenge might take. Even if we content ourselves, in the next chapter, that faith can be true to reason in the ways there at issue, we still have the possibility that some other aim *distinct* from the aim of thus staying true to reason—say, just for example, the aim of appropriate engagement in social issues of the day—might be slotted into P12 and used to achieve the challenger's desired result.[1]

This issue may be dealt with as follows. First, notice that we have already seen, in Part I, how skeptical religion incorporates and indeed enlarges upon concerns from various areas of life—including our social life—that

---

[1] It might seem that there is another complexity here. It may be said that because of the great breadth of the good being considered (of being true to reason), the nonsatisfaction of the relevant instantiation of P12 entails the nonsatisfaction of P9 *given that the latter is a principle of reason* (and also, and by the same token, the nonsatisfaction of the other principles, about which we have already satisfied ourselves). P9 is, as it were, one of the shadows cast by P12, when the latter is filled out as we are filling it out, a shadow that must be dispelled before we can be certain that the threat of P12 itself has been completely banished. However, this apparent complexity is only apparent. Principles P9–P12 divide up the relevant terrain between them. P12 is a separate principle from P9 and from all the other principles, and whether it applies must be regarded as a separate matter, to be separately considered—even if the aim discussed under its auspices is as broad as the aim of being true to reason. Since the shadows genuinely cast by P12 in this case are not being ignored but have been, or will be, independently dispelled, we may take the falsehood of the claim, to be considered in the next chapter, that faith involves a betrayal of one's commitment to reason as indicating the failure of what is distinctive about a P12 challenge phrased in terms of such a betrayal.

will animate the conscientious moral agent. The person who exhibits a faith response to ultimism, in other words, is already pursuing aims she ought all things considered to pursue that can with any plausibility be taken as lying outside the domain of a commitment to reason. Thus if faith survives the challenges of the next chapter, we can be pretty sure that P12 will not stand in the way of its being negatively justified. That said, it is still true that our strongest confirmation of the claim that P12 cannot in any further way be used to show that faith is unjustified will come later, in Parts III–V, as we gather our support for the *positive* justification of faith. If there are strong arguments *for* faith, as I will be arguing there, representing every area of our lives, then it follows that any independently specifiable aims that might be mentioned here are not only not hindered by faith but *furthered* by it. So while Part II shoulders most of the burden of problems associated with negative justification and expressible in terms of P12, our final denial of the latter's applicability will also be informed by the investigations of Parts III–V.

What about P9, the only remaining principle of negative justification? My way of dealing with P9 also brings us in contact with other parts of the book. Here the central issue concerns which dispositions or actions best support what P9 calls the aim that "apparently sanctions" faith. And what we need to notice is that for the discerning skeptic, and so for us as we discuss her situation, the relevant aim, whatever it is, will be the *same* aim that is referred to when we attempt to show that one or another aim we ought to accept is *furthered* by faith—that is, when we apply our criterion of positive justification (more on this below). Such a coincidence is not to be expected in every case of faith-evaluation; sometimes the general principles of negative justification, including P9, which are applicable to every case of faith (whether religious or nonreligious), can be applied quite independently of any considerations concerning positive justification.[2] But things are otherwise here. The aim apparently sanctioning skeptical faith for the reflective skeptic of our discussion who decides to adopt a faith response could hardly be other than the aim that, in that discussion, is regarded as the aim that *really does* sanction or call for (and therefore positively justify) such faith. This means that we cannot properly discuss P9 in

[2] Take the example of someone who has faith that he can escape a kidnapper by swimming across a wide lake, and who acts on this. It may be that he should actualize a faith response in such a case because of, say, the importance of the aim of supporting one's family, but that this aim is not on his mind: *his* aim is to get his share of money from an embezzling scam that is underway. Just because the former aim is not on his mind, if we were thinking only about negative justification and applying P9 here, we wouldn't have to introduce talk about positive justification at all: the aim that generates positive justification is here *not* the same as the aim "apparently sanctioning faith."

connection with our case without introducing aims that I will be putting forward in defense of the claim that skeptical faith is positively justified.

So how should we deal with this overlap? We could, I suppose, develop all of the aims in question and then discuss P9 by reference to each of them, asking whether hope or acting-as-if or some other action or disposition distinct from faith is more appropriate to that aim than faith itself, leaving for Parts III–V the defense of the claim that faith is superior to all such actions or attitudes in respect of that aim. But evidently the claim that faith is superior to other ways of pursuing the aims in question *entails* the claim that it is not inferior! So the most expeditious way of dividing up the terrain here will involve allowing our verdict on P9 to emerge from our later application of the criterion of positive justification.

It is clear, therefore, that our discussions of negative and positive justification—here in Part II and in Parts III–V—must be seen as connected in a variety of ways. I move now to fill in some remaining details about these connections.

2. Negative and Positive Justification

To identify these details properly, we need to have before us the criterion of positive justification to which I have already several times referred. Here is what I have been talking about:

> P16. A faith response is positively justified if (1) it is negatively justified and (2) some aim that should all things considered be pursued by us can only or best be pursued by making such a response.[3]

Notice that P16 purports only to provide a *sufficient* condition of faith's positive justification. Perhaps there are other ways in which one might seek to support the latter—say, through an application of decision theory. But in this book (in part because of how I want to appropriate the relevant parts of the philosophical tradition; in part because our twenty-first-century skeptic will want to beware complex and perhaps unrealistic

---

[3] It might be thought that "only or best" allows a very low probability of success. The best can in absolute terms be weak. Is this enough for positive justification? But here I rely on the aim in question being, as indicated, one that *we ought all things considered to pursue*. If I am rationally committed to the pursuit of some aim, then I am rationally committed to choosing some way of pursuing it, and even if all the ways including the best way are somehow problematic, wouldn't my choice be inferior to what it could have been if I choose a way that is *less* than the best?

theory), I appeal to certain simple arguments in connection with clear intuitions about what ought to be the case. Now these arguments, developed in Parts III and IV, in conversation with figures spanning the history of philosophy of religion, might individually and without recourse to our principles be taken as providing positive justification for faith, but I also want to tease out from them the various aims to which those principles can be applied, thus to support my conclusion about positive justification the more precisely and convincingly.

P16(2) is clearly of central importance here. In Parts III–V we will discover numerous aims that strongly appear to satisfy it, that apparently should be pursued by us and are such as can only or best be pursued by making a faith response to ultimism. In each case, in one way or another, it will become evident that alternative ways of seeking to satisfy the aim—ones not involving faith—are inferior to faith itself, which means, given our discussion in the previous section, that for *each such case* it will become evident that P9 is inapplicable. And all of these aims taken together, in conjunction with the arguments supporting them, will (as we already saw in the previous section) show that, for any such aim, P12 too is inapplicable. But if P12 and P9 are both inapplicable, then—given our points earlier in this chapter about P10 and P11—it immediately follows that a faith response to ultimism is negatively justified. And, of course, if this is so, then P16(1) is satisfied.

And P16(2)? Well, we have just seen that the claim that it is satisfied will be strongly supported many times over in Parts III–V. But what about the "all things considered" clause contained in it? Even if the suggestion that we should pursue some aim is strongly supported, can we really say that it is supported *all things considered*?

The final detail to take note of here involves another connection between our discussions of negative and positive justification. If we have powerful reasons for supposing that some aim should be pursued by us, these could surely fail to go through—fail to provide all-things-considered support—only if some *conflicting* aim has at least as much of a claim on our attention. But that is to say that if indeed we have the aforementioned support *and P12 has been shown to be inapplicable through a multiplication of aims supporting faith,* there is nothing that could lead us to withhold the affirmation "all things considered." Which is to say that, given the work of Parts III–V, P16 *as a whole* must be satisfied by a faith response to ultimism, and such a response must be both negatively and positively justified.

Let us turn now to the important contribution of the next chapter to the creation of those happy circumstances.

CHAPTER 5

How Skeptical Faith Is True to Reason

1. Pure Skepticism More Pure than Pure Faith?

What many will consider the strongest challenge to faith claims that the aim of staying true to reason should all things considered be pursued by all skeptics contemplating faith, and that this aim can only or best be pursued by not having faith. If this is true, then, of course, by P12, faith is unjustified. Now this "staying true to reason" may sound like a metaphor that needs to be cashed out. But I suggest that the challenge is plausibly viewed as intending it quite literally: any twenty-first-century skeptic who sees aright the situation she is in as she contemplates having faith (and, of course, perhaps many do not see it aright) will regard faith as a *betrayal* of reason, as an act and policy of unconscionable disloyalty. For such an individual, so says the challenge, pure skepticism must seem clearly preferable to faith.

But exactly why should we suppose that faith represents such a betrayal of reason? Why must faith and reason be estranged? And what exactly is the great good represented here by being *true* to reason, which we should all things considered pursue? For that matter, what is *reason*?

Let's address the latter two issues first. Reason, in challenges of the sort in question, appears usually to be regarded as something like the general human capacity for deliberate (and at least potentially successful) truth-seeking and problem-solving in pursuit of understanding, together with various narrower dispositions of mind that are activated when that capacity is exercised. Being true to reason would presumably involve making its goals one's own—desiring and pursuing them for their own sake—and not deviating from the path this sets one upon. Presumably by extension it would also involve thinking and otherwise behaving in accord with established results of the exercise of reason.

Some such construal will allow us to make the strongest case for our challenge. For it is precisely an unflinching commitment to truth and understanding that has brought the skeptic to her skepticism; hence if it can be shown that this would be undermined by a move in the direction of faith, we would have a very serious and pressing problem indeed. Without this commitment the skeptic is (whether she recognizes it or not) adrift at sea, with her very identity as an inquirer in shambles. Quite apart from this disastrous consequence, we must surely acknowledge, as I myself did at the outset of *Skepticism* (p. xiii), that "something of great worth would be forever lost to us should we relinquish our ambition to know and understand—in particular, that a certain relation to truth, if it can be achieved, is of great intrinsic value, and human dignity, if it obtains at all, such as to warrant our pursuing an ever deeper understanding of how best to support it." What could possibly be presented on the side of faith to compete with this?

The final remark here is revealing: if there *were* a good as important as or more important than the good of being true to reason that could only or best be pursued by having *faith*, then this attempted proof via P12 of the claim that faith is unjustified—that pure skepticism is a better, more worthy response to ultimism than faith—would not go through. And it might seem that, for all we have said so far, the arguments yet to be developed in Parts III–V might conceivably expose such a good. But let us grant at this stage that there is no such good: later discussion, I am happy to stipulate, reveals no good on the side of faith as important as or more important than the good of being true to reason. (It is indeed hard to see how there could be such a good, since the very act of pursuing it, at least if conscientiously undertaken on rational grounds, could be construed as part of an attempt to be true to reason.) In other words, let us grant that there is a very great good here which the skeptic is in no position to give up, an aim—to maintain her commitment to truth and understanding—that she has *all things considered* good reason to pursue. My strategy will involve not the production of another aim to compete with this one, but rather a demonstration that by grafting faith onto her skepticism, the skeptic need not pursue this aim any less well.

Why does the challenge suppose otherwise? Well, it may be said that in faith one must portray the world to oneself, and act, in a manner quite at odds with what the intellect has revealed. Reasoning indicates that ultimism is just as likely to be false as true, or that the relevant likelihoods cannot be determined, and yet in her acts of imagination and assent, and in acting upon this assent, the person of faith emphasizes only the possibility of *truth,* setting aside the possibility of falsehood. Such an attitude not only misconstrues the facts on matters that must be of the greatest importance to a lover of wisdom, but encourages the development of wishful thinking and attitudes of pretense and, in general, sloppy and nondiscriminating habits of mind. These things must wear away the sharpness and alertness and fair-mindedness that anyone seeking truth and understanding will prize, and so they represent a betrayal of reason. Being *true* to reason in such a case requires, instead, holding the possibilities of truth and falsehood in ultimism equally before one's mind and giving equal weight to each (or else acquiescing in indeterminacy), waiting for more evidence before acting. And this is something one evidently cannot do while having faith. A veritable wave of Enlightenment opinion released by figures like Locke and Hume in the seventeenth and eighteenth centuries, and ridden by Clifford and Russell in the nineteenth and twentieth, may be expected to bring this negative verdict on faith crashing to our shores.

But let us see whether the intellect itself supports what is here claimed in its defense, when we look with as much sharpness and alertness and fair-mindedness as we can muster at the details of the challenge. Perhaps the first thought worth recording is that this challenge is a very general one: if the argument given is correct, then it seems to rule out faith of *every* kind (for every kind of faith involves the assent that is being criticized). Yet surely there are cases where it is reasonable—consistent with a commitment to truth and understanding—to have faith. In *Prolegomena* (p. 132) I gave many examples of faith:

> I might have faith that I put enough money in the parking meter, faith that I will pass a course, faith that I have right now the *ability* to pass the course, faith—after societal collapse—that a new and better government is forming, faith that I will get a job, faith that the individual for whom I am campaigning will win the election, faith that someone will discover and prove the falsity of a murder charge on account of which I lie rotting in jail, faith that poverty will be wiped out or that democracy will spread throughout the world or that my friend is not the criminal that some pretty striking evidence suggests he is, and so on and so on. And, of course, I might also have faith that God exists or that the Buddha told the truth about enlightenment, or that there is an ultimate and salvific reality of some sort or other.

Do we really want to say that in each of the cases listed, having faith would amount to a betrayal of reason? Notice that in none of them are we talking about trying, self-deceptively, to form *belief* of the proposition in question, only about offering the nonbelieving assent of faith. Isn't it evident that there may sometimes be good reason to do *that*? If, for example, I find myself without the belief that I will be able to pass the course, or that my friend, to whom I am loyal, is not a criminal, might there not in certain circumstances still be good reasons—maybe even moral reasons—for having *faith* that it is so? If that is so, then reason itself may sometimes recommend having faith. In these cases, whether faith is in accord with reason cannot be determined until all of reason's voices have been heard, and the challenge, as urged above, is listening (at best) only to one of them.

The response just outlined is a tempting one. Perhaps we should think twice about challenges to religious faith given what we naturally find ourselves saying about *other* sorts of faith. But I do not wish to place a great deal of weight on this response. For there are differences between religious faith and other sorts of faith: it may be said, for example, that the former, unlike the latter, concerns the deepest, most important matters, or that it involves a total life commitment—and that these differences make all the difference. So let us consider again the challenge set before us, assuming that it is intended to apply only to religious faith. And I suggest we begin by looking at the claim that in setting aside the possibility of falsehood in ultimism, the person of faith "misconstrues the facts" on matters religious. Which facts are these?

We seem to have two main possibilities: either facts about how the world is in respect of ultimism or facts about our *evidence concerning* how the world is. Of these, it is the former that is most strongly suggested by the challenge. If that suggestion were correct, and if, moreover, the person of faith "misconstrued" those facts in the sense of *believing* in a manner contrary to them, then we would clearly have a problem. But notice that neither of these conditions obtains. For, given our assumption that religious skepticism is justified, we have to allow that we don't know how the world is in respect of ultimism—none of us knows either that ultimism is a fact or that its denial is. And so we are not in a position to say, with respect to any view concerning ultimism, that it construes the facts on *this* matter correctly or that it fails to do so. Furthermore, the skeptic who adopts faith, remaining a skeptic as she does so, is not inclined to believe that ultimism is true, even if she sets herself to imagining that it is and mentally assenting to this possibility. Hence we have no reason at all, so far forth, to say that the person of faith "misconstrues the facts" on matters religious.

But religious faith, it may be said, still badly and unconscionably misconstrues the facts, even if "misconstrues" is taken in a weaker sense than one implying belief, and even if those facts are only facts about our evidence. After all, the available evidence, as has been noted, is indecisive and so we have no basis for taking ultimism to be true (those are the facts), and yet the person of faith assents to a contrary picture (and that is the relevant misconstrual of the facts).

But if, as we must, we understand "taking ultimism to be true" to mean "either believing or having faith that ultimism is true," then the inference in which the former phrase is here embedded simply begs the question: it may be granted that where the available evidence is indecisive we have no basis for *believing* ultimism to be true, but whether the same conclusion holds for faith is just what we are investigating.

However, there is a more fundamental problem for the revised objection than that. For the person of faith does not assent to any picture according to which the available evidence is decisive instead of indecisive. She is not committed to taking the *available* evidence to be strongly in favor of ultimism, only the *total* evidence. (She allows that the evidence available to us is weak, but imagines that if *all* the evidence were taken into account—the available evidence together with whatever relevant evidence may lie outside it, presently unrecognized—it would be seen to support ultimism.) Now the truth of the proposition that the total evidence favors ultimism is quite compatible with (a) the available evidence being weak and with (b) the falsehood of ultimism being epistemically possible. Thus there is no reason to suppose, if (a) and (b) are the relevant facts, that what the person of faith imagines and takes on board is contrary to the facts. Indeed, if you were to interrupt someone consciously practicing skeptical faith to ask her about the force of the available evidence relevant to ultimism, she would immediately and quite sincerely and quite consistently with her faith commitment reply that it is weak and indecisive. The more we think about how large may be the class of unrecognized evidence relevant to *ultimism*—how much evidence may currently be unavailable to us because it has been overlooked or neglected or is presently or permanently inaccessible to finite and immature creatures like ourselves—the larger the possible gap here between "available" and "total" will come to appear. And this makes it possible to have religious faith while fully and wholeheartedly granting that the relevant available evidence is weak and indecisive.

What our skeptic imagines if she has faith is therefore not at all *contrary* to what the intellect has revealed. However, it will be noticed that it nonetheless in a sense *goes beyond* what the intellect has revealed: if I imagine that ultimism is true, and assent to this, I am giving my assent to something that reasoning does not fully support as true. Can it now be claimed that *this* is a problem—that to go beyond what the intellect has revealed in this way is still to go against it? This would now have to be taken as meaning something other than "against or contrary to our evidence": given what we have seen, we will have to understand "contrary to reason" in a larger, more general sense than that. So what might the new claim be?

Perhaps it will not be new at all but only the other half of the original complaint—that a welcoming of faith's assent in such circumstances encourages the development of wishful thinking and, in general, sloppy and nondiscriminating habits of mind unsuited to the pursuit of reason's goals. Does proper reasoning reveal that *this* is true of skeptical faith, even if it refutes the claim that to have such faith one must "misconstrue the facts"?

It seems not. Wishful thinking of the sort at issue here apparently entails hiding unpleasant or undesirable truths from oneself in a process involving the production of *belief* that things are otherwise. I might, for example, convince myself that my pet theory of origins is true, ignoring all counterindications; *that* would certainly be "wishful thinking" of a sort that expresses a vice if loyalty to truth and understanding is a virtue. But we have just seen how all of this is inapplicable to faith. The person of faith, eschewing belief, manages to project and assent to brighter possibilities without in this way hiding from herself, for example, the fact that the available evidence does not support ultimism. Therefore she cannot correctly be said to be indulging in wishful thinking.

Perhaps it will be said that even if this is so, there is still a weaker sense in which inappropriately wishful and slanted thinking is going on here. Clearly the person of faith is thinking of positive things when she mentally assents to ultimism, and surely these are such as anyone would wish to be true! Because of this there is still an unattractive element of pretense or make-believe (of "Let's pretend") in the faith I am defending. Faith seems indeed simply to evince a wish to mentally escape from unpleasant realities that an intellectually braver, more mature soul would face head-on; it involves us in playing a children's game called "Let's pretend that everything is okay."

Here we are ourselves playing with a caricature of faith, but let's give these ideas about pretense a closer look. Notice, first, that (as already suggested a time or two) there is no possibility at all here of pretense *to others,* since faith that *p* does not require affirming that *p* when asked whether *p* (and indeed, precisely because it would be misleading, the discerning skeptic will see such affirmation as rationally forbidden). But might there still be a worry about pretense to oneself? It seems not. As reflection on examples will reveal, to pretend that *p* in this sense minimally entails representing *p* to oneself as true *while believing it to be false.* I cannot *pretend* that aliens are invading unless I am pretty sure they are not. When one says "Let's pretend," one is saying "Let's treat this as true even though we know it's false." This is why pretense is so naturally associated with intellectually nonserious activities, including children's play. (When we are engaged in intellectually serious activities, trying to come to grips with reality, there may seem to be little time for entertaining recognized falsehoods.) Now the person who decides to adopt religious faith of the sort I have been talking about does not believe ultimism to be false; she is only in doubt about that. And the activity in which she engages by doing so is an eminently serious one (more on this in just a moment). Hence she cannot and does not pretend that ultimism is true.[1]

But what about the escapism of regularly imagining and endorsing, mentally going along with, good possibilities on an ultimate scale, even though the evidence doesn't support them? (We needn't call it "pretending" to sense the problem, our critic might say.)[2] There are a number of assumptions here about the context for faith's assent which should themselves be challenged. Why suppose that the person who adopts a faith stance is doing so in order that unpleasant realities need not be faced? Why should her motivation not be in part provided by the fact that, with an attitude of faith, she can *more effectively* face and deal with the unpleasant realities in her life, as reason instructs her to do? If her faith makes it easier to enter, emotionally, into positive possibilities, why must these concern only herself and her own needs? Not to put too fine a point on it: why must faith be self-centered and immature, as is suggested here? We have

---

[1] Perhaps it will seem that that the notion of pretense does not have to be given as strong a sense as I am here supposing to belong to it. We may pretend that something is so even when we are simply *unsure* as to whether it is or will be so. For example, if my grandchild is worried about his mother driving home in the midst of a snowstorm, might I not say to him "Let's pretend that she is all right and will make it home okay"? (This example was offered to me by Bill Wainwright.) But as Paul Draper has commented in conversation, the grandparent of this example had better hope that his grandchild understands the word "pretend" in the same way he does! That the Draper comment is amusing already tells us that the proposed weak sense of "pretense" is not the one we ordinarily use. (For additional support, see the various discussions of pretense in *The Architecture of the Imagination: New Essays on Pretense, Possibility, and Fiction*, ed. Shaun Nichols [Oxford: Clarendon Press, 2006], which—as the title of the book suggests—tend just to assume the stronger sense.)

[2] A further challenge not considered in the text might at this point distinguish between pretending that ultimism is true and pretending that I *believe* ultimism is true. Am I, in having faith, doing the latter even if not the former? Some support for moving in this direction may seem to come from Alvin Goldman, who argues that suppositional imagination—of the sort I have argued is involved in propositional faith—must be viewed as a species of *enactment* imagination, because in making a supposition, *I enact belief:* that is, I try to create in my mind "at least a rough facsimile of such a [believing] state" through imagination. (See his "Imagination and Simulation in Audience Responses to Fiction," in *Architecture of the Imagination*, pp. 42–44.) But for this to seem a problem one would have to forget *how* rough a facsimile imagination must be in the case of beliefless faith (cf. my Introduction's comments on the nature of propositional faith). In any event, that the word "pretense" does not apply, via Goldman, to my conception of faith in any except an innocuous sense divested of all its problematic features can be seen, again, from the fact that the clearheaded person of propositional faith, recognizing the important differences between belief and faith, thinks of herself as instantiating an *alternative* to belief and presents herself as such if in any way the question arises, instead of insisting—as anyone who in an objectionable sense was pretending to believe would do—that her state is really one of belief.

already seen (in Part I) that the content of faith is such as to lead in quite different directions. An unbiased account might therefore call the sort of thinking involved here *hopeful* thinking, placing the accent on the possibility of a universal good, strenuously pursued, instead of *wishful* thinking, with the latter's suggestion of self-centered escapism.

We might now seek to give a slightly different slant to the objection about slanted thinking. By indulging her desire for an overall good world, concentrating on that possibility to the exclusion of others, isn't the person of faith going to find it progressively more difficult to seriously entertain and carefully assess alternative metaphysical possibilities—which possibilities anyone committed to truth and understanding must, however, seek to give equal weight? Indeed, ultimistic faith would appear to be subject to the same criticism I leveled at its sectarian cousins in Chapter 1: to adopt it, one must "set aside all questions about the possibility of truth in competing claims." Is it not therefore just as intellectually stultifying as what I rejected there?

Let me begin my reply by examining this alleged analogy, in respect of openness (or rather closedness), between ultimistic faith and sectarian faith. Should I reject the former, on openness grounds, if I reject the latter? This idea does not hold up to scrutiny. For in the former case there is room for just the sort of intellectual exploration of diverse religious possibilities that in the sectarian case is ruled out. And we must remember that to pursue religious goals at all, one must set aside alternatives to ultimism like naturalism, whereas—this was demonstrated in Part I—it is not the case that to be religious one must adopt a particular understanding of ultimate things and set aside all others. So there can be a rationale for *this* "setting aside" that is not available to the sectarian. Finally, this setting aside is done after the question whether the issue of "ultimism versus alternatives" can currently be settled has been investigated and answered in the negative (that's what *Skepticism* was all about). Whereas in the case of the setting aside of sectarian alternatives, (i) there is a greater likelihood, because of their very specificity, that sectarian alternatives can fairly swiftly be assessed (this was argued with respect to the particular case of traditional theism in Part III of *Skepticism*), and (ii) much such investigation remains to be done. For these reasons, I suggest that an argument from analogy of the sort suggested by the challenger is not going to work here.

Some of the points I have just raised also permit a reply to the present objection's more general claim, which might proceed *without* the analogy—the claim about a positive slant and less than appropriate (i.e., full) attention and openness to alternatives to ultimism like naturalism. The skeptic who is following the path represented by my discussions in previous books *already has* given full and careful attention to the belief that ultimism is false, and has been led thereby to the conclusion that such belief cannot presently be justified. In such circumstances, it is perfectly consistent with her commitment to truth and understanding for her to turn her attention elsewhere, while keeping an eye open, of course, for new and more successful arguments justifying anti-ultimistic belief. And faith, though not compatible with a vigilance and evenhandedness in respect of such arguments as thoroughgoing as was exhibited by the skeptic before, *is* compatible with keeping that eye open. Faith is also compatible with the other element of openness discussed in Chapter 1, namely, a readiness and willingness to accept new beliefs as justified should their justification be made evident. Thus where the nature of faith and the context for the skeptic's faith decision are properly understood, we can see that the degree of openness and attention to alternatives consistent with her decision is fully adequate to a commitment to truth and understanding.

And here there are also some other interesting twists. For even though *alternatives* to ultimism are set aside by the skeptic who has faith, an intellectual investigation of the various *forms* of ultimism will, as we saw in previous chapters, be woven into the skeptic's distinctive religiousness. So intellectual inquiry will continue; it's just that its focus will change. Given that one must necessarily be selective in investigation and that much attention has already been given to ultimistic and anti-ultimistic arguments, also by the skeptic herself, it is hard to see how this focus—this "slant"—could be faulted. Indeed, one might argue that because naturalistic options have been so dominant in (at any rate Western) thinking over the past few centuries—as everyone knows, their trajectory has tended to parallel that of modern science—and because before that, rather parochial religious concerns held sway, a new and apparently one-sided program of research into a wide range of religious options both old and new is needed to rectify this intellectual imbalance.[3] We may therefore conclude more sharply that not only is the degree of openness and attention to ultimism's alternatives capable of being mustered here fully adequate to the skeptic's commitment to truth and understanding, but her new investigative focus is to be *applauded* as potentially forwarding the cause of understanding precisely where, heretofore, it has been sorely neglected.[4]

---

[3] Notice that the religious research program would clearly have consequences of interest to those who wonder about the credibility of naturalism. For if it turns up possibilities that can adequately be defended, naturalism will lose its sheen. And if it does not, naturalism will tend to be confirmed; for this is just what we should expect on the assumption that it is true.

[4] Here it is interesting to note that if this investigative focus is to be applauded, then so is the skeptic's religious practice—because of its instrumental value in relation to the former. Even in the absence of belief, assenting to the ultimistic claim and holding its content

So it seems that the weaker, more nuanced variations on the "wish-fulfillment" theme we have been considering are no more successful than their brash predecessor. But before leaving that theme entirely behind, let me briefly respond to a possible extension of arguments already discussed, phrased in terms of motivation, and then also to what was said earlier, when we first considered why going "beyond" the intellect in faith might be deemed problematic, about sloppy, nondiscriminating states of mind.

Does the skeptic, by choosing to have faith, set in motion a process that will result in the *undermining* of her motivation to take alternatives to ultimism seriously? While keeping "one eye open" for arguments that might unseat her faith by showing the probable falsehood of ultimism, will she be inclined swiftly to close it if such arguments actually appear, having been lulled into a love of blindness by the pleasures of faith? I would answer here as follows. Thinking that the world might overall be good is pleasant in a way, but it would be a good deal more pleasant for the skeptic if she believed this! In talking about faith I have been seeking to make room for another sort of attitude, where one has a commitment to a proposition p but does not *think that* or *feel that* p is so—has, indeed, no confidence with respect to it at all—and is thus not being carried along by an apparent reality, but rather always purposely choosing to project that p and assent to it, and always aware that p may be false. This imagining and this assenting of faith are rightly called tenacious and committed because it takes work to maintain such attitudes in the midst of a world in which awful things are happening, and in which less demanding attitudes are tempting. So it is hard to see why one should think it *overall* pleasant to think in the manner of faith of the world being overall good. Indeed, since by the same token we can say that new objections to a religious worldview will not have a hard time making themselves felt, we have, overall, confirmation of the idea that "one eye will remain open"—that faith is not a place where one can very easily hide from objections to faith.

Finally, on the intellectual sloppiness and nondiscriminatory states of mind alleged to be associated with faith. Here again we are easily the victims of prejudice because of the less than desirable reputation of a *believing* religious faith. (This reputation is not unearned. Tertullian, for example, after making his famous Athens/Jerusalem comment in *Objections to Heretics* 7, goes on to say this: "Once we have Jesus Christ, we need no further curiosity; once we have the gospel, no further inquiry.") The faith response I am defending, as to a large extent we have already seen, is not subject to such difficulties. Of course our skeptic who chooses faith

---

before our minds will help to work against despair over the prospects of success in the task of religious investigation.

has chosen to set aside any further skeptical questioning in order to have it, but this is only because the goods faith makes possible are impossible so long as she engages in such questioning. And precisely because she does not believe, and may recognize that not all situations are equally deserving of faith, and because she may apply such standards as I have developed to determine which ones are, she can avoid the sorts of undiscriminating habits of thought of which the most recent objection complains. That objection seems therefore to be without any plausibility when more carefully examined.

2. A Practice of Self-Deception?

The idea that religious faith should be rejected by reason has carved deep grooves in much Enlightenment and post-Enlightenment thought, and it is accepted as a matter of course by many twenty-first-century intellectuals. So all the arguments I have provided about how faith can be nonbelieving and thus transcend the intellectual difficulties besetting a believing faith may still leave some readers unconvinced. I accept that in the eyes of some I have more work to do. To them I commend not only the chapters yet to come, but also this section and the remaining sections of this chapter, in which I seek to voice as strongly as possible certain new or revised complaints our defender of pure skepticism is in a position to make, and to show that these too can fairly easily be answered. Perhaps by the end of all this, if not here near the beginning, the quite distinct rational standing of the attitudes I am defending, and thus the need for any intellect both sharp and alert, as well as flexible and discriminating, to take them more seriously, will have been made apparent.

In the present section I want to entertain and discuss the worry that some of the negative qualities from which I sought to distance faith in the previous section must reappear more threateningly when we take into account how faith is *operationalized*. Our focus, so far, it may be said, has been mostly on the *propositional* side of faith. But what happens when the skeptic takes up such an attitude and seeks to build on it the religious life depicted in Chapters 2 and 3? Thinking and acting in ways suggested by ultimism may indeed lead to a kind of self-transformation over time, as I argued there. But shouldn't we find certain aspects of this transformation problematic? For example, won't it be part of acting on her faith that ultimism is true to resist alternatives if and when they forcibly present themselves? And how could any true lover of understanding be led to do so?

I have clarified in *Prolegomena* (p. 124; and here see also note 9 of Chapter 2) that acting on skeptical propositional faith involves doing whatever seems appropriate to the truth of ultimism given one's other purposes and the rest of one's worldview—which worldview, for the skeptical person of faith, includes the proposition that evidence sufficient for either religious belief or disbelief is presently unavailable but might become available, and which purposes include for her the purpose of conforming behavior to the openness aim. In these circumstances, acting on faith can hardly involve resisting alternatives to ultimism (or to one's faith attitudes) that forcibly present themselves. One rather maintains faith unless and until it is shown to be unjustified; one remains ready to adjust to new information should such appear and be confirmed.

This "readiness" requires a sensitive construal. We need a distinction between preventing the presence of alternatives, always felt at some level, from barging into one's field of vision in a manner that makes faith impossible, and reflexively rejecting them whenever they arise, even when they come founded upon apparently powerful new arguments. The person of faith seeks to do the former and to avoid the latter; in this balance—which can be difficult to maintain, thus suggesting again the virtue of faith—she preserves a rational religious commitment, resisting the *intrusion* of alternatives while also possessed of a higher-level alertness and sensitivity to the possibility that changes in her attitudes may be required.

But perhaps we should now return to the issue of self-transformation. Is it not at least very likely that this will include a transformation of one's cognitive attitude *from faith to belief*? The repeated act of assenting, turned gradually into a disposition, together with participation in a religious community, may seem uncomfortably close to the complex of behaviors some religious writers—most famously, Pascal (see Chapter 9)—have *prescribed* for those wishing to acquire belief. Such behaviors, so they say, will turn one's state of mind into one of belief quite naturally. Why shouldn't we expect that this will happen for the skeptic, too, ridding her of skepticism and skeptical religiousness alike through a gradual process of self-deception? I have been speaking of a possible form of ongoing religiousness consistent with rational commitments, but here it appears that either the skeptic's beliefless faith will lead to a transgression against reason or it will cease to exist as such. And either way, my claim is revealed as false.

This objection gains whatever plausibility it may seem to have only by completely severing our skeptic's activities from their context. The skeptic's faith might lead to the mentioned "transgression against reason" if she were *seeking* belief, intentionally deploying assent and so on as a *means* of acquiring it, in *response* to advice of the sort referred to by the challenger. (Of course, even if this were her orientation, following the Pascalian recipe might not lead to the desired result: human belief states can be stubbornly unresponsive to attempted manipulation.) But her orientation is in fact a very different one. She approaches her assent on the basis of such arguments as I have detailed, and also others yet to come, and so from the side of reason—not from the side of an unreflective and traditional religious sensibility. She sees how immature and shortsighted it would be to yield to any desire for belief. And the religious activities (e.g., religious investigation) she undertakes as part of her skeptical religion are designed to strengthen that very distinctive sort of religiousness. So we should not expect her to be swept down the path of self-deception.[5] Now that is not to say that no skeptic who adopts the faith I am defending will ever succumb to intellectual temptations along the way, perhaps ones bound up with a seeming desirability in some belief state. But this is just a special instance of a familiar fact—that we are subject to temptations to give up on difficult commitments. There is no more reason here than in any other case of a difficult commitment to suppose that one who sees the importance and value of the commitment is unlikely to persevere in it.

But, forced back to the drawing board, testers of faith may soon come up with another objection grounded in the nature of operational faith. Suppose that the person of faith is not over time led by her practice, through a kind of self-hypnosis, into the belief that ultimism is true. Still, there are troubling possibilities at another level: the level of beliefs about *evidence*. If propositional faith is to do its job in relation to operational faith, its use of the imagination must be not simply occasional but pervasive, inflecting all one's thoughts, emotions, and actions. But it is unlikely that one could sustain such thoughts, emotions, and actions for long without systematically occluding or "forgetting" one's belief that the available evidence makes the denials of both ultimism and the claim that the total evidence supports ultimism epistemically possible. (How can one carry on with religious practice for any significant period of time while fully aware of how doubtful the relevant propositions are?) To do this, however, would seem again to involve a kind of willful self-blinding—a state in which one more or less willfully conceals from oneself the fact that the propositions to which one assents have the epistemic status in question. And that, for obvious reasons, must be deemed highly objectionable from the standpoint of reason.[6]

---

[5] Here we should also notice how studies of imagination have shown that even in very young children caught up in imagination, there is no tendency for this to be mistaken for—or to turn into—belief. See *Architecture of the Imagination*, pp. 6, 73.

[6] I am grateful to Bill Wainwright for his vigorous development and defense of this position at the 2006 meetings of the Society for Philosophy of Religion, in response to a paper of mine, and also in e-mail correspondence thereafter. Much of the content of this section's dialectical give-and-take is drawn from or based on that discussion.

But to sustain her religious practice, our skeptic does not need even to imagine that the *available* evidence is anything but weak. She might indeed be holding before her mind, in a blend of admission and imagination, the conjunction "The available evidence is weak but the total evidence supports ultimism" and finding her religious life sustained thereby! Of course it may be that much of the time the first conjunct of that conjunction—the fact about the available evidence in support of ultimism being weak—is *not* before the mind of the religious skeptic as she goes about her religious activities. Perhaps it will make it easier to get on with her religious life commitment if she does not spend much time thinking about it. But to see that this is in no way problematic from the standpoint of reason we need only notice that there is a difference between *not thinking about a proposition* such as the proposition that the available evidence is weak in order to get on with some commitment, and *concealing it or its truth* from oneself in any dishonest, self-deceptive manner. The former state *can* sometimes be linked with the attitude of the person of faith when, in the course of operationalizing her faith, she concentrates on ultimism in a positive way and mentally assents to it, internally repeating such phrases as "so be it" to keep the relevant state of affairs from slipping out of focus. (There may be little room in such mental circumstances, and given the specific purposes she pursues, for thinking about the available evidence being weak.) But the latter, self-deceptive state in no way—logically or causally—follows from the former state, and it is certainly absent in one who recognizes the force of skeptical arguments regarding ultimism.

Indeed, such "not thinking" as may be associated with the skeptic's faith state is no more than a by-product of thinking about *other* things. (The person of faith does not say "Okay, I've got to ignore the available evidence now," but rather says "Okay, I'm having faith now," and when in the latter state is naturally not thinking about the available evidence.) If one finds this objectionable, then one should as well find objectionable the behavior of a pilot who, concentrating on the flying of the plane in the midst of a storm, is not thinking about the possibility of a crash. Must the pilot really be *concealing* this possibility from himself in any dishonest, self-deceptive manner? If there is good reason to adopt such an attitude as faith, then there will also be good reason to countenance such an innocent by-product as the "not thinking" at issue here. And, again, if thoughts about the available evidence do come to mind, they need not be rejected or ignored, but only paired with the above-mentioned possibility about the total evidence.

Now of course if the one who has faith believed it to be true that the available evidence supports the *denial* of ultimism, then the stronger claim about occlusion might apply too. But since she is a skeptic, she does not believe this. The only other way, as it seems to me, that a troubling occlusion could follow from the point about pervasiveness is if, by some means independent of the aforementioned belief, reflecting on the state of the available evidence made the skeptic pessimistic about ultimism turning out to be true. Why, otherwise, should it be difficult to persist in assenting to ultimism or in attitudes presupposing such assent while aware of what the available evidence shows? And here it is rather important to remember that the belief about available evidence of any skeptic persuaded by my arguments is held as part of a *larger evolutionary picture* of things that includes the distinct possibility that the human race may be rather far behind the line where spiritual things are concerned, at a very early stage of spiritual development. The latter possibility makes it possible that the murkiness of available evidence relevant to ultimism is just what we should expect even if ultimism is true! Thus when the belief that the available evidence fails to support ultimism is held in *this* way—*in this context*—it will certainly not leave the skeptic pessimistic about ultimism turning out to be true. (The larger the possible gap between "available" and "total," the less threatening facts about the former must appear.) Indeed, if there is anything here that needs to be "occluded," it is the idea that we already have what it takes, as a species, to determine how things are on ultimate matters. And such occlusion, as confirmed by *Skepticism,* is not intellectually vicious but virtuous. We may conclude, then, that what is required for the success of the argument opposed to faith, in this as in the other cases, is unavailable.[7]

3. *Mill on Religious Imagination*

What we have been learning in this chapter, and especially again in the previous paragraph, is how different is the context in which *we* are discussing the idea of a tension between faith and reason from those in which that subject has generally been discussed in the past, especially throughout the supposed Enlightenment of the West. No talk here of religious *belief* or of detailed religious propositions. Instead we are dealing with a *nondoxastic*

---

[7] It may be added that should a further response be required, it could be developed by assuming that the occlusion referred to and its effects indeed occur, and then setting against that all the intellectual *benefits* to be associated with faith (I touched on this point in the previous section and will return to it in Part III). In arguing thus, we would not be claiming that there is some *independent* benefit to be associated with faith that outweighs its betrayal of reason (this strategy was set aside at the beginning of the chapter), but rather suggesting that by virtue of its *intellectual* benefits, it does not, on balance, amount to a betrayal of reason at all.

conception of faith appropriate to the new perspective afforded by a skeptical shift from past to future and also the diachronic conception of religion, which leads us to expect religion to evolve. The rules are changing. And though it is natural for opponents of religion initially to assume that the new idea will succumb to arguments that undid the old, against the background of that shift, and after we have run those arguments in as many ways as we have, perhaps it is time to admit that the new faith, unlike the old, may succeed in passing the tests of reason.

Some elements of this new faith, as it happens, were anticipated by John Stuart Mill in his *Three Essays on Religion,* though his work on them is somewhat sketchy and has been thoroughly neglected. Mill, of course, was an Enlightenment figure, about as rational an individual as one could care to meet, and one in whom no trace of religious believing was ever found. He couches what he has to say about an alternative to belief in terms of *hope.* But it is clear that he is talking about a *religious* alternative, and one with more of a bite—more of an active component leading to a life orientation—than hope as usually construed, which is no more than an involuntary complex of possibility belief plus desire.[8] In fact, his alternative is grounded in imagination—which is of course at the heart of the approach defended in this chapter. Perhaps it was only his acquiescence in the common assumption that religious faith must include religious belief that led Mill to speak of his attitude and orientation in terms of hope instead of in terms of faith.

I won't spend any time trying to link Mill's notion of hope more firmly to my notion of faith. But I do want to look at what he says about religious imagination, both to dislodge a way of crystallizing and further confirming what I've been saying about the rational blamelessness of the religious exercise of such imagination, and about a shift to the future being required here, and to turn up one last objection, representative of those found attractive by contemporary critics of Mill.

Mill's comments on imagination and religious hope come in two of his *Three Essays:* briefly in the second, "Utility of Religion," written in the mid-1850s, and at greater length in the third, "Theism," written around 1870 near the end of his life.[9] In "Theism" he suggests that the view that religious imagination is contrary to reason presupposes a certain

---

[8] Specifically, desire that a state of affairs obtain and belief that it is in some respect good and not impossible (not *logically* impossible—one might *hope* for things one regards as epistemically impossible). For more on hope, see *Prolegomena,* pp. 142–143; there will also be quite a bit more about hope in Part IV of this book.

[9] See John Stuart Mill, *Three Essays on Religion,* 4th ed. (London: Longmans, Green, Reader, and Dyer, 1875).

principle: "the rational principle of regulating our feelings as well as our opinions strictly by evidence." Call this the symmetry principle. Then he interestingly remarks that the question whether the symmetry principle is true—or, more broadly, the question of which principles "ought to govern the cultivation and the regulation of the imagination"—has hardly been addressed in philosophy, and "will hereafter be regarded as a very important branch of study for practical purposes, and the more, in proportion as the weakening of positive beliefs respecting states of existence superior to the human, leaves the imagination of higher things less provided with material from the domain of supposed reality." In other words, as more of us become religious skeptics, there arises a need to decide whether those ideas of transcendent things we used to regard as clearly true can still play some subsidiary role by "increasing the happiness of life and giving elevation to the character" or must altogether be rejected.[10] Those who object to religious imagination are treading on new terrain, perhaps without noticing it. As I put it above, new thoughts are required here and an openness to the evolution of religion. This is an example of Mill ahead of his time: indeed, as this chapter bears witness, it is only now that such questions about the imagination are beginning to be seriously addressed.

So what of the symmetry principle? Mill seems to hold that it is correct *only if* imaginatively dwelling on evidentially unsupported ideas must disturb "the rectitude of the intellect and the right direction of the actions and will." He thinks the consequent here is false and accordingly holds that the symmetry principle is false. In support, he offers the example of a "cheerful disposition." This, Mill says, is "always accounted one of the chief blessings of life" and yet what is it "but the tendency, either from constitution or habit, to dwell chiefly on the brighter side of the present and of the future?" He then elaborates:

> If every aspect, whether agreeable or odious of every thing, ought to occupy exactly the same place in our imagination which it fills in fact, and therefore ought to fill in our deliberate reason, what we call a cheerful disposition would be but one of the forms of folly....But it is not found in practice that those who take life cheerfully are less alive to rational prospects of evil or danger and more careless of making due provision against them, than other people. The tendency is rather the other way, for a hopeful disposition gives a spur to the faculties and keeps all the active energies in good working order....In the regulation of the imagination literal truth of facts

[10] Ibid., pp. 244–245.

is not the only thing to be considered. Truth is the province of reason, and it is by the cultivation of the rational faculty that provision is made for its being known always, and thought of as often as is required by duty and the circumstances of human life. But when the reason is strongly cultivated, the imagination may safely follow its own end, and do its best to make life pleasant and lovely inside the castle, in reliance on the fortifications raised and maintained by Reason round the outward bounds.[11]

So the symmetry principle is unreasonably severe. And Mill finds the results to be favorable for a hopeful form of religion. But not all have agreed, especially when the imagination in question is religious imagination. Consider, for example, what Alan Millar says in his contribution to *The Cambridge Companion to Mill:*

> I think Mill goes too far. It is one thing to be hopeful about what for all we know might be the case when we think there is at least some chance that it may be so. It is another to indulge hope where we have no reason to think there is such a chance. This latter speculative hope is what Mill enjoins, yet there is an obvious danger. The hopes which he seeks to encourage are those which release vital resources and energies in the pursuit of worthwhile ends. But directing such resources and energies behind hopes which are entirely speculative diverts them from more realistic hopes and may get in the way of reconciling one to a situation which in reality may be less pleasing than that hoped for. Clearly this can happen. Imagine parents who in the absence of any evidence continue to hope that their long lost child is alive. Such a hope might be sustaining, but it might equally detract from coming to terms with the loss.[12]

Millar is in effect objecting to Mill's defense of religious imagination against the symmetry principle by arguing that religious imagination *does* have a tendency to disturb "the right direction of the actions and will." But his objection is not well thought through, and in any event cannot be applied when the religious imagination is ultimistic.

First ask this question: Why assume that devoting resources and energies to religious faith must mean *diminished* attention to other important causes—presumably ones in some way bound up with the improvement of

---

[11] Ibid., pp. 246–249.

[12] Alan Millar, "Mill on Religion," in *The Cambridge Companion to Mill,* ed. John Skorupski (Cambridge: Cambridge University Press, 1998), p. 198.

the world? Here Mill himself has an answer, since in all of his comments about religious imagination, its capacity to provide support for the moral life is front and center. He speaks of "the enlargement of the general scale of the feelings; the loftier aspirations being no longer in the same degree checked and kept down by a sense of the insignificance of human life," which produces "increased inducement to cultivate the improvement of character up to the end of life."[13] And again, "human life, small and confined as it is...stands greatly in need of any wider range and greater height of aspiration for itself and its destination, which the exercise of imagination can yield to it without running counter to the evidence of fact."[14] It is precisely *through* (what I am calling) religious faith that Mill thinks we may benefit those other moral causes Millar alludes to, for it will make us more inclined to engage in them. In other words, devoting energies here will result in renewed zest for living and thus *magnify* or *replenish* energies in all other departments of life instead of in any way competing with them.

Mill, of course, has in mind a religious imagination focused on theistic and perhaps Christian ideas. Now notice how what he has to say must come to appear still more plausible when we are thinking not of some narrow object of *that* sort, which may suck us into specific commitments at odds with other good things, but rather of skeptical *ultimistic* religion. As we saw in Part I, when we're talking about a religious faith focused quite generally on ultimism, then we do indeed have something that is not in competition with other good causes but rather *supports* them in various ways. Millar's point here is therefore quite clearly false when applied to the exercise of ultimistic imagination.

There is yet another problem with the objection Millar makes. He suggests that religious faith may "get in the way of reconciling one to a situation which in reality may be less pleasing than that hoped for." But how is this to occur? More specific issues of the sort represented by the parents and child of his example may indeed suddenly be resolved one way or another (perhaps the child turns up dead), and then faith previously directed to one possibility may make it more difficult to be reconciled to the fact that the other has been realized. Even so, I would say, one need not infer that the faith was unjustified: perhaps it was needed to do justice to the situation that *previously* existed. But the more important point is this: we shouldn't expect the *religious* issue to be resolved anytime soon! Now perhaps such a view is unduly pessimistic where the traditional theism of Mill's time (and still so much of ours) is concerned. But certainly it is not unduly pessimistic where the more general claim of ultimism, which "for

[13] Mill, *Three Essays*, pp. 249–250.
[14] Ibid., p. 245.

all we know might be the case," is concerned. As has been noted more than once, we are still quite immature as a species, and a correct understanding of ultimate things may be a long time coming—if it comes at all. And as we saw in Chapter 1, ultimism is the most *stable* of religious propositions, since with less content comes less vulnerability. Indeed, no religious proposition is more likely to remain undisturbed by apparent proofs of falsity long into the future than simple ultimism. So again Millar's point is inapplicable.

There seems, then, to be no good reason to accept the symmetry principle in the present context, no reason to think that ultimistic imaginative faith is as much a betrayal of reason as its detailed believing ancestors. Indeed, all of the arguments offered in this chapter can be lined up against it—and all the more effectively now that, with Mill's help, we see more clearly what a new thing it is that is emerging in the evolution of religion.

4. A New Challenge

There is one more challenge that needs to be taken up before we conclude that religious faith with a skeptical heart is able to meet reason's demands. And this is a rather different sort of challenge (though from a certain perspective it can appear that its basic point has been staring us in the face all the way through this discussion). It is a challenge that, paradoxically, takes its point of departure from the *success* I have had reconciling the faith I am defending with reason. If my faith really can meet reason's demands, so it asks, is it really *religious* faith anymore? As I myself have argued, religion is above all and by definition concerned with ultimates. Not only is propositional religious faith directed to a proposition about an ultimate reality, but operational faith—if genuinely religious—must reflect one's ultimate commitment. In *Prolegomena* (pp. 30–32) this essential feature of a religious commitment was described in terms of the latter representing one's deepest focus of action and dedication in the realm of action; being what determines or most strongly influences the course of the religious person's life and also perceived as most important in it; having deep and wide effects in that life; being reflected—this is her aim at least—in all of the religious person's dispositions; being central to a religious person's life, that to which she seeks to give her fullest attention. All of this suggests that in the religious person's life, her religious commitment has primacy. However, in this chapter religion has been turned into a child of reason. That is to say, on the view I have defended, it is the skeptic's commitment to *truth and understanding* that is most fundamental, and religion is to be accepted only if it can be made consistent with this commitment. If push came to shove, the skeptic would indeed give up her religious faith to meet the demands of reason. How, then, is her religious commitment an ultimate commitment? Thus, it may be said, whatever it is that I have vindicated at the bar of reason, it cannot be religious faith! There is a necessary conflict between reason and religion that is fueled from the religious side even if not from the rational. Religious faith *cannot* be true to reason, for then it would not be religious faith anymore.

It may be agreed that we at least seem to have a problem here. If I am right (and of course there is more to come on this in the rest of the book), then when we properly seek an understanding not only of the world but also of the attitudes by which we should address it, "skeptical faith" appears in bright flashing lights. The religious commitment is, in a sense, generated through our exercise of the rational one. And if, contrariwise, reason showed that ultimism is false, or else that one of our other principles from the previous chapter applied (principles generated by reasoning), then the skeptic's faith would be lost. *On the other hand,* the skeptical religious commitment, as I have described it, can seem from a certain angle the broader of the two, and it unifies the various parts of one's life. It appears to represent at any rate the deepest explicit focus in the life of one who adopts it: as we have seen, it is that in terms of which everything else deliberately is understood, to whose purposes everything else is referred. And all the attention it gets in such a life certainly seems to suggest that it is perceived as most deeply important.

So what to do? We might spend some time distinguishing different types of metaphysical ultimacy—compositional, explanatory, generative, teleological, comprehensive, perhaps—and try to apply these by analogy or metaphorically to commitments, parceling them out among the commitments involved here, seeking in this way to allow both the rational and the religious commitments to preserve ultimacy in certain respects. But I suspect that we would still find ourselves tempted, in certain moods, to apply all of these types of ultimacy to the rational commitment, and in certain other moods, tempted to apply them all to the religious one.

My own proposal is that we find a way of yielding to both temptations: the way to answer the objection claiming that we have made too close a connection between faith and reason is to *look for an even closer connection.* Skeptical religion, as I am understanding it, really is a child of reason— reason's blood flows in its veins. If my arguments in the remainder of the book are right, then religion of a certain kind is what reason bids us embrace as we move into the next stages of evolution. Thus understood, a religious form of life *expresses* one's commitment to reason's goals (truth and understanding), and indeed the religious expression of that commitment is rationally required. If this is true, if religion is the way that a commitment to reason ought to be manifested in a life, then all those ultimistic terms can apply to religion even though its pedigree is a rational one. If reason leads one to see that this form of life should provide one's deepest focus, if this is a *conclusion* of reasoning, then everything here is imbued with reason even though the religious commitment is, in the sense of *Prolegomena,* one's ultimate commitment. The challenge assumes that somehow the religious commitment and the rational commitment must in the end come apart, but precisely that is what I am (and will be) arguing is not the case. Reason—the drive toward truth and understanding—is, as it were, the stuff of the skeptic's life, and a certain kind of religion is the form it comes to bear. No doubt reason takes this form only contingently, but it still does take this form! The faith I am defending is, in the end, at one with reason. And if these two are at one, then they are not estranged.

PART III

Renewing Faith (1)
How Skeptical Proof Subsumes
Believing Argument—Evidentialism

WE HAVE WITNESSED how a variety of seemingly strong challenges to religious faith in the name of reason end up falling flat when the faith in question is the skeptical faith I am defending. It will be intriguing now to take this to the next level: might the arguments *supporting* religion—now that we have a form of religion appropriate to our time—be as strong as the challenges were weak? I think the answer is yes. Indeed, if ultimistic faith is really as rational as I have been (and shall be) claiming that it is, then any attack on it in the name of reason must ultimately be self-defeating. Then any clearheaded examination of a faith response to ultimism should lead to an unexpected assessment: not only is it possible to be true to reason while adopting such faith, *it is impossible without it.*

Of course we cannot be entirely sure of this surprising turnaround for religion until much more work has been done, and the task of completing this work is the task assigned to us in the remainder of the book. We must undertake an extended push toward the light at the end of the apparent conflict between faith and reason; having once rid ourselves of tunnel vision, we will more fully be able to see how those two are one. Now we will find ourselves completely out of the tunnel only when we have itemized and systematized all the various considerations involved, observing how aims from various areas of life that it is incumbent on us to pursue can best be pursued by having faith. (These aims are, at once, aims that—as indicated in Chapter 4—we need to know about in order decisively to answerthe last challenges to faith's negative justification, and the aims on which we can successfully build our arguments for faith's positive justification.) But we can start gathering the supportive considerations and identifying the relevant aims now—and we will find them, I suggest, in some most surprising locations, namely, in the main contexts of classical argumentation for theistic religious belief. In perfect accord with the evolutionary thrust of this book, some old arguments that didn't work when theism was the target can be adapted to the successful defense of ultimistic faith. Arguments for theistic belief, in other words, can successfully be *recast* as arguments for ultimistic faith.

Here in Part III this claim is borne out in connection with the traditional theistic proofs (ontological, cosmological, and teleological) and their best-known defenders. These earlier philosophers would of course be unlikely to smile on my attempts at appropriation: their arguments, they might say, are just fine as arguments for the truth of theism, thank you very much! But the problem with this attitude is that it is unjustified, as shown in *Skepticism* (see especially Chapter 14). The famous theistic proofs are all plowed under by the modes of religious skepticism. Some will of course hope for new shoots to grow. But my own conclusion about theism and its proofs must be a negative one. It is interesting that this conclusion is embraced even by many theistic *believers* (its forcefulness is one of the reasons for the existence of the various arguments of theistic *nonevidentialism* discussed in Part IV, developed by thinkers who tend to be disillusioned with proofs). You don't have to be a religious skeptic to see that the traditional theistic proofs—however modestly they may be deployed, with whatever concessions to an inductive or abductive sensibility—leave something to be desired.

But this is just where the observant religious skeptic considering whether skeptical religion is justified may arrive at a critical realization, leading her to break in: "They leave something to be desired *as support for the truth of theism.* However, it may be that they can more fruitfully be turned to other ends. Indeed, if we look at these arguments (or central aspects thereof, or the concerns that animated their authors) from a slightly different perspective, we will see how a religious attitude can still be supported by means of them, even if it is not the attitude of theistic belief. There are some interesting latent possibilities here that need to be developed—shoots that with a bit of watering can grow into a tree capable of sheltering the nonbelieving and nonsectarian form of religion appropriate to our time."

Now a historian of theistic argumentation might be inclined to point out that I am not the first to see how the theistic proofs may be associated with more than simply the impulse to establish the truth of a religious proposition. Many (perhaps most famously, Karl Barth, in his work on Anselm) have tried to show that the aim behind them is not really to convert atheists but rather to lead theists into a deeper understanding of the object of their belief. But my approach, while learning from views like this, also seeks to move beyond them. My sort of move, if successful, would not just identify the religious sensibility behind the arguments, giving us some insight into the mental states and spiritual trajectory of believers, but fashion this information into *arguments of another kind,* arguments that still justify a form of religion—albeit a nonbelieving one. (In going this far, it would take us farther than the arguments as usually understood, with their narrow focus on establishing the truth of a proposition, ever explicitly seek to go.)

It is because of this fact that I am inclined to say that my appropriation of the traditional theistic proofs is a *generous* appropriation. It is generous not only in the sense that much is taken from the proofs, but also because in this appropriation the central apologetic ambition of those who formulated the relevant arguments is respected and even, in an unexpected way, permitted to be realized. Our discussion of faith can be seen as providing a proper home for these arguments, in which their untapped potential is realized and they are given new life as defenses of a form of religion open to all, thus permitting the aspirations of their authors, most broadly construed, to be realized—and this despite the claim on our allegiance of the very religious skepticism those authors saw themselves as needing to combat.

But enough of advertisement. Let us see how all of this looks when worked out in detail, beginning with the ontological argument formulated by Anselm.

CHAPTER 6

Anselm's Idea

1. Where Ontological Reasoning Should Lead Us

The ontological proof devised by Anselm (some six centuries before its name was invented by Kant) claims that the nature of God as ultimate—absolutely perfect or unsurpassably great—logically precludes God's nonexistence. In Anselm's famous phrase, God is "that-than-which-a-greater-cannot-be-thought," and according to him, if that-than-which-a-greater-cannot-be-thought existed only in the mind, as the foolish disbeliever supposes, and not in reality, then that-than-which-a-greater-cannot-be-thought would be that-than-which-a-greater-*can*-be-thought (for then it could be thought to exist in reality as well as in the mind, which is greater than existence merely in the mind)—and this implies a contradiction. Hence, by reductio, what the foolish disbeliever supposes is false, which is to say that that-than-which-a-greater-cannot-be-thought exists not only in the mind but also in reality.[1]

Notice first that this can hardly constitute a proof of the existence of *the theist's God:* even if one shows that there exists a being that deserves to be called unsurpassably great, one cannot conclude that God exists, and this despite the fact that (according to theists), *if* God exists, then a being unsurpassably great exists. Anselm needs the converse of the latter proposition: that if a being unsurpassably great exists, then God exists. But this is not available. For there are other possible ways of filling out his general notion than by reference to a personal being. Although Anselm might

---

[1] See *Proslogion* 2, in *Anselm of Canterbury: The Major Works,* ed. Brian Davies and G. R. Evans (Oxford: Oxford University Press, 1998), pp. 87–88.

wish us to think otherwise, "that-than-which-a-greater-cannot-be-thought" cannot be taken as equivalent to "*the personal-being-*than-which-a-greater-cannot-be-thought."

But set that aside. There are several ways of showing, in strictly argumentative terms, the inadequacy of Anselm's line of reasoning and also of others in the same family—such as a second ontological proof focused on the noncontingency of the Divine that many would claim is also to be found in Anselm.[2] I will not linger over the issue, having already shown, in *Skepticism,* that arguments for religious belief lack the requisite force, all things considered—and having explicitly addressed the best-known contemporary version of the ontological argument, which seeks to learn from Anselm's second proof, in Chapter 1 of that work. But let us nonetheless briefly consider the basic Anselmian argument of more long-standing fame sketched above.

It will work as a proof for the circumspect nonbeliever of today only if the conclusion that an unsurpassably great being exists can be made to follow by reductio from what such a nonbeliever, having her wits about her, would be willing to grant. Now whatever may have been true in Anselm's own day, no contemporary nonbeliever *but* a fool would grant that *that-than-which-a-greater-cannot-be-thought* exists in the mind. The most that any nonfoolish nonbeliever today will concede is that the *idea* or *thought* or *understanding* of that-than-which-a-greater-cannot-be-thought exists in the mind. And what can Anselm do with that? If circumspect himself, he will not say that the idea or thought or understanding of that-than-which-a-greater-cannot-be-thought cannot exist in the mind alone—for this is trivially false. Indeed, Anselm's critical move of claiming that that-than-which-a-greater-cannot-be-thought cannot exist in the mind *alone* is now completely blocked, for this move he could make only if the nonbeliever had been led to grant that such a being does exist at least in the mind, and our circumspect nonbeliever will grant no such thing. In short, no reductio leading to the conclusion that a being unsurpassably great truly exists can be fashioned out of what any sensible twenty-first-century skeptic has reason to allow concerning the relation between that-than-which-a-greater-cannot-be-thought and the mind.

This point need not be developed any further since virtually every contemporary commentator will be prepared to grant that, for this or some other reason, Anselm's argument is ineffective today. The point I do want to develop here is that even if this is so, even if there is no clear route from awareness of the idea of an unsurpassably great reality in one's mind to

---

[2] J. L. Mackie has an interesting discussion in his *The Miracle of Theism* (Oxford: Clarendon Press, 1982), chap. 3, as does Richard Gale in his *On the Nature and Existence of God* (Cambridge: Cambridge University Press, 1991), chap. 6.

awareness of its being instantiated, reflection on the former awareness and on its relation to our lives can be religiously and philosophically enlightening, and as such quite in tune with Anselm's own approach of using "pure reasoning, so as to show the rationality of the faith he is seeking to heighten in his readers."[3] We don't have to take Anselm's idea all the way from the mind to reality, as he supposes, in order to see how it provides rational support for religious attitudes; we can remain within the ambit of the mind alone, gazing upon the idea itself and suspending judgment as to its instantiation.

But notice first that if Anselm's idea is to be viewed as a religious idea, and if his arguments are to be thought relevant to the advancement of religious practice in our time, then we must assume his idea to have all of the content of ultimism: to be the idea of an ultimate reality *in relation to which an ultimate good can be achieved*. As we have seen, in his formula—that-than-which-a-greater-cannot-be-thought—Anselm explicitly suggests only the first half of ultimism, the "ultimate reality" part, but to make him relevant to our concern, to see how his reflections can be transformed into arguments supporting skeptical religion, we must imagine him thinking of the whole. Interestingly, this does not really require any adjustment to our picture of the context of his reflections, if we understand that context correctly. (Here the points of writers like Barth can be seen as relevant.) For Anselm is writing as a deeply religious man, caught up in prayer, seeking to get clearer about what it is in relation to which he and his fellow monks are supposing their salvation lies. As Marilyn Adams puts it, the "overarching common aim" in his monastery was "to become persons who could see and enjoy God's face."[4] Further, it is important to note that in the central idea of the ontological argument he thinks he has found something capable of proving not only that God exists but also everything else that Christians believe about God—which of course includes the salvific efficacy of a proper relation to the Divine.[5] He would have no trouble explicitly accepting into his reflections the full content of ultimism; indeed, we must suppose, when we hear his rendition of ultimacy, that the salvific idea is tacitly present.

So let that enlarged content be what we think of ourselves as gazing upon when we contemplate the idea of that-than-which-a-greater-cannot-be-thought. What will we see if this contemplation is sustained for any

[3] Introduction, *Major Works*, p. xi.

[4] Marilyn McCord Adams, "Anselm on Faith and Reason," in *The Cambridge Companion to Anselm*, ed. Brian Davies and Brian Leftow (Cambridge: Cambridge University Press, 2004), p. 32.

[5] See *Proslogion* preface, *Major Works*, p. 82. See also G. R. Evans, "Anselm's Life, Works, and Immediate Influence," in *Cambridge Companion to Anselm*, p. 12.

length of time? Well, consider what Anselm himself sees when he is not trying to prove that God exists or getting distracted by the details of Christian
doctrine (explicitly thinking not just of the-personal-being-than-which-a-
greater-cannot-be-thought but of the-personal-being-revealed-as-Trinity-
than-which-a-greater-cannot-be-thought):

> [My soul] strives so that it may see more, and it sees nothing beyond
> what it has seen save darkness. Or rather it does not see darkness,
> which is not in You in any way; but it sees that it cannot see more
> because of its own darkness. Why is this, Lord, why is this? Is its eye
> darkened by its weakness, or is it dazzled by your splendour? In truth
> it is both darkened in itself and dazzled by You. It is indeed both
> darkened by its own littleness and overwhelmed by Your own im-
> mensity. It is, in fact, both restricted by its own limitedness and over-
> come by Your fullness. For how great is that light from which shines
> every truth that gives light to the understanding!...Truly I do not
> see this light since it is too much for me; and yet whatever I see I see
> through it....My understanding is not able to attain to that light. It
> shines too much and my understanding does not grasp it nor does
> the eye of my soul allow itself to be turned toward it for too long. It
> is dazzled by its splendour, overcome by its fullness, overwhelmed by
> its immensity, confused by its extent.[6]

Anselm of course is speaking as a committed believer, and it might be
thought that nothing here makes any sense except for a believer. But that
is false. Penetrating as he does to the core religious idea so often hidden
beneath the layers of detail religious traditions have built up, and noticing
both its sublimity and the limits of his own mind in relation to it (instead
of lauding an apparent *discovery* of his mind, as when expounding the ontological argument), Anselm is putting before us something that both the
believer and the nonbeliever can feed on. Indeed, even if Anselm were a
skeptic, quite unconvinced by the traditional ontological argument or any
other apparent evidence for supposing that the Ultimate "truly exists," he
could be saying similar things. Let us listen to the Anselmian skeptic:

> Look at this amazing idea—just look at it. And since you're trying
> to apprehend the idea of something that is the unity of deepest fact
> and deepest value, you're going to need to let your emotions be-
> come engaged too. You're thinking about something that, if it ex-
> ists, is in a sense the fullest possible extension of everything that has

---

[6] From *Proslogion* 14, 16, *Major Works*, pp. 95–96.

ever impressed its reality upon you or mattered to you. Every curving mountain ridge, every baby's newborn cry, every leap of your heart, and every being that does or could elicit it—the reality you are thinking of is somehow responsible for all of this and manifests everything good and real in it ten thousand times more deeply. And now remember also the salvific content of the idea—that we are thinking of something that, if it exists, involves the positive transformation and fulfillment of our existence, perhaps already realized but in ways we cannot recognize because in our limitations and immaturity we haven't been seeing things as they truly are. How can one not be put in a state of awe if for any length of time one truly seeks to hold this idea before one's mind and imagine it in its fullness? How could it fail to be the most magnetically attractive of all ideas? Wouldn't one's mind have to be an even meaner and less spacious thing than it is already revealed as being by our inevitable failure in any attempt to embrace this idea fully—that is, meaner and less spacious than it needs to be or ought to be—if we did not *make* the attempt and if we were not led into *wonder* by the failure?

One might not have thought that a religious skeptic could speak like that! But simply the *idea* of ultimism, properly apprehended, is enough to provoke such thoughts—and precisely here we begin to see how the central feature of the Anselmian approach can remain religiously viable even if the traditional ontological argument is, as arguments go, an utter failure. Shorn of its usual trappings, ultimism can appear startlingly attractive even to someone used to recoiling at the crudities of much sectarian religion, and can quickly bring her to the brink of genuine religiousness. Just properly thinking about this idea—something even a nonbeliever can do—should because of the greatness and profundity of the idea and the receptiveness of a finely tuned imagination be sufficient to move us far in the direction of religious attitudes.

At this point it may be objected, however, that it is only when the Anselmian skeptic (or one of us, under his influence) is in the throes of such a reverie that his state of mind will bear any resemblance to a religious one. When he remembers that he is, after all, a skeptic—that it is only if such a reality *exists* that all the wondrous things he imagines are true and that he has no reason to suppose that such is the case—he will, at least insofar as he is rational, snap out of the reverie and back into a fully nonreligious state of mind in which no more than a thin hope of the existence of such wonderful things is possible.

But the Anselmian skeptic can reply that the very arguments that make him a skeptic, giving him no reason to suppose that ultimism is true, also deprive him of any reason to suppose it is *false,* and so leave the content of his reverie epistemically possible. And this is the key to a new Anselmian approach. Perhaps there is no such ultimate reality—perhaps it is not even logically possible for there to be an ultimate reality in relation to which an ultimate good can be realized (Chapter 2 of *Skepticism* canvasses some arguments suggesting that it might not be). Nevertheless, at our early stage of development and of religious exploration, and given various amenable facets of human experience, we must equally say that such a reality might well exist: nothing available to us justifies the belief that it does not. And if it is as much as epistemically possible that so amazing a fact obtains, then the very fact that it would be so amazing if it did obtain reveals that a response "thicker" and more self-involving than mere hope (which, as we saw in the last chapter, is reducible to involuntarily acquired belief and desire) is required of us.

Why must it be thought of as doing so? Well, let me begin my answer by developing the notion—quite Anselmian in its basic texture[7]—of an "alignment" in our own being with what would be the case if there were something combining metaphysical and axiological ultimacy (I shall sometimes call this, more simply, an alignment with something ultimately real and valuable), and also the notion of desiring for its own sake *to be* thus aligned with something ultimately real and valuable, should such exist. Let's start with the alignment idea. An alignment of the relevant sort obtains just in case one's dispositions and behavior are *in accord with* or *appropriate to* or *befitting* the state of affairs in which the aforementioned reality exists. However, this definition is still unsatisfying, in part because it leaves unresolved a tension between the admittedly attractive idea of some objective coherence or harmony between the stream of one's own life and other aspects of a Divinity-infused world, and alignment ideas that are relativized to human purposes and desires. (Won't a decision as to whether our dispositions and behavior are appropriate to a Divine reality have to think in terms of appropriateness *given* this or that human purpose or desire?) But perhaps we can bridge the gap here by idealizing a bit, by thinking in terms of the purposes possessed by a human being with twenty-first-century capacities but also flawless practical rationality who was aware of the existence of something ultimately real and valuable, and defining alignment with such a reality in terms of the presence of those same purposes in the skeptic and also the complete appropriateness thereto of the skeptic's dispositions and behavior.

---

[7] As the editors of the *Major Works* write in their introduction, Anselm was "profoundly drawn to the idea of 'order.' The right order in things, the 'oughtness' of truth and righteousness, of right willing and divine intention, form over and over again the basis on which he builds a solution to a problem" (xxi).

Now it may seem unlikely in the extreme or even impossible (given our skepticism)[8] for any of us in the messy here and now to be in that idealized state, but it does make sense to think of us as seeking to *approach* such a state ever more fully (more on this in a moment). And it does not seem difficult to think up at least some excellent candidates for dispositions that would belong even to the idealized state. For example, it seems clear that no one could be aligned with an ultimate salvific reality who never felt wonder and awe in connection with the idea of its existence, or who did not desire a life filled with good actions, or whose moments of wonder and awe were confined to the occasional reverie and unintegrated with the rest of her life; and it seems clear that it would contribute to an alignment with such a reality if one cultivated dispositions contrary to these.

So much for the alignment notion. What about desiring for its own sake to *be* thus aligned with something ultimately real and valuable, should such exist? This I take to be a desire directed to a complex state of affairs articulable by a conditional. The expression of such a desire would have the form "I desire that if p, then q." Here: I desire that if there is something ultimately real and valuable, then I am aligned with it.[9] Of course this is not the expression of a conditional desire: it is not "if p, then I desire q." Nor does the desire in question entail a desire that there *be* something ultimately real and valuable (the desire that p), or the desire that there be such a reality and that one be aligned with it (the desire that p & q)— though it is compatible with the latter desires and might commonly be realized together with them. Here it is also important to note carefully that we are talking about someone who desires the relevant state of affairs for its own sake. We are not talking about some prudential inclination to win favor from the gods or to better one's life in some way. That would involve desiring the alignment in question for its possible *instrumental benefits*. (I am not saying that there is anything wrong with such a desire and indeed we will be encountering it later in connection with Pascal; but something else is involved here.) One desires the relevant state of affairs for its own sake when one believes that a state of affairs in which one exists

---

[8] I am thinking here of the unavailability to the skeptic of sustained belief or knowledge that the Ultimate exists, which might be thought to be involved in being aligned in one's being with its existence. However, it is interesting to note that, if we keep our statements of purposes general, then in a sense even the skeptic's skepticism, especially if mixed with propositional faith, can be seen as representing a cognitive state that aligns him with something ultimately real and valuable (in the manner to be discussed), since it is the result of seeking the best available cognitive state.

[9] This may sound somewhat odd given the usual analysis of conditionals into propositions about sufficient and necessary conditions, but notice that the oddness disappears when we convert "I desire that if there is something ultimately real and valuable, then I am aligned with it" into the equivalent "I desire that it not be the case that there is something ultimately real and valuable and I am not aligned with it."

and the Divine exists and one is aligned in one's own being with that of the Divine, were it to obtain, would have great value in itself, quite apart from anything good to which it might lead (whether for oneself or anyone else), and is drawn to the idea of being in such a relation to the Divine, should the latter exist, on that account.

And now what I want to suggest is that we will see that it is good and proper for precisely such a desire to figure prominently in our own repertoire of mental states and will either possess such a desire or see the rational appropriateness of cultivating it, insofar as we give adequate consideration to what is involved here. Think about this for a moment. (I mean that literally: words like "ultimately real and valuable," though they carry a tremendously impressive content, may simply bounce off our minds like other words, failing to penetrate or leave a deep residue of understanding, unless we spend some time with Anselm meditating on their content.) How could a clear-thinking person fail to find intrinsically inappropriate a state of affairs in which she exists and so does something that is ultimately real and valuable but in which the dispositions and behavior of the bit of reality she represents are *out* of alignment with—not in accord with, unbefitting—the latter reality?

Intuition can take us a long way here, but there are also at least two ways of filling out and defending more concretely this notion of a sense of "intrinsic inappropriateness," or the idea that we should positively evaluate desiring, for its own sake, to be rightly aligned with something ultimately real and valuable, should such exist. Consider moral virtue. A rational person will cultivate moral virtue, and there are several virtues that involve the relevant beliefs, attractions, and action dispositions. Indeed, *all* of the virtues do, insofar as all in their own way instantiate a love of the good for its own sake. The latter is at least a very appealing interpretation of virtue, rearticulated recently by Thomas Hurka and also by Linda Zagzebski, who powerfully challenges the rather thin view of virtue according to which a virtue is reducible to action dispositions and perhaps a certain form of the pursuit of well-being.[10] Paragons of virtue clearly love goodness—whether goodness-as-compassion or goodness-as-honesty or whatever—for its own

---

[10] See Linda Trinkaus Zagzebski, *Virtues of the Mind: An Inquiry into the Nature of Virtue and the Ethical Foundations of Knowledge* (Cambridge: Cambridge University Press, 1996), and Thomas M. Hurka, "Virtue as Loving the Good," *Social Philosophy and Policy* 9 (1992), 149–168. The consequentialist view that virtue is reducible to action dispositions serving well-being appears in each succeeding edition of James Rachels's well-known ethics text, *The Elements of Moral Philosophy* (New York: McGraw-Hill, 1986). Under the force of recent criticism, some openness to an alternative perspective is expressed in Brad Hooker, *Ideal Code, Real World: A Rule-Consequentialist Theory of Morality* (Oxford: Clarendon Press, 2000).

sake, valuing and cultivating the desire and feeling states that go along with that. And it is hard to imagine that this is not part of their virtue.

But suppose such a view is cast into doubt. We need not be deterred by this or caught up in wrangling over the issue. We need only define another concept, virtue*, that *does* entail such states. Anyone who reflects upon it will notice the superiority of what it refers to and endorse its value and importance immediately! Whereupon he will either resolve for himself the former dispute (interpreting virtue as virtue* on the not implausible principle that any human trait than which there can so easily be a greater could not count as virtue) or he will in any case recognize the importance of cultivating virtue*—which is all the present argument requires. The point is that it is a pure and lovely thing to love the good for its own sake, and anyone committed to the good, the true, and the beautiful will be led to praise and to pursue such a state upon appropriate reflection. Anyone seeking virtue (and hereafter I myself assume that virtue is virtue*) wishes to love the good ever more fully and better and to embody this love ever more richly and exquisitely in her life. The idea of something *deepest* in possible value must therefore present itself to such an individual as representing what would be most worthy of love and imitation, were it to exist.

But add now to our emphasis so far on moral virtue an appreciation for the importance of *intellectual* virtue. A person of both moral and intellectual virtue is, as we might say (for the moment ignoring possible connections between these two), drawn to both the good and the real, and this makes the attraction to alignment with what is *ultimately* real and valuable only more obvious: alignment with anything combining what is deepest in the realms both of fact and of value, should such exist, must be most deeply attractive to anyone of both moral and intellectual virtue.

But, in addition to these general points about virtue, we should also note, as earlier suggested, that there are particular virtues embodying the dispositions at issue here. Think of honesty. It is surely an expression of honesty (or an obvious extension thereof) to wish not only one's words but also all one's actions and dispositions to be conformed to the way things are (and note that honesty instantiates a love of the good for its own sake only if one wishes this to be the case not just for any instrumental benefits it may produce but also because of its intrinsic value). So an honest person who recognizes what is at stake here will desire, for its own sake, to be aligned with what is ultimately real and valuable, should there be any such thing. Appropriate reverence seems also to be a virtue, by which I mean not just a general love of the good all over again, which *every* virtue exhibits in its own way, but something more like a disposition to be struck, impacted, moved at various levels of one's being by the thought of good, valuable, impressive, important things (whether real or only possible, and the more so the more good, valuable, impressive, or important they are), and to be influenced by such experiences to accommodate oneself to the things in question, allowing the shape of one's life to reveal the shape of their impact.[11] This would seem clearly to entail recognizing the importance of desiring, for its own sake, to be aligned with what is ultimately real and valuable, should such exist.

Perhaps there are other particular virtues about which a similar story could be told, but already we see the strong support that exists for the idea that a person who sees the importance of cultivating virtue—and so all twenty-first-century skeptics, insofar as we see aright—will recognize what we might call the *intrinsic importance* of cultivating a desire to be aligned with what is ultimately real and valuable, should such exist. But support can also be found by pursuing inquiry in a slightly different direction.

Remember that it is a desire for *understanding* that we have associated with a commitment to reason (see the beginning of Chapter 5). A desire for understanding, and in particular for the fullest understanding, amounts to a desire for a kind of *intellectual* alignment with what is most deeply *real*. A person committed to reason will see such alignment as deeply and intrinsically valuable. But there are various ways in which what is most deeply real could be instantiated and a person committed to reason will want the alignment in question no matter which of these is actual—will, for each such way, desire that if it is realized, her intellect is aligned with it. Now *one* way in which what is most deeply real might be instantiated involves it being not just ultimately real but also ultimately *valuable*. It follows that the person committed to reason will desire that if *this* way is realized, her intellect is aligned with it. But now for the critical premise: whatever supports the value of the alignment represented by this conditional state of affairs referring to the intellect surely must support *every* kind of alignment with the valuable reality in question, both intellectual and non-intellectual. Thus the person committed to reason will desire that if there is something both ultimately real and ultimately valuable, she is in *every* way—intellectual and non-intellectual—aligned with it, which is what was to be proved.

What about that critical premise? Should we really accept it? In support, one might reason as follows. The intellectual alignment in question is deemed by the one who is committed to reason to be intrinsically valuable. She wants this connection with the real for its own sake. But why

---

[11] For a recent work on reverence, see Paul Woodruff, *Reverence: Renewing a Forgotten Virtue* (Oxford: Oxford University Press, 2001). According to Woodruff, "reverence is the well-developed capacity to have the feelings of awe, respect, and shame when these are the right feelings to have" (p. 8). My explication is somewhat different from Woodruff's, while entailing what his refers to.

should one sort of alignment with the real be intrinsically valuable and others not? Wouldn't someone who cared deeply about intellectual alignment but who couldn't care less about *mis*alignment in other aspects of her being be missing something—perhaps even the larger context in which the valuing of the former makes sense? (Might intellectual alignment have a value derivative from the value of a more general alignment?)[12] It may help here if we bring to mind how the wise are commonly thought to be those who both have a certain sort of understanding *and act on it,* and how yet another virtue, the virtue of *integrity* in one's being (in the sense of integration), would seem to require pursuing no less than this.[13]

If, on the basis of such points as I have raised, we accept the intrinsic importance of cultivating a desire to be aligned with what is ultimately real and valuable (should such exist), we have put in place one part of what the skeptical Anselmian argument needs. But how can we get from here to what the reader will by now have suspected is the other part, the idea that we should all do whatever we can to approach an alignment of the sort in question in the here and now? How do we take a desire that *if* something ultimately real and valuable exists, one be aligned with it (that if *p* then *q*), and translate it into—show the equal propriety of—a desire and aim that one be as well aligned with such a reality as one can be in the actual situation, in which one is quite uncertain of its existence (that one directly approach the realization of *q* as fully as possible)?

In general, we may say that two factors are relevant to making such a move: the likelihood that *p* and the importance (and corresponding rational strength of the desire) that if *p* then *q*. If the likelihood of *p* is high, then this will smooth the transition all on its own: if one desires that if *p* then *q* and thinks it very likely that *p*, then one will surely want to do what one can to realize *q*, for this state of affairs one wishes to *accompany* that betokened by *p*. But here, obviously, we cannot say that *p* is very likely: it is quite uncertain whether something combining ultimate reality and value exists. Nevertheless, this is epistemically possible: it might very well be the case that *p*. Keeping this in mind, let's introduce now that other

---

[12] The value of seeking the deepest possible connection to all of reality is both illuminatingly discussed in and vividly expressed by Robert Nozick, *The Examined Life: Philosophical Meditations* (New York: Simon & Schuster, 1989).

[13] It may be thought that in this way we are simply drawn back into the previous virtue argument. But we are not. Though there is clearly a connection, there is also a distinction. For earlier, virtue was said to be capable of doing the supportive job all on its own (and different virtues as well as different points about virtue were being made). Whereas here new virtues are being brought in to help *complete* an argument begun on other grounds, which even someone who is uncertain what to say about virtue might uphold, namely that a commitment to reason involves a love of understanding for its own sake.

factor—the *importance* that if p then q. Where p is epistemically possible, this factor assumes considerable significance. For if the importance is great enough, it must smooth the transition despite the absence of a clear likelihood that p: if one is not at all sure that p but it is very important that if p then q, then one will, again, rationally do what one can to realize q, and be the more intent on this the more important it seems to one that if p then q.[14]

Now what I want to argue is that we are in precisely this second situation where p says that something ultimately real and valuable exists and q says that one is aligned with it. It is epistemically possible that something ultimately real and valuable exists and highly important that if it does, we are aligned with it. Indeed, it seems that here we can claim the *highest* importance. It follows that we should all find it very attractive to approach as fully as possible the alignment in question—indeed, this should appear *maximally* attractive and important.

What gives us the right to speak of the highest importance here? I suggest that to establish this right we can use the very same arguments used above to establish that the state of affairs in question is important at all. For we spoke there of a reality *deepest* in possible value and *most* worthy of embodiment. We said that it should be most deeply attractive to anyone of both moral and intellectual virtue. The person of reverence must, in the nature of the case, be most deeply struck and affected by the idea of such a reality. Indeed, the value and importance of alignment with something both ultimately real and valuable, if such exists, must be a (creaturely) value and importance than which a greater cannot be thought! And the desire and aim to approach such an alignment may therefore rationally be commensurately strong—and this even where the existence of such a reality is only epistemically possible.

Of course we should recognize in all of this—as in all the ensuing chapters of Parts III and IV—a certain qualifier: other things being equal. But it will not take long to deal with this here (though longer to manage it altogether). Given what we have seen, a necessary condition of cashing out this qualifier in a way that will support any criticism of the skeptical Anselmian argument and aim is that some other and *contrary* aim be found which we have some reason to pursue. (The same goes for arguments and

---

[14] As an analogy, consider the whole intellectual enterprise. Suppose that postmodern (or other skeptical) arguments gained even more of a grip than they already have and we all felt it was quite uncertain that there is an objective truth about the world that can be known and understood. In such a case the *importance* that *if* such understanding can be achieved it be pursued would suffice to make it clear what we should do, and would be taken as such by all philosophers.

aims uncovered in subsequent chapters.)[15] But as we will see in the remainder of this book, the various distinct aims that might be mentioned here *themselves* support pursuing the alignment in question, with the result that other things are indeed equal. I can only issue a promissory note to that effect at the moment, but it is one that the reader will be able to cash progressively and ever more satisfyingly (perhaps even with interest) as the rest of the book unfolds.

In conclusion, then, let me offer a summary and an application to Anselmian reasoning and skeptical religion of what we have discovered so far. Recycling Alvin Plantinga's famous reformulation of the ontological argument's premise but in an *epistemic* tone of voice, we have to say that unsurpassable greatness is possibly exemplified.[16] Of course it is also possible that it is *not* exemplified. But if both of these states of affairs are epistemically possible, then because of the enormous intrinsic value and importance of being aligned with something ultimately real and valuable, should such exist, the rational skeptic who sees this will go along with the affirmative possibility. (It would be entirely in the spirit of Anselm to do so.) What we have in Anselm's idea is a unique possibility. He was wrong in supposing that a reality corresponding to it could be deduced from it. But, given our circumstances and what seems unavoidably true about reason and value, this unique possibility should nonetheless be *treated* as reality. The risk of a most intrinsically inappropriate form of life is just too great and also too important to allow for any other reaction—this we can see simply by reflecting on the relevant epistemic possibilities and value considerations and the incredible idea that the Anselmian reflection has placed before our minds. (Indeed, we should conclude that avoiding such a reaction would itself be intrinsically inappropriate to these things.) And the rational skeptic will "go along with the affirmative possibility" by adopting and practicing skeptical religion, since the best way of fulfilling one's aim of as fully as possible approaching a state in which one is aligned in one's own being with anything ultimately real and valuable is by *acting on* the notion that there *is* something ultimately real and valuable in the best way one can—and precisely the latter state is the state instantiated by the one who adopts and practices skeptical religion.[17] Of course the notion of alignment we have been working with and our way of dealing with it has

---

[15] The ceteris paribus clause does not explicitly appear in connection with other reasons in this and the following chapters, but it should always be understood as tacitly present.

[16] For Plantinga's much-discussed but controversial and inconclusive form of ontological argumentation, see his *The Nature of Necessity* (Oxford: Clarendon Press, 1974).

[17] The central idea here is not dissimilar to a view defended by Richard Swinburne in his *Faith and Reason* (Oxford: Clarendon Press, 1981), p. 117, though Swinburne's point is more narrowly focused on theism.

been very abstract, but nothing could be more in the spirit of Anselm's approach. And even very abstract arguments can be seen to be sound.

2. A Second Skeptical Ontological Argument?

Our Anselmian ontological reflections have already exposed an argument on the basis of which the religious skeptic can become a *religious* skeptic, and, in connection with it, an important aim, relevant to the positive justification of faith, which our twenty-first-century skeptic should have. Let us call these the Alignment Argument and the Alignment Aim, respectively. There is something pleasingly analogous to the purely conceptual and a priori nature of the argument Anselm produced in our emphasis here on the *intrinsic* appropriateness of seeking the alignment in question, which can be contrasted with the more "a posteriori" nature of arguments to be developed later in the book, which often focus on *instrumental* appropriateness.[18]

But there is a basis for at least one other (and distinct) argument here too, and it is perhaps the more easily and naturally linked up with our Anselmian skeptic's panegyric to the Divine idea above. I call it the Imaginative Fulfillment Argument (and the aim associated with it is the Imaginative Fulfillment Aim). Here we are asked to consider what it is about being human that *generates* such panegyrics when ultimate things come into view, at least for those who are undeterred by a prejudice or misunderstanding provoked by the excesses of much that belongs to religion-as-it-is. The kind of being we are has an imagination that, as reflection on Anselm's reflections (and, more generally, on religion in human culture) will reveal, is sufficiently spacious and grand to *hold* the idea of the Ultimate—though it trembles on the edges of human understanding—and also is bent toward pursuing an expanded understanding capable of embracing this idea ever more fully, though this may never be achieved. And it is in and by means of the sort of religious life imagined here, with its no-holds-barred exploration of ultimate things, that this imaginative capacity is best able to express itself and most likely to realize its (surely admirable) aim.

---

[18] Of course, depending on one's definitions of "benefit" and "well-being," one might think it a benefit or a furtherance of one's well-being to which faith is instrumentally related to possibly bear a relation to a Divine reality that is intrinsically appropriate to its existence. Here, however, I am thinking not of one for whom *this* is the reason, but rather of one for whom intrinsic appropriateness—regardless of the benefits that may be involved—is itself reason enough.

Now one might wonder whether indeed the whole of the religious life is required to best pursue this aim. Why, in particular, do we need more than faith-that, with its imaginative projection of ultimate possibilities onto the screen of reality? But while for it to do so is theoretically possible, one cannot expect ultimate imagination to exist off on its own, in some sealed compartment separated from the rest of life (faith-that without faith-in). Indeed, one would not really be giving free reign to such imagination if one did not allow it to seep into the pores of all one's activities and interactions, in an attempt to expand one's self-understanding and to see what can be made of the world. The operational, "faith-in" element of religion expresses and also extends the daring imagination of faith-that, permitting it to flow freely into all the interstices of life. Furthermore, an expanded understanding of the sort the imagination seeks may be approached only by *intellectually* acting on one's faith-that—meditating, contemplating, experimenting with various more detailed conceptions that may come to light in pursuing what in Chapter 2 I called the "downward" dimension or direction of the religious life, moving ever deeper into reflection on the ultimate idea. As can be seen, it is indeed the whole of the religious life that is required to allow one to really *live* in the world of ultimate imagination referred to here.

Now if the ultimate idea were obviously false, we might appropriately think of such living, because of the comprehensiveness suggested here, as taking things too far—as imbalanced and closed off from reality. Then reason might rise up and demand that we instead believe and act on the proposition that what religion imagines does not really exist. But as it is, we may once again point out that the denial of the just-mentioned proposition is epistemically quite possible; its truth cannot be ruled out by present-day inquiry. It cannot be ruled out that we are destined for ultimate things, and that the imaginative activity in question will turn out to be fundamentally realistic, only hastening our arrival at that destination. For the skeptic, therefore, no such deterrent as is here mentioned can be placed in the way of affirming what will seem true upon reflection (though it easily goes unnoticed): that there is something noble in an imagination-based life of the sort in question, in which a finite individual is found always straining to the limits, which now (given the sort of being she has evolved to be and despite her finitude) do not appear at any point this side of the idea of ultimacy. As the word "noble" suggests, we are again dealing with intrinsic value here: seeking imaginative fulfillment in the life of skeptical religion is good because it develops an admirable human capacity and realizes intrinsically valuable states of mind.

Let us consider these mental states and their value more closely. I suggest that a relevant element they have in common might be called *expansiveness* or (perhaps more misleadingly) *transcendence*. What we have here are elevated and broadened states of mind that "mimic" in some small way the qualities of their object, for example, in envisaging a truly universal human good—more on this in later chapters—and pursuing within an ultimate frame of reference what might seem quite unrealistic possibilities of human or earthly improvement, seeking to bring every aspect of life into organic unity within that largest frame of reference. But if so, they must by definition bring intrinsic value into the world. By facilitating, in the words of one of Anselm's titles, "a rousing of the mind to the contemplation of [the Divine]," skeptical religion, which as must always be remembered breaks the tie between religion and narrow objects of traditional loyalty, permits the richest possible development of the human personality to take place—richest because closest to even though still infinitely distant from what is ultimately real and valuable. More than any other states of mind, this precisely because of their richness and because they are grounded in a life-commitment, the states of mind it nourishes enable a human being to rise above—to transcend—the limits of his station. By connecting that station and everything else in the whirling circles of his life to the largest imaginable frame of reference, they involve him in probing every crevice in which creative new thoughts about his situation and resourceful new possibilities for advancing the creation of peace and unity within himself and the world might be found, and to stubbornly expect such thoughts to be fruitful and such possibilities to be realized. They finally enlarge his station until it is intimately inclusive of all things. How could such a condition fail to be admirable and worth pursuing?

To summarize, then, our second Anselmian argument. Especially given that the epistemic possibilities are as they are, it would be a travesty—intrinsically inappropriate to *our* nature—to pull the imagination back from its natural goal and keep it cooped up in some cramped and (relatively) darkened corner of existence, to prevent our imaginative life and related aspects of our conscious existence from being as fully extended and continuously brightened as they can by this amazing idea that has come before the human mind.[19] Instead we should encourage this. Now the best way for us to do so is to find a home for human imagination somewhere between a diffident pure skepticism (or an insubstantial and periodic hope) and the overly extravagant indulgences of a believing religiousness. And precisely this skeptical religion provides, with its ability to stimulate and also to develop and deepen the religious imagination that

---

[19] Anselm, apparently, would agree. Reflecting on a paradox of plurality and oneness in the Divine, he says "I find it especially delightful to reflect more frequently upon such an impenetrable mystery" (quoted in Adams, "Anselm on Faith and Reason," p. 34).

it is so evidently in our nature to exercise, while avoiding the suffocating credulity of traditional religion.[20]

Now it may seem that the aims envisaged by the Alignment Argument and the Imaginative Fulfillment Argument can be realized at all only if ultimism is *true*, for only then is there a religious reality for one's being to be aligned with or for one's imagination to uncover. And so the religious skeptic who takes these reasons on board is in a fairly startling manner making herself a hostage to fortune. But while there are certainly goods that are realized by the religious person only if ultimism is true, not all of the goods associated with these reasons are among them. As already suggested, given our epistemic situation and the nature of the Divine, it is definitely intrinsically appropriate, and it is so *now*, for one to live in a manner that befits the existence of an ultimate salvific reality—something one regards only as possible. It is indeed a requirement of virtue that one do so. And it is so even if reality is in fact barren of any such thing. What we see in the development and pursuit of this aim are traits of character that would be admirable even if the basic religious claim were false. As for the imaginative aim: here, even more obviously, there is plenty of good that can be achieved even if ultimism is false—good realized in the present by the person who pursues it on account of the deeper, richer expression of her own nature that such activity uniquely facilitates and so (as we have seen) on account of a kind of virtue all its own. And the contribution of skeptical religion to the pursuit of these aims is quite real, though—because of the immaturity of much extant religion—easy to overlook or misconstrue.

All of this we are forced to recognize simply by appropriate reflection on the *idea* of ultimism's truth, and in thus beholding the rational power of his idea, we see Anselm's continuing contribution to the discussion of religion.

---

[20] The word "suffocating" is worth pausing over for a moment: in skeptical religion we can give free rein to the big "what if" of the imagination in a manner that is denied to traditional religion, for not only do we allow that there may be no ultimate, salvific reality at all, thus making clear that our faith *is* a work of the imagination, but we remain entirely open as to the details of its nature, thus permitting the imagination to fly off in every direction, gleaning insights from every wind and becoming enriched in myriad ways. Here it may be worth noting that Anselm himself is only in some respects an inspiration for such an attitude. Associated as he was with traditional Christian religion, it was only within fairly narrow bounds that he could exercise "faith seeking understanding"—note the many passages in which a revealed Word, the Incarnation, the Trinity, etc., are assumed—and his operational faith was of course a believing one.

CHAPTER 7

Leibniz's Ambition

1. *The Lure of Cosmological Understanding*

In the previous chapter it was discovered that from Anselmian reflection or, more grandly, the ontology of religion at least two reasons can be drawn that singly or in conjunction provide strong rational support for religious faith. We might call an argument citing either or both of those reasons an Anselmian argument for skeptical religion or, more provocatively, a skeptical ontological argument. In the present chapter I show that similar results can be achieved in connection with Leibniz's cosmological argument and the issues and concerns suggested thereby.

A central notion to be appropriated for our purposes here, as might be expected, is Leibniz's famous "principle of sufficient reason." In his *Principles of Nature and Grace, Based on Reason,* he introduces this principle and its purpose in his work as follows:

> So far we have spoken only at the level of *physical* inquiry; now we must move up to the *metaphysical,* by making use of the *great principle,* not very widely used, which says that *nothing comes about without a sufficient reason;* that is, that nothing happens without its being possible for someone who understands things well enough to provide a reason sufficient to determine why it is as it is and not otherwise. Given that principle, the first question we are entitled to ask will be *why is there something rather than nothing?*[1]

---

[1] Gottfried Wilhelm Leibniz, *Principles of Nature and Grace, Based on Reason,* 7, in *G. W. Leibniz: Philosophical Texts,* trans. Richard Francks and R. S. Woolhouse (Oxford: Oxford University Press, 1998).

As is well known, Leibniz holds that we are entitled to conclude, in response to this fundamental question (understood—the context indicates—as a question about the existence of the universe), that God exists. Since there must be, for the existence of the universe as for anything else, a sufficient reason, and since this "can never be found in the series of contingent things" itself, it follows that there "must be a necessary being, which carries the reason for its existence within itself"—and "that final reason for things is what we call God."[2]

Now many have wondered whether Leibniz's necessary being deserves to be called God, but it is important to see that, on his view, closely related considerations immediately prove that that being possesses not only necessity but also all the other features—in particular, the axiological features—of the Divine. In *Principles of Nature and Grace*, we are told (immediately following the above reference to the necessary being as God) that "this simple, primal substance must contain eminently the perfections which are contained in the derivative substances which are its effects."[3] In the *Monadology*, which gives a slightly more detailed account of many of Leibniz's views, we read that imperfections come from the "limitations or boundaries of things" and that God, being completely unlimited, is therefore "absolutely perfect."[4] We should also notice (as this quotation suggests) that Leibniz, in wielding the principle of sufficient reason in this context, is aiming to cut through to an explanation not just of the fact that there is a world, but of the fact that *this* world exists instead of other possible worlds—and here too claims about value are brought in. The sufficient reason for the latter fact is that our world is "the best, which God's wisdom brings him to know, his goodness brings him to choose, and his power brings him to produce."[5] Indeed, the work of Leibniz, from early to late, on matters as diverse as monads and money, is filled with considerations of value, rooted ultimately in the Divine. In all of his ambitious quest for understanding, which was wide-ranging indeed,[6] and which was perhaps more public-spirited and sensitive to the need for social and political improvements than his complacent-sounding talk about our world

---

[2] Ibid., 8.

[3] Ibid., 9.

[4] *Monadology*, 40–42, in *Leibniz: Philosophical Texts*.

[5] Ibid., 55.

[6] One biographer refers to him as an "innovator able to lead the specialists" not only in philosophy but also in "law, history, politics, linguistics, theology, logic, technology, mathematics, [and] science." (E. J. Aiton, *Leibniz: A Biography* [Bristol: Hilger, 1985], p. ix.) Robert Adams says that Leibniz dreamed throughout his life of a "quixotically massive proposed encyclopedia of definitions, axioms, and theorems that would facilitate accurate and relatively uncontroversial reasoning on every topic." (See Robert M. Adams, *Leibniz: Determinist, Theist, Idealist* [Oxford: Oxford University Press, 1994], p. 200.)

as the best possible has led many to think,[7] the notion of a metaphysically and axiologically ultimate and salvific reality (conceived by him in personal terms) figures centrally.[8]

But, alas, as is well known, Leibniz's reach—his ambition to convincingly arrive at an absolutely complete and thorough explanation of things—somewhat exceeded his grasp: his famous cosmological argument in particular (and the principle of sufficient reason utilized therein) is subject to formidable objections, and no one has yet managed to state it in a manner that is anywhere close to free from controversy.[9] Consider, for example, how the things we encounter in everyday life and in the most developed and respectable areas of science are always details in a larger picture, coming as part of a package or collection—just try to identify one such thing that sits alone, without neighbors. Because of this it is not surprising (if we make any room at all in our metaphysics for relations and causation) that they should be found to exhibit such relations to *other* things as the relations of "being caused by," "being explained by," and "provided with a sufficient reason by." Simply put: we know there are other things around that can do the explaining. But this "part of a package" point cannot (or cannot uncontroversially) be applied to the total series of contingent states. Hence the reason in question for expecting explanation is unavailable in the latter case.

Now this is of course where Leibnizians will want to emphasize that there is another reason for expecting things to be explained: it is, we are told, really in virtue of their *contingency*—the fact that it is possible for them not to exist—that the things around us should seem to us to require explanation by reference to external events or states of affairs (or at least to be possibly thus explained, in a logical or metaphysical sense of "possibly")—and contingency is shared by the aforementioned series. But this, it seems to me, is the wrong inference here: from their contingency we can infer that an external explanation for common things, including the fact of the world's existence, is not by definition ruled out in the way that it would be if these things were necessary instead of contingent. But it is a long way from "an external explanation is not by definition ruled out"

---

[7] On this see Nicholas Rescher, *The Philosophy of Leibniz* (Englewood Cliffs, N.J.: Prentice-Hall, 1967), p. 160.

[8] That Leibniz viewed his perfect and necessary being as salvific is evident. "Everything is made the best possible, both for the general good and for the greatest particular good of those who are aware of it and who are content with the government of God" (*Principles of Nature and Grace*, 18).

[9] See, for example, William Rowe, *The Cosmological Argument* (New York: Fordham University Press, 1998), and Peter van Inwagen, *Metaphysics* (Boulder, Colo.: Westview Press, 2002).

to "an external explanation applies." And it is very hard to see how that property of contingency—of "being such as can not-obtain"—as opposed to the empirically discovered property of existence-within-a-collection or (better yet) *origin*-within-a-collection could get us all the way to the latter destination. If we think this easy to see, it may be because we mistakenly suppose that by admitting it is possible for *x* not to exist, we do more than simply recognize the *kind* of existence *x* has, a recognition that is even compatible with *x*'s existing eternally: that instead we thereby are admitting a kind of *instability* or *insecurity* in the existence of *x*. Or perhaps under the cover of philosophy we are yielding to a belief in God independently underwritten by traditional religious influences to which we still are subject. Of course there is another, seemingly more sophisticated route one might try here: noticing that a necessary fact does not require an external explanation and that contingent facts are non-necessary, one might be tempted to infer that contingent facts *do* require such an explanation. But that way lies only the fallacy of denying the antecedent.

Such problems and controversies (and we haven't even mentioned the relevance of such things as Divine hiddenness and earthly horrors to the security of the Leibnizian conclusion), especially in the context of the broad skeptical argumentation of *Skepticism,* should prevent us from lingering over the thought that Leibniz might have successfully fulfilled his ambition of generating a complete understanding of the world that we are justified in believing to be correct. Perhaps Leibniz himself would today wish to adopt a different approach. Maybe a more realistic Leibniz, properly chastened by skepticism but retaining the desire to understand, would develop his arguments differently. While putting forward his various ingenious ideas as possibilities to be explored, he might defend a religious attitude on other (though related) grounds. He might say that ultimism is to be presumed true on practical grounds, for the sake of a proper pursuit of understanding. As Robert Adams has noted, "Leibniz was quite willing to appeal to arguments of practical or moral force, specifically including presumption," in matters of religion. According to Adams, although the "presumption" intended by Leibniz seems most often to have been bound up with belief, in at least one place there is the suggestion of something that does not quite add up to belief.[10] Whatever the case, whether the idea of a chastened Leibniz (or Leibnizian) as a person of skeptical, beliefless faith is just too much to take or whether it is acceptable, I myself want to suggest and support the idea that even if we cannot safely arrive at the conclusion of a necessary God from facts about a contingent world any

[10] Adams, *Leibniz,* pp. 197, 203.

more than we can do so from facts about the idea of an unsurpassably great being, here again we can aim for an evolutionary adaptation, finding support for skeptical religion by moving in different directions from a similar starting point.

That starting point, as already suggested, concerns the *promotion of understanding*. Leibniz looked at the world and wanted to understand it thoroughly.[11] Such an understanding he valued most highly. And his principle of sufficient reason told him that no understanding of the world is adequate that excludes religion. We can look at the same world and reflect on our position in the world as seekers of understanding (including the deepest, most general understanding), and we too can make some connections between all this and religion, even if they are not Leibniz's connections and even if the religion we contemplate is different from his. We can notice that we do seek understanding in various ways and at various levels of our lives and, naturally enough, deeply value the understanding that we seek, and that an understanding comprehensive enough to bring fact and value together is also worth seeking. And we can notice further that the human quest for understanding is fraught with difficulties and beset by obstacles of various kinds, among them such as have prevented the human species from developing intellectual investigation (including specifically religious investigation) very far. Noticing all of this, and thinking about it in connection with skeptical religion, we may come to realize that although traditional religion has not produced a successful intellectual hypothesis by means of which the world is explained, skeptical religion may provide the practical framework within which all of our explanatory and (more generally) understanding-focused activities, from the most limited to the most expansive or sweeping, are best carried out. Slightly altering Leibniz's view that no understanding of the world is adequate that excludes religion, we may say that no *general context for the seeking* of understanding is adequate that excludes religion. Stating the basic idea here more fully, and transforming Leibniz's principle of sufficient reason into a principle of rational sufficiency, we might judge that no human form of life should be deemed adequate or rationally sufficient by our twenty-first-century skeptic unless it allows her to pursue all her understanding-related aims, including the aims involving cosmology, in the best available way. Adding

---

[11] Notice the aim of an unrivaled depth of vision reflected in the following extract from his famous discussion of the monads: "Everything is full...every portion of matter is not only divisible to infinity...but is actually subdivided without end, every part into smaller parts....Every portion of matter can be thought of as a garden full of plants, or as a pond full of fish. But every branch of the plant, every part of the animal, and every drop of its vital fluids, is another such garden, or another such pond" (*Monadology*, 61, 65, 67).

the premise (from above) that the best available way of pursuing these aims is going to be skeptically religious, we may conclude that no form of life is rationally sufficient unless it is skeptically religious.

Now this suggestion, which purports to turn on its head the usual, Chapter 5–type criticism of religion as by nature intellectually weak or stultifying,[12] of course requires a lot of unpacking and defense. It is at least as ambitious, someone might say, as Leibniz's own suggestion. (Well, anything else could hardly hope to be true to him.) Let us see now how this ambitious use of Leibniz's ambition can be developed and justified, making use, as we go, of some strands from earlier discussion.

2. *Religion and the Promotion of Understanding*

Here again is the basic argument—we might most naturally call it the Understanding Argument and the aim it enshrines the Aim of Understanding:

1. No human form of life is rationally sufficient unless it allows one to pursue the conjunction of our various understanding-related aims (including cosmological aims) in the best available way.

But

2. The best available way of pursuing these aims involves adopting skeptical religion.

Therefore

3. No human form of life is rationally sufficient unless it is a way of realizing skeptical religion.

The first premise here must certainly be said to be very plausible indeed, much more plausible than the principle of sufficient reason with which Leibniz operates. Think, for example, of our discussion about what a "commitment to reason" involves, or about how an understanding

---

[12] This criticism has received a lot of press again recently. (Consider, for example, the flurry of discussion over Richard Dawkins's *The God Delusion* [London: Houghton Mifflin, 2006]). But always the focus is, shortsightedly, on traditional religion, which, with all its imaginative shrinkage and abuses of the imperative of understanding, represents religion only as we have seen it so far.

of worldly things in so many ways promotes human flourishing in the world—flourishing that in the twenty-first century is still sadly lacking in many quarters. Most generally: we should pursue understanding and, in our lives, do whatever we can to facilitate its pursuit in order to realize our extrinsic goals most effectively; and in order to determine what those goals *should be;* and ultimately we should pursue understanding as a goal in itself (here I refer to the highest, deepest, most comprehensive understanding). With each level we improve ourselves and potentially the world, adding to the complexity and the value of our lives.

So the first premise of the argument seems quite secure. It is obviously the second premise that will be controversial, and in the rest of this chapter I develop a series of considerations to defend it which show that it too is very plausible. These considerations are four in number.

(i) *Motivation:* additional or crucial motivation for pursuing understanding-related interests is afforded by being skeptically religious. This point can take different forms, depending on the kind of motivation that is highlighted—at least three forms, in fact.

The *first* of these says that additional motivation of a very general nature (applicable to any level or subject of inquiry) is afforded by skeptical religion because of a general feature of such religion that in Chapter 2 we described in terms of the most sensitive, discriminating, and wide-ranging "attentiveness and study" aimed at a fuller understanding of the Ultimate. As was said there, since in having ultimistic faith one is going with the idea that an ultimate good is latent in reality, and since it is unclear just where or how it is to be found or even just what, in its details, it may involve, one has good reason to cultivate a full and appropriate alertness in all one's moments, continually stretching one's capacity for fine-grained appreciation of what is going on in one's environment. Although the context for this investigation is a pursuit of the Ultimate, the investigation itself—given that this is *skeptical* religion, with its emphasis on an early stage of development—is thereby broadened and intensified rather than narrowed in any way, as one might have been led to expect must be the case with religion. In other words, the passion for inquiry that comes with (or at least is strongly cultivated in) skeptical religiousness spills over as additional motivation for inquiry for anyone, in any field of study whatever. This should make skeptical religion very attractive to any twenty-first-century skeptic who has made the seeking of understanding a priority in her life, no matter where or how she intends to pursue that priority.

A *second* form of the motivation point begins by drawing attention to the fact, already suggested by the previous point, that in skeptical religion everything is subsumed under the idea of a reality that, if ultimism is true, must be incomparably wonderful. The idea of such a reality is of course deeply attractive, drawing one in and broadening and intensifying one's investigative activity, as we have seen. And it may be expected to draw to inquiry and understanding-related activities even persons who would otherwise not care much at all about such things. For them it therefore would provide *crucial* motivation for such activities. This point can also be broadened. For there are many individuals and groups in the world of today who are, for various reasons not restricted to the vague apathy and indolence so far suggested, disinclined to pursue the sort of investigation that may be needed for the human species to approach a fuller understanding of the world. (Think here, for example, of complacent fundamentalists or cynical postmodernists.) Skeptical religion, for reasons already suggested, may be expected to rid them of this disinclination. Now, of course, not all will stand in need of this new sort of motivation for inquiry in order to have any motivation at all, and perhaps it would be good if none did, but given the actual facts about human nature and typical human preoccupations and present intellectual and religious trends, it is still undeniable that the rate of careful investigation and inquiry must go up with the rate of interest and participation in skeptical religion. This should be noteworthy for anyone unwilling to sanction a form of life that realizes less than the best available context for inquiry.

But there is also a *third* form of the motivation point. For it can be argued that skeptical religion, if universally adopted, would provide for all of us additional—and for some of us crucial—motivation to actively pursue inquiry *of a particular sort,* the deepest, most comprehensive sort: namely, religious inquiry. Among the sorts of inquiry that, from a purely intellectual perspective, must appear important to anyone concerned for understanding is religious inquiry, inquiry aimed at determining whether there is an ultimate and salvific reality, and what sort of nature such a reality might have. Of course, since successful prosecution of such inquiry might also yield the understanding science seeks—given that inquiry into what is metaphysically ultimate is entailed here, and this might turn out *not* to be religious but rather a scientifically explicable and accessible reality—there could be "spin-off" benefits for science from such inquiry. A number of times I have said or suggested that the human species may yet have a long way to go in the quest for spiritual understanding. I think it quite possible that in a few thousand years' time, most present notions about the detailed nature of ultimate things will seem quite primitive and undeveloped, and will have been replaced by more adequate conceptions, which can themselves fuel further and deeper inquiry. Of course more adequate forms of religious investigation will need to be practiced if this sort of development is to be possible. It is one of the great goods of the nonsectarian faith I am championing that it motivates and facilitates such investigation. As we have seen, humble and open and wide-ranging religious investigation that engages all aspects of our being is central to this faith: here faith truly seeks understanding.

This sort of seeking and investigation is a necessary means of doing justice to the depth and richness and significance of the idea of a reality at once ultimate and salvific. As I have indicated, we have as a species not come close to doing justice to this idea so far. Thus the fact that skeptical religion provides motivation for such investigation must make it the more attractive to any twenty-first-century skeptic who values the deepening of human understanding.

(ii) *Balance:* with the advent of skeptical religion we would find the exclusively or primarily secular investigative concerns of the present and recent past balanced by proper investigation of religious matters, especially neglected before. Here we are saying not only (as under [i]) that the latter sort of investigation may yet have a long way to go and is important, and that motivation for carrying it out must therefore appear desirable, but that a disproportionate amount of attention in organized human inquiry so far has been given to matters *other* than those falling under religious inquiry as explicated above. The need to rectify this imbalance gives religious inquiry added importance, or makes it important in a distinctive way, and thus gives us even more reason to endorse skeptical religion as a way of promoting understanding.

Here we are harking back to a point already made in a different context, when in Chapter 5 we addressed the objection that skeptical religion only encourages "slanted thinking"—a one-sided preoccupation with religious selections from the metaphysical menu. What we pointed out there, and what we may use again here for a somewhat different purpose, is that especially because of the influence of modern science, naturalistic metaphysical options have been rather dominant in (at any rate Western) processes of investigation over the past few centuries. Furthermore, prior to that, rather parochial religious concerns held sway. Where investigation was done, it was commonly under the watchful eye of some religious tradition or other (in the West, we need only think of the well-known intellectual influences and baleful constraints of severely conservative forms of Christianity and of political structures imbued therewith). Therefore, a new and intensive and continuing program of research into a wide range of religious options both old and new is needed to rectify this intellectual imbalance. Notice that this need not lead to a new imbalance if we remember—as highlighted in the first version of the motivation point above—that skeptical religion sponsors not only such explicit concern with inquiries explicitly relevant to its ultimate goal, but also a deepening of the sort of attentiveness and study that is compatible with and evinced by inquiries directed to the more proximate goals of everyday life and science.

(iii) *Unification:* there is a need, if we are to settle for nothing less than the most comprehensive understanding, to seek to bring the sort of knowledge available through natural science into harmony with what we know from experience about such things as consciousness, value, and will, and one important way of seeking to satisfy this need is by pursuing skeptical religion. No such unified understanding as I have mentioned here seems presently available or is even much pursued by contemporary investigators, who are often under the spell cast by the idea that science is all. This lamentable feature of the present state of affairs is clearly expressed by Thomas Nagel in his recent review of Richard Dawkins's book *The God Delusion:*

> It is natural to try to take any successful intellectual method as far as it will go. Yet the impulse to find an explanation of everything in physics has over the last fifty years gotten out of control. The concepts of physical science provide a very special, and partial, description of the world that experience reveals to us. It is the world with all subjective consciousness, sensory appearances, thought, value, purpose, and will left out. What remains is the mathematically describable order of things and events in space and time.
>
> That conceptual purification launched the extraordinary development of physics and chemistry that has taken place since the seventeenth century. But reductive physicalism turns this description into an exclusive ontology. The reductionist project usually tries to reclaim some of the originally excluded aspects of the world, by analyzing them in physical—that is, behavioral or neurophysiological—terms; but it denies reality to what cannot be so reduced. I believe the project is doomed—that conscious experience, thought, value, and so forth are not illusions, even though they cannot be identified with physical facts.[13]

Even someone who is unsure about the merits of the reductive program (as opposed to denying them, like Nagel) or about whether the alternative

---

[13] Thomas Nagel, "The Fear of Religion," in *The New Republic* (online edition, issue date: 10.23.06), p. 2.

of unification can be achieved should see the point, in light of the awareness Nagel brings to us, of uniting our *inquiries* into related matters, so
as to give proper attention to the intriguing *possibility* that there is some
overarching understanding in which all these things are harmonized. One
might imagine a research program that takes as its hypothesis the claim
that this can be achieved, exploring every way of confirming that hypothesis. And skeptical religion presents itself as embracing what is in effect
just such a research program. It acts on the faith that the richest possible
understanding, in which fact and value are united, is correct, and strains
to see how the various disparate elements of experience might be brought
into harmony under such a conception.

Now Nagel recognizes that one way of trying to effect a unification of
the sort to which he alludes involves the traditional religious idea of God.
He does not hold out much hope for such an attempt, referring instead
to the possibility of ideas that have not yet occurred to us.[14] I am naturally
much in sympathy with this proposal, but I want to point out what persons
overly influenced by the familiarity of traditional religious ideas (including critics of traditional religion like Nagel) tend to overlook: that there
may be new *religious* ideas among the unforeseen ideas of the future that
promote the development of our understanding, ways of filling out that
underinvestigated idea of ultimism which lead us further in the direction
of an understanding of how to reconcile fact and value. In any case, by
losing the "fear of religion" to which Nagel refers—indeed, by embracing
religion fully in its skeptical form—we may do more to promote the unification of understanding that Leibniz sought and that we should seek than
would be possible otherwise. Certainly the skeptically religious way is one
important way of pursuing it.

(iv) *Moral support:* providing, as we have seen, additional or crucial motivation for undertaking various intellectual tasks, skeptical religion also
makes an important contribution to the forms of psychological *fortification* that are needed to see them through. The aim of understanding—
certainly if as thoroughgoing a pursuit as a Leibnizian must advocate—is
bound to be challenging. It is easy to give up or to have one's efforts in investigation diluted by the attention one is tempted to give to other, lesser
concerns. But a religious commitment and community continually keep
the heat on, prodding one to move forward in a focused way, keeping
before one's mind the idea of a grounding for the investigative adventure
and the possibility of actually achieving what is envisaged in the goals of

[14] Ibid.

inquiry, not to mention the deep worthwhileness of pursuing them. Non-believing religious faith, that is, inspires a continuing respect for objectivity. It imaginatively places the world within an intelligible framework: the world can be known, will be known, and is worth knowing. Further, it steers one past distractions, makes available strategies for combating despair, and also—because of the openness of the world-picture and the temporal sensitivity and humility it provokes one to cultivate—helps one ward against overquick conclusions and complacency. (Faith, as we might say, gives reason the *patience* to do its job effectively.) In sum, given our immaturity, the goals we are inclined to pursue, and the difficulty of making intellectual progress in a complex world like ours, inquirers at every level will benefit from the moral support for adequate intellectual inquiry afforded by skeptical faith, and these benefits will be the more important as the subject matter becomes more comprehensive and complex. (This last point leads to an interesting result: scientists and philosophers may have more reason to avail themselves of faith than unsophisticated types, rather than less!) All of these things are of enormous value in an investigation aimed at the truth about things and must surely be taken by anyone who values understanding as facilitating its pursuit in important ways.

So much for our four considerations. What they permit us to see is this: skeptical religion takes nothing away from the investigation-promoting factors that would be operative in us should we remain pure skeptics but rather significantly enhances our prospects of success as seekers of understanding. Though perhaps not always when taken singly, certainly when taken together the considerations here outlined therefore lead us to the surprising conclusion that a form of religion provides the best available context for the pursuit of understanding. Its central and only controversial premise having thus been supported, we may endorse our basic argument above—with its Aim of Understanding—as sound. Anyone who shares the Leibnizian ambition, recognizing the imperative to promote understanding, should adopt and seek to extend the pursuit of skeptical religion.

3. *Skeptical Responses to the Skeptical Ambition*

But, with due deference to injunctions that our own emphasis on understanding should lead us to accept, we must now carefully consider whether any of the arguments I have just given faces important difficulties so far unnoticed. Are any of the considerations outlined above perhaps weaker than I have made them appear? In the remainder of the chapter I want to examine several suggestions to that effect.

(1) "You have said, in describing the motivating power of skeptical religion, that this is a form of motivation that remains effective no matter how one's intellectual tasks may be construed. But there are many purely nonreligious forms of inquiry. And some of them certainly require the full attention of the inquirer if they are to be successfully prosecuted. But in that case the religious focus of an adherent of skeptical religion (which comes to light more fully in your other points) must certainly sometimes operate as a significant *distraction* and as a factor that *undermines* motivation to pursue inquiry. Think of the distractions represented by specifically religious pursuits for, say, a physicist or a mathematician. (Mightn't Pascal, for example, have been motivated to achieve much more in mathematics if he hadn't been distracted by religion?)"

This objection assumes that a religious focus means that one must be thinking explicitly about religion and only about religion all (or most) of the time. It also assumes that full attention to physics or mathematics entails exclusive attention thereto. Both assumptions are false. A religious focus means that all of one's thinking goes on within a religious frame of reference and is integrated thereby. This is quite possible even if one spends extended periods of time thinking explicitly about physics or mathematics and only physics or mathematics. Relatedly, giving one's full attention to physics or mathematics over long periods of time can be a *way* of giving attention to religion if one of the reasons one has for doing physics or mathematics is that it might open up insights into ultimate things. As can be seen, both assumptions overlook the presence of levels and means-ends relations in our mental life and pay insufficient attention to the distinctive features of skeptical religion outlined in Chapters 2 and 3.

Now, of course, a religious person (even a skeptically religious one) will also spend much time thinking explicitly about religious matters or engaged in explicitly religious activities. But, especially given what we have just seen, these need not threaten as full a preoccupation with physics or mathematics as we would normally consider compatible with proper attention to other goods—goods that, as future arguments will show, are often themselves most fully found in explicitly religious pursuits. An adherent of skeptical religion might very well at some juncture think that her ultimate interests will be as well served by simply doing some more physics or mathematics as by seeking to tease out, say, new understandings of the Buddhist concept of Emptiness. Again, the objector is thinking too much about conventional or traditional forms of religion (though even here we might point out that many of the most accomplished scientists have been quite conventionally religious).

And this is relevant to Pascal. The reason that Pascal was so distracted by religion, if he was, is to be understood by reference to shortsighted thinking and a consequent passion for defending a sewn-up religious picture of the world of a sort sponsored by conventional religiosity but to which skeptical religion is explicitly opposed. Many of Pascal's scripturally based convictions, it might usefully be noted, have come to appear quite quaint in the light of subsequent critical biblical scholarship. Pascal was in his own way strongly influenced by skepticism, as Terence Penelhum has shown,[15] but his response to its difficulties was to follow his heart into a form of traditional Christian theism (together with its investigation-dulling dispositions) rather than to broaden his conception of appropriate religiosity and fully embrace the appropriate injunctions of humility as skeptical religion admonishes us to do.

(2) "With respect to both the motivation and the fortification points: how can faith have such psychological power when it is not grounded in belief? Isn't it precisely the *belief* of the traditionally religious that motivates and fortifies them in their peculiar pursuits? How can we expect such a powerful psychological force to be carried over into a form of religion in which one is *divested* of belief?"

The basic idea of this objection was already encountered in Chapters 2 and 3 and dealt with there. I particularly recommend the point that a vivid imagination can perform a role in emotion quite analogous to that of full-fledged belief. But I want to say more than that as well. While belief is indeed psychologically powerful, capable of causing a kind of complacency as I have often emphasized, when it comes to the motivating and fortifying power of religion we have to think about not just the cognitive attitude at the bottom of it but the larger way of life it informs. Likewise, when it comes to assessing the motivating and fortifying potential of skeptical religion, we have to think about more than simply the disposition involved in imagining that ultimism is true, as the objector appears to be doing. Perhaps if that were the sole element of skeptical religion, we would lack what is needed for the usual motivating and fortifying potential of religion to be present in any significant force. But that element is only one part of a larger form of life structured by *all* the features of propositional faith and also by *operational* faith. Just as in the case of traditional religion, one finds a unifying focus and a tightly woven way of life involving multiply layered and integrated religious practices (ideally) carried out with community support. It is total immersion in such a form of life that has the motivating and fortifying potential in question. And this "total immersion" occurs as much in a skeptical form of religion as in any other. Voluntarily submitting herself to something larger than simply

---

[15] See his *God and Skepticism: A Study in Skepticism and Fideism* (Dordrecht: Reidel, 1984).

the ultimism-directed thought of this moment or that, the individual is moved swiftly forward along the stream of the religious life and quickly past the eddies that might otherwise have sucked her in and prevented her progress.

(3) "In suggesting that religious motivation and fortification are needed, or at any rate that where they are present the prospects of human understanding are enhanced, are you not neglecting the power of certain *other* forms of support for inquiry? Wouldn't, for example, a purely philosophical disposition—the love of understanding for its own sake—be enough? After all, philosophers (and scientists too), when lit up by a passion to know and understand, will carry on in intellectual tasks almost obsessively, despite the obstacles to success skeptics are continually erecting on their paths."

There is truth to this, but it is incomplete. Cultivating the passion of philosophy may provide part of what is needed—a drive to persist, even in the face of difficulty. But what is required here is a *package* of things including such a drive, certainly, but also something to oppose too narrow a focus and our natural tendency to exaggerate the significance of findings or to believe prematurely. It must further be said that it is quite possible for the light of passion to go out (perhaps because the light of reasoning exposes skeptical obstacles ever more clearly). The larger one's goals with respect to knowledge and understanding, the less reason there is to think they can successfully be carried out: this certainly has relevance to the cosmological reflection of the Leibnizian. And so there remains the strong possibility of despair in the course of a whole life even for one motivated well enough *right now* by desire or love or whatever.

Furthermore, some of the things we need to understand are not as flashy and exciting as what normally comes to mind when one thinks of philosophical or scientific passion. *Self*-understanding, for example, is hugely important, but may not immediately commend itself to one unless it comes as part of a package that specially motivates it—a package of the sort delivered by skeptical religion. What is needed here is an entire way of being that highlights a passion for understanding but also all the other things the investigative life requires, and this, as we have seen, is just what skeptical religion affords.

(4) "Even if faith is needed in this context, why must it be specifically religious faith? Why wouldn't a more general investigative faith—a freely and persistently willed imagining of success in the pursuit of understanding, for example—do the trick just as well?"

As we have seen, *various* desiderata must be kept in focus, so one would need independent acts and dispositions of faith for each of them. At a certain point, it will obviously be advantageous, from a purely psychological point of view, to have an overarching framework in which all these things are unified instead of propositional bits and corresponding acts of imagination floating separately, as it were, in thin air. If, for example, one is directly imagining success in this and/or that aspect of some limited inquiry, questions may arise about what might *make* it so, questions that are stilled when one has the more powerful faith directed toward an adequate framework proposition like ultimism. (There seems to be a natural human intellectual tendency always to push things to the limit, and to rest only in ultimate things.) What will be most effective in this context is not separate forces to oppose each of the obstacles to investigative success directly but a counterbalancing commitment—again, an entire way of being—that directly and indirectly (e.g., through the desires it cultivates) presents a unified front against the enemies of the intellect.

(5) "Even if a religious attitude is required for the benefits in question here, why must it be faith instead of a more modest hope, which is compatible with pure skepticism?"

Well, contrary to the aphorism, hope does *not* spring eternal; it requires a commitment to support it. Furthermore, hope, as normally construed, is so weak as to be something one may have even when first identifying and surveying the problem here! (I *hope* that all will be well in our pursuit of understanding, but how can I make it more likely that it *will* be so?) Suppose, however, that our concept of hope is beefed up so as to include the more positive thoughts and commitment required to provide a solution to that problem. Then it turns out to be equivalent to faith! Either way, then, this objection fails to threaten what I have said about motivation and fortification.

(6) "Concerning now your point about *balance:* it might seem right to focus more on religious questions to redress the problem you have described, but to suppose in faith that there is an ultimate religious explanation is to go too far. Indeed, such a supposition gets things backward, postulating at the *outset* what should, at best, be a conclusion at the *end*. How can this approach be in line with the spirit and fundamental dispositions of inquiry? Isn't it simply imbalanced in another way, stacking the deck in favor of religion?"

There may appear to be a problem here, but it is only an appearance—one that will vanish when we remember the general nature of ultimism, and also the special requirements of proper religious inquiry. Because ultimism is such a general framework proposition, embracing it in faith is not at all going to stack the deck in favor of any specific and detailed religious account of the sort that might seem to represent the sought-for conclusion of inquiry and whose acceptance might move one to cease inquiry. Indeed, and more strongly, taking ultimism on board by faith and also living accordingly is necessary for the deepest and most adequate forms of religious investigation to take place. In matters of religion we, paradoxically, need to take a stand—and moreover, a *positive, affirming* stand—if we are to investigate the issues most adequately (in the way that will seem best from the perspective of a deep love of truth and understanding).

Why is this? Why not leave the job to someone who offers no form of assent to religion's claim at all, whether voluntary or otherwise? Well, for one thing, to keep our attention directly or indirectly on the pressing task of developing and exploring alternative religious possibilities (including, of course, many not heretofore conceived) and to carry out this task properly and dedicatedly over the long haul requires considerable investigative zeal as well as unusual thoroughness and wide sensitivity. But why shouldn't a pure skeptic be able to summon the requisite attitudes? Perhaps she could do so: I would certainly not say it is impossible. What I would say is that *extra* psychological support for investigation is available to the skeptic who, while not losing her skepticism, chooses to adopt skeptical religion; and that a skeptic who clearly sees the task that lies ahead and wishes to display a love for understanding that is the best possible will avail herself of this support. As we have seen, even in the absence of belief, assenting to ultimism and holding its content before our minds will help to work against despair and distraction by antireligious influences. Further (and this is a point of deep importance), it would seem that at least such an attitude is necessary for some of the forms of investigation that will need to be pursued: a more detailed understanding of religious possibilities will in the nature of the case be arrived at only by those who enter into the spirit of religion in some way. And so a skeptic who really loves and pursues the truth about religion must be prepared to do so.

Perhaps it will be argued that some disposition falling short of faith and certainly less than the total complex set of dispositions involved in skeptical religion would suffice to produce the desired result here. Perhaps something like a working hypothesis, an assumption for the sake of inquiry, would do. I think this suggestion underestimates the complexity and subtlety of the facts that we need to appreciate from the inside in order to significantly deepen our understanding of religious possibilities. But suppose we accept it. It takes nothing away from the support provided for skeptical religion by our point about balance and the points I have been making here in its support. For these are meant to work *in concert* with the other considerations of motivation, fortification (or moral support), and unification. And this they can do even if, because of the possibility of substituting a nonreligious attitude for religious faith in the activities aimed at restoring the balance in question, they would not work on their own. If a distinctively religious response is supported by the other considerations concerned with the promotion of understanding, then that the form of life in question would also be sufficient (even if not necessary) to help restore the desired balance must give us even more reason to adopt skeptical religion than we otherwise would possess.

(7) "Regarding the point about *unification:* the assumption that we need somehow to bring consciousness, value, and will, as ordinarily construed, into our overall picture of things is unjustified. Consciousness is reducible to the brain and its processes, will is just a certain special kind of determined behavior, and value is simply a function of desire—itself explicable as a brain process. Indeed, a proper picture of inquiry and its legitimate objects depends on leaving value out of the picture. We can make do well enough with fact alone, and it is naive to suppose otherwise."

I suggest that it is rather this sort of objection that is naive. One way of showing this would refer again to our relative immaturity and the presumption, at this stage of inquiry, of any declaration to the effect that we have already plumbed the depths of consciousness, will, and value, and found nothing independently substantial there. But another would simply consider certain unavoidable ways of talking and thinking.

We can perhaps develop this approach most pointedly in connection with the notion of value (earlier in the chapter I sometimes used "value" as a kind of shorthand for "all the neglected things Nagel emphasizes"; here it is used exclusively in the ordinary way). The very expressions "proper," "legitimate," and "make do well enough" cry out for a more substantial understanding of value, not reducible to desire. Is the objector talking about *his* desires (why should we care?), the desires of *most* of us (this seems just false, and most competent speakers would also find it clearly irrelevant), the desires we *would* have if we reflected in a certain way (but then we still seem to need a reason to think it *good*—in some sense irreducible to anyone's desires—to reflect in that way; and what exactly, if we have rejected the independent standing of the normative, is a *reason?*) . . . ?

Now this critique may seem unfair since of course I am the one who put those expressions into the objector's mouth, but I did so in order to show how very difficult it is to live by a resolution to think of everything as reducible to non-normative fact and description. As already suggested in this book (see especially Chapter 2), value considerations more substantially construed must be as prominent for us as they were for Leibniz. They are unavoidable. And as our objector's comments show, they underlie even the whole enterprise of inquiry, at every level and in every form. In inquiry, in our search for understanding, we are trying to figure out what is going on at various levels of our ongoing experience and in various contexts, for its own sake and/or because we want to satisfy certain needs, whether for food, shelter, protection, intimacy, amusement, or whatever.

And the value-drenched notions embedded in such inquiry—notions of effort, desire, having a reason, instrumental value, intrinsic value, and so on—cannot be given a reductive interpretation without skewing our language all out of recognition. Passionate inquirers, lovers of wisdom and understanding, who attempt to use a completely reductive vocabulary literally cannot believe (and perhaps cannot even understand) what they are saying! The point is that no one is able to arrive at a completely "transcendental" position here. We refine what we all have in common in the way of sensory, introspective, memorial, and rational/intuitive tendencies of mental behavior, including the tendency to generate and build on nonreductive intuitions of value. And if these devices for making cognitive contact with the world aren't good enough, none of us is getting anywhere in that regard.

But there is another point to be made here. Even if we somehow could make sense of the attempt to reduce everything to the realm of the non-normative, we would be turning our backs on what makes human inquiry human in the first place, were we to adopt such an understanding. As argued in *Skepticism* (pp. 172–173), because we find it so difficult not to form and revise beliefs using the belief-forming practices mentioned above, including those involving a more substantial notion of value, a certain basic picture of the world has been generated. This picture becomes part of the very fabric of our being, affecting our sense of identity and of connectedness to others and also our goals, including intellectual goals. The very impulse to inquire, as this suggests, is deeply conditioned by aspects of our "basic picture": how could one desire truth or nobly determine to seek the truth, whatever it may be, without thinking it *good* to do so in a nonreductive sense of "good"? And what we want to know as inquirers is not whether our basic picture is correct but rather how it is to be filled out. The picture itself has become virtually inescapable: we find ourselves *in* the world, *shaped* by the picture, and all our serious investigative questions presuppose it. It follows that the reductive enterprise being criticized here misses the whole point of inquiry as it has arisen and taken hold in human life. Especially given our immaturity (and now I reintroduce that point) and the little we have done to rule out a nonreductive interpretation of the relevant phenomena, it would therefore be absurd for any human being pursuing understanding to try to get along without value. The unification project advocated by Nagel should win the allegiance of us all.

So much for objections. Their transparent failure to undermine the previous points about how skeptical religion promotes motivation and fortification, balance and unification, together with the initial persuasiveness of those points, make it clear that it is simply a baseless prejudice to suppose that religion must be intellectually stultifying. Indeed, skeptical religion commends itself precisely on account of its intellectual, understanding-promoting benefits! The Understanding Argument (together with the corresponding Aim) gleaned from reflection on Leibniz's great projects can therefore take its place alongside the Alignment Argument and the Imaginative Fulfillment Argument we distilled from Anselm as a reason strongly supporting faith. Leibniz's ambition for a successful defense of theistic religion may not have been realized, but, as we have seen, by setting it aside and exploring the more general ambition from which it contingently sprang, we can discern a strong and distinctive argument for skeptical religion.

CHAPTER 8

Paley's Wonder

In this chapter we descend from the heady heights of unsurpassable ideas and unsurpassed intellectual ambition to consider the contributions of William Paley, whose gaze was focused squarely on the details of the concrete natural world. Paley's characteristic response to these details was a kind of admiring wonder at their order and exquisite beauty. Of course they also inspired him to a certain lofty intellectual ambition of his own: Paley is the best-known and most often cited representative of the *teleological* or *design* argument for theism, itself perhaps the best-known and most often cited of the so-called theistic proofs. What I want to show here is that this proof and the related attitudes of its most famous defender lend themselves to the support of skeptical religion in much the same way as do the ontological and cosmological proofs and provers already discussed.

1. *The Vicissitudes of Teleological Argumentation*

Paley's argument is that the high degree of apparently goal-directed order in nature requires (or at least makes highly probable) the existence of an intelligent orderer or designer—a designer with a grandeur commensurate with the awe induced by its effects. Commonly, as at the very beginning of his *Natural Theology,*[1] in which these matters are most fully discussed, the argument is developed by analogy with goal-directed order as we find it

---

[1] See William Paley, *Natural Theology* (Boston: Gould and Lincoln, 1851). Page references in the text are to this work.

in human artifacts like the watch. Wouldn't we accept the watch as having a designer because of the complex mechanism that neatly produces the result of telling time? Well, then, says Paley, we should also accept that nature has a designer when we note the complex mechanisms to be found in it and the results they neatly produce. "There cannot be design without a designer; contrivance, without a contriver; order, without choice; arrangement, without anything capable of arranging; subserviency and relation to a purpose, without that which could intend a purpose; means suitable to an end, and executing their office in accomplishing that end, without the end ever having been contemplated, or the means accommodated to it" (10).

That theism might be defended by reference to the order in nature had occurred to numerous writers before Paley: there are clear antecedents for many of his points even in Cicero's *The Nature of the Gods,* not to mention Plato's *Timaeus.* But Paley developed the claim about natural order with unprecedented thoroughness. He saw design and contrivance everywhere and wrote it all down with lavish and loving attention to detail. (The result is, among other things, a clear outline of late-eighteenth-century anatomy.) His most characteristic tone in all of this is one of wonderment. As a biographer puts it, "he approached his subject with a childlike awe and bubbling exuberance...he was continually stunned by the beauty and efficiency of nature."[2]

To give the flavor of his *Natural Theology* (what he says about the eye is perhaps overfamiliar, so I focus on some of the multitude of other examples): "The *spine,* or back bone, is a chain of joints of very wonderful construction. Various, difficult, and almost inconsistent offices were to be executed by the same instrument. It was to be firm, yet flexible, (now I know no chain made by art, which is both these...)" (55). "The reciprocal enlargement and contraction of the *chest* to allow for the play of the lungs, depends upon a simple yet beautiful mechanical contrivance, referrible [*sic*] to the structure of the bones which enclose it" (62). "The works of nature want only to be contemplated. When contemplated, they have everything in them which can astonish by their greatness....At one end we see an intelligent Power arranging planetary systems...and, at the other, bending a hooked tooth, concerting and providing an appropriate mechanism, for the clasping and reclasping of the filaments of the feather of the humming bird....The hinges in the wings of an earwig, and the joints of its antennae, are as highly wrought, as if the Creator had nothing else to finish" (294–295).

---

[2] D. L. LeMahieu, *The Mind of William Paley* (Lincoln: University of Nebraska Press, 1976), p. 79.

Paley is clear about the consequences of embracing the teleological argument for the practice of religion: "If one train of thinking be more desirable than another, it is that which regards the phenomena of nature with a constant reference to a supreme intelligent Author. To have made this ruling, the habitual sentiment of our minds, is to have laid the foundation of everything which is religious. The world thenceforth becomes a temple, and life itself one continued act of adoration. The change is no less than this; that whereas formerly God was seldom in our thoughts, we can now scarcely look upon anything without perceiving its relation to him" (293–294).

But *should* we embrace the teleological argument? The answer, just as in the case of the other two theistic proofs already discussed, must be no. The teleological argument faces problems at least as severe as those afflicting its ontological and cosmological cousins. Though new mutations of Paley's argument—as well as versions of teleological or design argumentation more distant from his own—continue to appear, none of these succeeds in justifying traditional theistic belief. The general argumentation of *Skepticism* is again relevant, obviating the need for detailed discussion of this claim, but I also provide some brief justification for it here.

Paley's own reasoning, even if it can survive the point that it is not because of their complex mechanisms that we suppose watches to have intelligent designers but because of our background knowledge about watch production, is still refuted by the combination of Hume's (or his character Philo's) well-known criticisms in *Dialogues Concerning Natural Religion* and the work of Darwin, who fleshes out the Humean speculations concerning natural causes of order with his own patiently detailed theory of evolution through natural selection. Darwin's basic idea is now widely accepted, but it is sometimes forgotten that it does not need to be provably true to undermine Paley's argument. What everyone will and should accept is that Darwin has in his *Origin of Species* persuasively described a previously unconsidered mechanism by which the human body—not to mention the hummingbird and earwig—*could* through the processes of nature have come to bear those features that to Paley suggested the direct involvement of an intelligent orderer or designer.[3] And the epistemic possibility that Darwin's mechanism, or something like it, is at work in nature

---

[3] And his ideas (or extensions thereof), as many have convincingly argued, can handle as well the most recent revival of Paley, represented by the so-called intelligent design movement and its claims about irreducible complexity. (See, for example, Niall Shanks, *God, the Devil, and Darwin: A Critique of Intelligent Design Theory* [Oxford: Oxford University Press, 2004].) Intelligent design is controversial even in the camp of orthodox Christians. (See, for example, Kenneth R. Miller, *Finding Darwin's God: A Scientist's Search for Common Ground between God and Evolution* [New York: HarperCollins, 2002].)

is all that is required for Paley's designer to cease to do the work formerly assigned to him in theology.

There is also the problem of evil, in its many forms. This is made use of by Hume and also by more recent writers to suggest that the cosmic designer, should there be one, must at the very least lack certain desirable personal qualities. That nature is full of suffering—"red in tooth and claw"—is knowable and should be troubling for the theistic teleologist quite apart from Darwin (though Paley, for one, seems relatively unperturbed).[4] But Darwin's theory gives a new and painful twist to the screw. As Philip Kitcher writes: "Evolutionary arms races abound. If prey animals are lucky enough to get a favorable variation, then some predators will starve. If the predators are the fortunate ones, then more of the prey will die messy and agonizing deaths. There is nothing kindly or providential about any of this, and it seems breathtakingly wasteful and inefficient. Indeed, if we imagine a human observer presiding over a miniaturized version of the whole show, peering down on his 'creation,' it is extremely hard to equip the face with a kindly expression."[5]

Darwin's chilling effect on traditional teleological argumentation provides a nice example of the big changes in our understanding that, as our species continues to evolve, we must expect regularly to encounter. By moving in thought from Paley to Darwin, we see how something seemingly utterly convincing and clear in one generation can be put into an entirely different and contrary perspective in the next. And, as emphasized in *Skepticism*, because of the immaturity of the species, our own future may be full of such changes and new perspectives.

This, of course, has relevance to more recent versions of teleological argumentation not obviously affected by Darwin, such as the presently popular "fine-tuning" argument, which focus on larger-scale manifestations of order than those that especially interested Paley—order that, if it exists, is out of the range of evolutionary theory. Even if the phenomena these arguments cite are such as we should expect to be explained (and they may not be—some of these arguments, for example those citing the bare fact of temporal order, approach the level of generality found in Leibniz's cosmological argument), why should we suppose that explanatory alternatives to the traditional God have already been adequately explored? Indeed, in some cases we must ask how sure we can be that the cited phenomena exist at all. Often grounded in physical cosmology, which even one of their ablest advocates has characterized as "a very unstable

---

[4] See his *Natural Theology,* chap. 26.

[5] Philip Kitcher, *Living with Darwin: Evolution, Design, and the Future of Faith* (Oxford: Oxford University Press, 2007), p. 126.

branch of physics,"[6] such arguments, whatever their merits may presently appear to be, simply cannot be trusted to survive the changes likely to occur in our picture of the physical universe over the next 100, 1,000, or, yes, 1,000,000 years or more that may well still lie ahead of us, with new Darwins around any corner. For example, the scenario of an infinite number of universes (or multiverse), which many view as taking the wind out of the sails of recent teleological arguments, may very well be more fully confirmed by future study in cosmology.[7] Thus, given that changes at such a high level of theoretical speculation are so likely, and relevant changes are epistemically possible, we are forced to conclude that the more recent teleological arguments, which depend on such changes *not* occurring, can no more provide justification for belief in God than their Paley forebear.

2. *Paley's Wonder and Skeptical Religion*

If this is the "state of the subject," then how should we respond? Many involved in these debates, like Richard Dawkins, would say that in light of the evident decline of Paley-style natural theology and the ascendancy of the physical sciences, we must give ourselves to a completely naturalistic perspective. But our twenty-first-century skeptic cannot do that. Both naturalistic and religious belief are placed out of reach for her by powerful arguments, arguments of a sort to which Dawkins and his ilk have yet to give proper attention. But by the same token she is forced to open herself to unforeseen possibilities. One of these, I suggest, is the possibility that Paley, like Anselm and Leibniz, can with a little imagination be seen as gesturing in the direction of skeptical religion. This vague gesture I want now to bring into focus and turn into a crystal-clear argument.

What we need to conjure is a *skeptical* Paley, hard as that may be to imagine, but one who retains the wonder and exuberant love of order and beauty in nature from which grew the original Paley's teleological

---

[6] See Richard Swinburne, *The Existence of God*, 2nd ed. (Oxford: Clarendon Press, 2004), p. 179.

[7] Even Swinburne, who once derided the scenario as completely unhelpful, is now more cautious (compare in this respect the second [2004] edition of his *Existence of God*, pp. 185–188, with what he says on this subject in the older so-called revised edition of 1991). Swinburne still insists on the greater simplicity of the theistic approach: "It is far simpler to postulate one God than an infinite number of universes" (p. 185). But here he seems to overlook that the comparison should properly be between one entirely nonmaterial God *plus* a material universe and an infinite number of material universes—really one material multiverse—including our own. It is far from obvious that the former picture should, all things considered, appear to us in the relevant sense simpler than the latter (note especially how there is only kind of reality, material reality, on the latter picture).

argument for the existence of God. Of course Darwin himself may come to mind here: once enamored of Paley but, even after recognizing his deficiencies, much in love with the natural world and not quite sure what to say about religion.[8] Or Dawkins: a fierce and not always fair critic of traditional religious belief, but surprisingly gentle in his treatment of Paley and transparently in awe of the complexity and detail his own studies of nature have revealed to him (here, of course, we have to imagine that the appropriate criticisms of naturalistic belief have also been absorbed).[9] I want to take the wonder expressed by such individuals, and no doubt felt in some measure by all of us, and use it to create an argument for skeptical religion that is stronger than Paley's argument for theism. How is this to be done?

First let us make sure that we are clear about the object of Paley's (and Darwin's and Dawkins's) wonder: it is the amazingly intricate, hugely complex, and stunningly beautiful order of the universe. The idea of beauty is perhaps the central idea here, which the others subserve. It is at any rate the one I wish to focus on in developing my argument. Dispassionate scientists like Dawkins can go on at surprisingly great length about the beauties in nature and the wonder of it all, as a host of popular science books—his and others'—in recent years attest.

Now what is it to think nature beautiful? And can such belief legitimately be viewed as uncontroversially true by someone like our twenty-first-century skeptic? In thinking nature beautiful, we form a value belief of some kind (clearly the label "beautiful" is commendatory), and if ordinary language is even the slightest help here, the value we believe to obtain is a distinctive sort of value irreducible to that of other values such as friendship or knowledge. Although a beauty experience, the often pleasurable and sometimes achingly powerful experience we may have when contemplating nature and its laws, commonly provides the *grounds* for such a belief, it is clearly not the *object* of the belief: in forming a belief about nature having the value involved in being beautiful I am thinking about nature, not about my experience thereof. (Of course I may also, and independently, have thoughts of the latter sort.) In this context we might also note that although beauty's apprehension is frequently pleasure-*generating*, it

---

[8] Any account of Darwin's life and work will bear this out. See, for example, Janet Browne, *Darwin's Origin of Species: A Biography* (Vancouver: Douglas and McIntyre, 2006).

[9] See, for example, *The Blind Watchmaker: Why the Evidence of Evolution Reveals a Universe without Design* (New York: Norton, 1996). Of Paley's *Natural Theology*, Dawkins has this to say: "It is a book that I greatly admire, for in its own time its author succeeded in doing what I am struggling to do now. He had a point to make, he passionately believed in it, and he spared no effort to ram it home clearly. He had a proper reverence for the complexity of the natural world" (p. 4).

would be a confusion to suppose that we value beauty exclusively *for* the pleasure it brings, much as it is a confusion to suppose that when I derive satisfaction from helping someone I desire to benefit in some way, those good feelings must be the object of my desire.

When one seeks to move past such fairly obvious points, however, disagreements are likely. While it is easy and tempting to be an aesthetic realist, holding that natural beauty supervenes on the properties of external objects (such as their shapes or order-instantiating relations to other objects), there will be those who deny that beauty is thus objective, who take what we see in nature when we think it beautiful as something we project *onto* nature. Is the belief that nature is in some respect beautiful necessarily enmeshed in such debates? Must it fall into the controversy sponsored by aesthetic noncognitivism? If so, and if the controversy cannot quickly be resolved, our reflection on what it is to think nature beautiful might only lead us to recognize the justification of a certain sort of aesthetic skepticism. And that would be unfortunate for any beauty-based argument hoping to persuade our twenty-first-century skeptic of the justification of faith!

At first it may seem that this problem cannot be circumvented. For beauty beliefs do seem in a certain sense naively realist; when in the throes of such belief I am (as suggested above) taking nature itself to possess a certain value, thinking of this in the way that it is appropriate to think of factual matters concerning which objectively true or false statements can be made. Of course it would be a mistake to conflate such believing with the results of opinion formation in aesthetics. The belief that nature is beautiful is one thing; the belief formed by *analysis* of beauty beliefs another; the belief we may form about the *intellectual status* of our beauty beliefs yet another. These levels are different in important ways. But unresolved controversy about the latter two levels seems to infect the first one as well, leaving us with uncertainty over whether the belief that nature is beautiful should be endorsed.

However, to see that this worry is superficial in the present context, one need only take note of the fact that we cannot *help* forming beliefs of the latter sort. We all quite unavoidably and innocently or naively are struck by the beauty of things in nature from time to time—though of course not always in response to the same things, such as mountain scenery or any other specific phenomenon that happens to win special attention at this or that stage in the development of human culture. And I have already indicated that we will be accepting unavoidable belief-forming practices and the basic view of the world they have generated as providing the parameters for inquiry (on this see the discussion at the end of the previous chapter). The point is that the belief that certain things in nature are beautiful at some level persists and is unavoidable even after various noncognitivist interpretational maneuvers have been undertaken or entertained. Certainly we can engage in skeptical talk about such beliefs. But I don't see that the situation here is structurally very different from our situation in respect of moral value beliefs or even sensory perception. Consider especially the latter. Our basic and unavoidable view of the world includes our interaction with objects external to ourselves, but here too nonrealism can be entertained. That it can be does not make sensory skepticism obligatory. Since value beliefs of the sort invoked in this chapter contribute as much to that view as anything else (this the spate of popular science books already mentioned does much to confirm), aesthetic skepticism is no more obligatory for our twenty-first-century skeptic than sensory.[10]

So let us take it that the powerful experiences of natural beauty and the beliefs we all form when in the grip of such experiences are at least sometimes to be taken at face value: nature, as science and everyday experience reveal it to us, really is exquisitely beautiful in many respects! Paley's link between this sort of fact and religion based on the claim that there is an infinite Divine reality (understood by him in personal terms) is that of inference: the truth of the theistic claim is supposed to *follow* from the facts about beauty. This link won't hold, as we have seen.[11] But another link to religion can be forged.

---

[10] Thanks to Bill Wainwright for pushing me on these matters. Anyone who disagrees with what I say about them can still arrive at an aesthetic argument for skeptical religion by making one or both of two adjustments: (1) translate what I say in this chapter about beauty into the language of aesthetic sensibilities (in particular, sensibilities allowing us to see the world as beautiful); (2) focus on how skeptical religion allows us to do justice to the power of our aesthetic sensibilities, which in the light of ultimism may be imagined as reliable even when the *belief* that they are reliable is unjustified.

[11] Nor will the link of inference some others have defended on behalf of beauty. See, for example, Mark Wynn, *God and Goodness: A Natural Theological Perspective* (London: Routledge, 1999). Wynn supposes, with F. R. Tennant, that nature "is uniformly beautiful whereas the products of human beings are rarely beautiful in the absence of artistic intent" (p. 20), using this conjunctive thought in an argument for the existence of God. But both sides of Wynn's claim (both conjuncts in his conjunction) are questionable—the second in his own terms, since presumably he must say that the products of human beings which lack the beauty resulting from special artistic intent still display the beauty uniformly present in nature. (This, by the way, suggests a distinction between beauty in nature and beauty of the sorts artists intentionally produce—which cannot be helpful to Wynn's attempted analogy.) But suppose that both points can somehow be defended. In that case we still have to say that, even if nature is in some sense uniformly beautiful, perhaps because of awe-inspiring temporal order everywhere, it has in many parts a beauty we would not expect from an unsurpassably great Artist, since the order involved is implicated in horrific death and disaster. (Here again the problem of evil rears its decidedly nonbeautiful head.)

To see how, we need first to notice that a certain alternative relationship between beauty and ultimism is a natural part of the perspective of skeptical faith. Imaginatively organize the relevant facts about nature in order of ascending beauty and complex harmony, finally adding ultimism to the mix. Look closely at this addition: at how it is related to the aforementioned facts, and how it is not related to them. What you will see is that, although you cannot deductively, inductively, or abductively infer the truth of ultimism as a conclusion from those facts, the truth of the former would in an important sense *complete the picture* begun by the latter.

This "completeness" has two main aspects. (1) Given the value associated with beauty, axiological ultimacy entails ultimate beauty, and thus through the addition of ultimism one attains a kind of *aesthetic* completeness; one moves all the way from limited beauty to unlimited instead of stopping somewhere along the way.[12] (2) Furthermore, if this is how we see things, we also have a kind of *explanatory* completeness, for the Ultimate as we have conceived it is not just axiologically but also metaphysically ultimate, and so by adding ultimism to the mix we are picturing finite beauty as in some way deriving from infinite. Notice that although worldly beauty is in a sense completed by Divine beauty here, and although there is even an explanatory component to this, what we have when all is said and done is still a product of the imagination; there is no justification for inferring the Divine from the world, even as explanation thereof. A Divine reality is not entailed or probabilified by facts about beauty—there might be some other explanation or none at all—but rather pictured as their completion.

Such, at any rate, will be the perspective of an adherent of skeptical religion aware of the facts about beauty: she will cultivate an imaginative orientation that takes the completed picture I have referred to as normative. This is our starting point. And now we need to notice the instrumental value associated with aesthetics which flows from adopting such a stance. By adopting such a stance, our adherent of skeptical religion can do (the conjunction of) several important things (things we all ought to do) in a better and fuller way than she otherwise could: (1) *honor* the world's beauty; (2) do justice to her most intense beauty-inspired *experiences;* (3) *extend* her appreciation of the world's beauty; and, not least, (4) contribute to cultivating a concern, within herself and perhaps in others too, for the

---

[12] I would not wish to *identify* the realm of the aesthetic with beauty; my treatment leaves open the possibility that there are other sorts of aesthetic value (and later in the book I bring them in).

preservation of the world's beauty and of all the valuable and vulnerable forms of life that depend on it.[13] (Call the aim that is pursued if one seeks to do all four of these things the Respect for Beauty Aim and the corresponding argument for skeptical religion, which emerges if my claim about this aim is correct, the Respect for Beauty Argument.)

I now show how skeptical religion facilitates each of the desiderata here mentioned and also, where needed, show that they are desiderata.

(1) *Through skeptical religion we can honor the world's beauty.* We honor the beauty of the world by intentionally experiencing it in a context in which it is imagined that worldly beauty is the nearer side of Beauty, and in which our life is ordered accordingly and thus brought into harmony with the overall harmony we are imagining to obtain. This notion of "honoring" or "paying tribute" (i.e., expressing deep respect and high regard) can be linked to proper reverence for beauty. The notion of reverence was introduced in Chapter 6, where we described it in terms of a disposition to be struck deeply by truly grand, important, valuable things and a willingness to allow the shape of one's life to reveal in some appropriate way the shape of their impact. In that case reverence was discussed in connection with a recognition of the importance of alignment with an ultimate reality, should such exist. Here the immediate object of reverence is rather the orderly beauty of the natural world. The more—and the more consistently—one is struck by this in the relevant fashion, the more appropriate is the full development of reverence toward it and some meaningful tribute of the sort in question.

Individuals of the sort I have mentioned—Paley, Darwin, Dawkins—are struck and moved in this fashion quite consistently indeed. Here is another example of such an attitude, this time from the writings of Einstein, who explicitly makes a connection to religion: "The most beautiful emotion we can experience is the mysterious.... He to whom this emotion is a stranger, who can no longer wonder and stand rapt in awe, is as good as dead, a snuffed-out candle. To sense that behind anything that can be experienced there is something that our minds cannot grasp, whose beauty and sublimity reaches us only indirectly: this is religiousness."[14]

Now Dawkins, for one, might question whether we can sense that there *is* something ungraspable and supremely beautiful behind the discernible

---

[13] Notice that the imagining of the picture described here does not entail the imagining of pantheism: in that picture we do not represent the natural world as seamlessly continuous with the Ultimate but rather the former's *beauty and the value thereof* as in a sense continuous with the value instantiated by the Divine.

[14] Albert Einstein, "What I Believe," *Forum and Century* 84 (1930), 193–194.

order of nature, and indeed, such a sentiment does seem to go beyond what twenty-first-century skeptics can confidently believe. But even he admits that it is epistemically possible,[15] and so must we all. And, more to the point, we can see that *imagining* things to be so and living accordingly is a very natural way for someone properly enamored of natural beauty to express and deepen the reverence he feels. Indeed, such a one could hardly pay natural beauty as he experiences it a higher and more meaningful tribute than by picturing it as deriving from, and perhaps in some limited and indirect way expressing, a truly unlimited and ultimate beauty.

But now we must pause to consider an objection: might not ensconcing our feelings about natural beauty within a religious context result only in a subtle *denigration* of the latter—quite contrary to the thrust of my argument? Aren't we then simply acquiescing in the thought that the admired hillside of a thousand green spires flooded with light (or, yes, even that intricately formed backbone that nature has produced over millions of years) is not good enough on its own but needs somehow to be linked to something *more*—something transcendent? And *isn't* nature quite good and great enough on its own? Indeed, isn't that the fact provoking our reverence in the first place?

This objection, as expressed, is misleading; I have expressed it thus to expose a tempting slip I want us to avoid. For it is not its physicality as such that makes us revere nature—a physical world could be a chaotic mess—but rather its beautiful order. The objection might mistakenly make us think that the essential contrast is between the physical and the nonphysical or supraphysical, instead of between two kinds or levels of beauty. (The "more" and the "transcendent" referred to here still represent beauty, even if it is not natural beauty.)

With the proper contrast in mind, let us turn to the objector's last two questions. I suggest that we should answer yes, indeed. Even if all of reality were reducible to some variation on the theme of physicality so richly played by green hillsides and intricate backbones, we would have an object worthy of veneration. The order and beauty exhibited by the natural world as we find it does not need to be connected to the idea of the Ultimate to invite reverence. Indeed, here we are not thinking at all about how we might reverence the Ultimate or the idea thereof but rather

[15] This is indicated by an interesting, highly relevant, comment Dawkins made during a discussion with Francis Collins (*Time* online, November 2, 2006, p. 5): "My mind is not closed, as you have occasionally suggested, Francis. My mind is open to the most wonderful range of future possibilities, which I cannot even dream about, nor can you, nor can anyone else. [But] if there is a God, it's going to be a whole lot bigger and a whole lot more incomprehensible than anything that any theologian of any religion has ever proposed."

about reverence for beauty; nor are we reverencing beauty *by* reverencing the Ultimate, but rather by picturing things within an ultimistic frame of reference.

All of these points about the greatness of natural beauty may gladly be admitted. But none implies or even suggests that it could not be *greater*. (Thinking about that wonderful but certainly not unimprovable backbone provides a quick way of seeing this!) If any did have that implication, then perhaps the denigration in question would follow from what I am advocating, for then we would be giving to something else the exalted status that belongs only to nature. But, again, it is implausible to suppose that the natural world's great beauty makes it the greatest reality there could be.

Nor does there seem to be any other way of making the denigration charge stick. Natural beauty is not swallowed up in the larger picture here, somehow rendered invisible or displaced, but rather is imagined as aesthetically and explanatorily tied up with the most significant fact about the whole. Because of this, we are permitted, through keeping that larger picture before our minds as we live our lives, to appreciate nature just as we did before while *also* paying a very deep *respect* to natural beauty. This respect, again, comes from thinking of natural beauty as deriving from, and perhaps in some limited and indirect way expressing, a truly unlimited and ultimate beauty. If our respect for natural beauty is great enough, perhaps it will seem to us that this is how it deserves to be seen.

(2) *Through skeptical religion we can do justice to our most intense beauty-inspired experiences.* We should not think only of beauty itself here. The experiences that commonly follow its perception are also important and relevant to my concern. In the passage quoted above, Einstein speaks about the beauty of nature, but also of beautiful *emotion*. This emotion, he says, comes from sensing a higher beauty, a mysterious greater order in which the world as we know it is embedded. We might think that Einstein is missing something here: isn't the relevant emotion the one evoked in us by the intelligible beauties of nature all around us, and isn't that emotion beautiful enough? But I think Einstein is rather *adding* something: we can take him as exposing an ambiguity in the notion of an "emotion evoked." There is, to be sure, the first-order emotion that naturally comes as part of what I earlier called the beauty experience. But there is also a second-order emotion for which the first supplies, as it were, a platform—a "beautiful emotion" commonly attending the beauty experience, which involves the apparent presence and play of some transcendent quality, a seeming extension or fulfillment of the beauty perceived in or through the original beauty experience. This seeming transcendent quality includes a fulfillment or ultimization in terms of both the apparent *intensification* of beauty

and the apparent *comprehensiveness* of its influence. When we experience the beauty of that hillside flooded with light, it may suddenly seem that the *whole world* is aflame.

What we're talking about here is really a sort of religious experience to which the beauty experience can give rise; among other things, a "sense" of unlimited depth—of never being able to fully penetrate through all the layers of meaning that beauty brings in its train. This, it seems, is the sort of experience to which Einstein's comment alerts us. Now someone returning from such an experience may, apparently like Einstein, think that she has indeed sensed an ungraspable sublime reality lying behind the beauty directly present in experienceable things. But perhaps, with our twenty-first-century skeptic, she will remain in doubt about this and allow that what has appeared may *only* be an appearance—that beauty might well be shallow, not deep, in the nature of things. This of course is the stance that I must advocate. But what I want us now to see is that, quite compatibly with such a stance, one may carry on in the train of thought that the beauty experience has begun by *imagining* that beauty is *not* shallow in the nature of things. The transporting experience itself calls upon us to do so, instead of neglecting the horizons it has opened up. As Robert Nozick suggests (though his discussion shows the urgent need for a positive alternative to belief), to neglect such promptings would only reveal a regrettable distrust in one's own positive responses to the world, and thus involve a "significant alienation from oneself."[16]

It is precisely in this situation that the life of faith, which imagines that the latent drive of all experienced beauty is indeed fulfilled, must recommend itself to us, as a way of doing justice to the depth and power and, yes, beauty of (what might be called) our trans-beauty experiences even when a conventional religious belief response seems unjustified. By "doing justice" here I mean that religious faith allows us to weave deep trans-beauty experiences fully and enthusiastically into the warp and woof of our lives, in a manner that gives them an orienting and integrating significance appropriately commensurate with their profundity, power, and persistence. And this must make religious faith attractive to all lovers of beauty, the more so the more they love it.[17]

---

[16] Robert Nozick, *The Examined Life: Philosophical Meditations* (New York: Simon & Schuster, 1989), p. 52.

[17] This point expresses my subtly but significantly different version of the idea, often found in theistic literature, that worldly beauty "points to" or "reveals to us" the infinitely greater beauty of God. (See, for example, Peter Forrest, *God without the Supernatural* [Ithaca: Cornell University Press, 1996], p. 135.) There is, in the first place, no warrant apart from familiarity for speaking specifically of a personal God rather than more generally about an

(3) *Through skeptical religion we can extend our appreciation of the world's beauty.* If beauty and beauty experiences are as valuable as we suppose them to be, then it must be important that we seek to *extend* our acquaintance with beauty. And surely they are that valuable. Don't we think of aesthetic appreciation as contributing to the highest and best ways of being human? But few of us are acting on this realization appropriately. Although our experience brings much of the value thus apprehensible to our mental door, much also stays outside: clearly we could discern and appreciate and integrate into our lives much *more* of the world's beauty if we paid more deliberate attention to it. It is one of the great virtues of skeptical religion that it constantly encourages us to do just this and also provides a framework for doing so.

We saw in Chapters 2 and 3 how skeptical religion promotes attentiveness and investigation in respect of all that we encounter, providing various possible structures for organizing such activity, and is constantly widening the circle of such investigated experience—all this so as to uncover any insights about an ultimate and salvific reality that might be available to us. The present point is really only a variation on (an enrichment of) these themes. Beauty experiences will be taken as possible intimations of the Divine by one who practices skeptical faith, and she will therefore be prompted by them to open herself more fully to all the detailed beauty of the natural world. One will be prompted by a proper attempt to live by the ultimistic proposition to strain to find beauty wherever possible, and even where otherwise, deterred perhaps by some parochial preference, one might have given up on it.

Something analogous to this religious effect can be seen in certain of the sectarian and believing forms of religion that we have found to be unjustified. All the world, so it may be declared, is the handiwork of a God who loves us, and we can come to know God more fully by becoming thoroughly acquainted with nature. Unfortunately, in such forms of religion, adherence to a variety of *other* specific claims often deters practitioners from deepening their acquaintance with nature very much. They may be told—and authority *will* be given priority over their own beauty experiences—that God is more readily known through some Scripture than in the book of Nature, or more easily and effectively addressed in church or synagogue or mosque than in any natural temple. And thus they are prevented from reading the book of Nature or exercising focused religious attentiveness in its temples.

---

infinitely beautiful reality. But, second, the suggestion of theism's inferability must again be resisted.

Skeptical religion, by contrast, does not have the luxury of particular revelations; it is seeking, indeed, to help us reach a social and intellectual maturity that such "revelations" often simply militate against. Perhaps it will grow toward a point where more particular claims about the Ultimate can be made, but if it does so, it will be only by means of the sort of wide-ranging investigation and scrupulous attentiveness that, among other things, seeks to bring as much of worldly beauty as possible within its field of vision.

(4) *Through skeptical religion, we can contribute to cultivating a concern, within ourselves and perhaps in others too, for the preservation of the world's beauty and of all the valuable and vulnerable forms of life that depend on it.* One of the few steps toward maturity that the human species—or a considerable segment of it—has taken in recent years involves a greater respect for (at least some) other forms of life and a greater emphasis on environmental concerns, including such things as concern for the preservation of biodiversity and for the prevention of harmful global warming. But the step that has been taken is a short one and is just the first of many steps that need to be taken. Indeed, the latter fact is the main fact that first step has drawn to our attention! So much remains to be done. As many are pointing out, E. O. Wilson among them, human beings are stripping the rainforests, causing oceans to warm and destroying their life, driving various species to extinction (thus depleting the biosphere, which thrives on complexity), and pumping chemicals it cannot absorb into the atmosphere.[18] In the process not just the existence or flourishing of other species but that of their own species is more and more dangerously threatened.

Wilson's recent book is addressed in the first instance to conservative Christians, whose apathy and distractedness—supposing that God will take care of things while they preoccupy themselves with moral minutiae—are not exactly helping one of the main culprits, his own country of the United States, to make a serious effort toward solving these serious problems. He urges Christians to remember the glories of nature and the love of nature as a Divine creation that even their own traditions might encourage, and in doing so to reorganize their priorities and curb behaviors harmful to nature, urging others also to do so. In presenting his appeal, he makes it quite clear that what we have been referring to in terms of the orderly beauty of nature is very much front and center in what is at stake. It is also made clear that by *appreciating this more,* we might be led, as a species, to do more to sustain it—and thereby to sustain life on earth.

---

[18] See E. O. Wilson, *The Creation: An Appeal to Save Life on Earth* (New York: Norton, 2006).

And now it will not be hard to see how the other pieces needed for my argument fall into place. We have already observed how skeptical religion strongly promotes just such an appreciation for the world's beauty as is here mentioned. We have also seen how—sadly for Wilson's project—it does so much more persistently and thoroughly and effectively than sectarian, believing forms of religion like orthodox Christian religion can be expected to do. Thus, since from such a deepened and extended appreciation for the world's beauty must flow more of the benefits in question, it seems that Wilson and all of us who value those benefits must look very favorably indeed on the spread of skeptical religion.

It may be here, however, within this context of apparent agreement with environmental concern, that skeptical religion is forced to confront a serious objection. Isn't the whole idea of religion—the present form included—just too sunny and optimistic and, yes, human-centered, in its talk of an ultimate good for *humanity,* to be of much use in the struggle for a more sensitive human presence in the world at large? It is all too easy for anyone involved in religion to lose a true appreciation for our status as one species among others, and to forget or to overlook or to take less seriously than one should the danger that confronts us all because of humans' obsessive focus on their own needs and their own fulfillment. Indeed, because of our preference for the dream it represents over the harsh realities that face us, we may allow religion to lull us to sleep over precisely such matters.

I feel this objection in a deep way. It raises matters of critical importance. But we need to keep things in proper perspective—the *new* perspective skeptical religion represents. The skepticism that drives it (at least in the present context) forces us to contemplate a radical alteration in our self-conception. It requires us to imagine ourselves as limited and immature in many ways, as part of a process of development whose uncompleted portion may be ridiculously larger than that which our species has already gone through. It openly faces the possibility that we may not venture much further along that line into the future—that our existence is but a wrinkle in the universe that, though perhaps only with some difficulty after the havoc we have wreaked, time will finally smooth away.

But it also asks us to imagine there being more to reality than the physical, as currently construed, a supremely good "depth" or "center" in the nature of things toward which all things tend that we simply do not yet have the equipment to grasp with any security, but that is dimly glimpsed (as a chimp might dimly glimpse some of our realities) in certain elevated moments—perhaps even including experiences of beauty. And the faith that skeptical religion combines with its skepticism grasps hold of this *second* imagining, though it never loses the lesson of the first because it never settles into the security of confident belief. It dares to set out in quest of ultimate things, and as we have seen (and will see) at various points, it may do so from a tenacious love of the many-splendored good and with a hope that its understanding—including its understanding of the good—will constantly be altered and enlarged. Its focus on ultimism indeed involves the idea of a reality "in relation to which an ultimate good can be attained," but especially given its deep agnosticism about the inner recesses of any ultimate reality there may be, the *distance* it sees between itself and its goal, there is nothing in it to motivate holding on to any preconceived idea of a particular good for humanity militating against the good of other beings that exist or may come to exist, or of a swift resolution of problems facing us to which we need not contribute.

Quite the contrary. The dream of religion—if indeed the ultimate dream—can be of nothing less than a good embracing all that exists. This dream is firm in the one who adopts skeptical religion, but her conception of how it might be realized and of her part in that is flexible, and is sensitive to all that the environmentalist holds dear. Indeed, if skeptical religion were properly realized anywhere, its adherents would have to be in the vanguard of environmentalism broadly construed—as a movement of concern for *all* the world's ills, of willingness to negotiate our place in nature with all who have a part in it, whether in the present or in the future, and of determination to correctly identify and resist all that we have made ugly instead of beautiful. And their faith should, all things considered, make it easier rather than more difficult for the skeptically religious to persist with this vision.

It is the "all things considered" part of that last sentence which is of central importance here. When we properly identify what skeptical religion is about and relate it sensitively to its context, paying attention to all the details that emerge rather than to prejudices against religion nurtured by the latter's limited past instantiations, the objection under consideration must melt away.

That concludes my discussion of the four desiderata involving natural beauty which skeptical religion helps us to further. I think we have seen enough to say that they are indeed important desiderata that we ought to pursue. Have we seen enough to say that they are more effectively pursued by practicing skeptical religion than otherwise (and, of course, for us "otherwise" translates to "by remaining purely skeptical")? Even if individually they might not have led to this assessment, can we say that the *conjunction* of these desiderata is better and more fully pursued by someone who adopts a skeptically religious orientation than by someone who, in whatever shade or grade, retains the tentativeness of a pure skeptic? I think we can say this. Just as in the previous chapter, the central point is that by adopting skeptical religion, we do not give up any of the ways to which we might otherwise have had access of realizing these good things (and here our answer to the objection just considered should be of special help), but simply *add richly* to what we can bring to the task. Since the task is great and, especially in the case of (4), may resist our best efforts, the means of pursuing it must be as substantial as we can muster. It is evident that this must lead us to endorse the Respect for Beauty Argument, together with the corresponding Aim, as other things being equal providing a *good* reason to adopt skeptical religion.

Looking back, we may find ourselves in wonderment over how much we can accomplish on behalf of religion using Paley as our point of departure—and this without giving any credence at all to his teleological argument. Even without that argument, surprisingly little needs to be altered in that passage in which Paley relates his teleological ideas to the conduct of the religious life: "If one train of thinking be more desirable than another, it is that which regards the phenomena of nature with a constant reference to a supreme intelligent Author. To have made this ruling, the habitual sentiment of our minds, is to have laid the foundation of everything which is religious. The world thenceforth becomes a temple, and life itself one continued act of adoration. The change is no less than this; that whereas formerly God was seldom in our thoughts, we can now scarcely look upon anything without perceiving its relation to him" (293–294).

3. *General Conclusion to Part III*

Thus we come to the end of our discussion of the traditional triad of theistic arguments, the great theistic proofs. As we have seen, though unsuccessful in their own terms, they can quite easily be appropriated by the twenty-first-century skeptic defending skeptical religion.[19] Anselm says

---

[19] In Chapter 7 of *Prolegomena* I distinguished two higher-level aims in philosophy of religion that are often inappropriately conflated: the aim of investigating to what extent (if any) religious claims may help to solve *theoretical problems* in other areas of philosophy, and the aim of determining whether *religious practice* is justified. For religion to be useful in the solving of theoretical problems, its claims need to be demonstrably true or probably true—here, for example, a successful proof of the existence of God would go a long way and be most impressive and important. But to support religious practice, we don't need arguments like that. For one thing, as we are seeing, we don't need arguments supporting religious *belief*, and we certainly don't need a proof or demonstration that any religious claim is true. If it is the faith response we are defending, that would indeed be the wrong

that there is something simply about the *idea* of the Ultimate that supports religious faith; Leibniz, that the *project of complete understanding* calls for it; Paley, that the *beautiful order of nature* should drive us to embrace it. As we have seen, each was right, though not quite as he imagined. And in imagining these things in a new way, we are able to move forward—from the faith of our fathers to a faith of our own, which can be embraced without hesitation by even the most severely rebellious daughter or son.

Such faith is imperative for us today (this is at least part of the story) because it provides the best way of showing that the things that mattered to Anselm, Leibniz, and Paley matter to us too. And they *should* matter to us. Isn't there something wrong with turning one's back on the idea of unlimited value, the aspiration of complete understanding, or the experience of seemingly infinite beauty? A faith that thrills to these sounds, resonating with their refrain, would no doubt lead to a kind of inner incoherence if we knew there was no ultimate salvific reality, but given skepticism the only way we can have *coherence*—taking proper account of all the things here mentioned and in these three chapters discussed—is by evolving the musical sensitivity of skeptical religion.

---

kind of argument. So we need to open our minds a little, get quite clear about which aim in philosophy of religion is governing our reflections, and seek arguments appropriate to that. What this part of the book has claimed, in effect, is that when we do, we will even find that we can use revised or rethought versions of arguments that fail as responses to the first higher-level aim of philosophy of religion to successfully pursue the second.

PART IV

RENEWING FAITH (2)

How Skeptical Proof Subsumes
Believing Argument—Nonevidentialism

A NUMBER OF influential figures in the history of philosophy of religion have felt the intellectual impotence of the theistic proofs as traditionally construed without being much perturbed by it—and this even when called upon to defend theistic belief. The arguments of these other thinkers seem united in the thought that to solve the rational problems facing theism, we must look elsewhere than to evidence. For most such arguments, the central point is that we should respond positively to certain *goods* that would or might be realized by believing theistically even when the available evidence for the truth of theism is indecisive.

Of course it will be clear by now that I do not think theistic belief is justified, and this regardless of whether its alleged justification is dressed up evidentially or nonevidentially (my reasons for thinking so are, again, laid out in *Skepticism;* on the distinctive difficulties facing nonevidential belief, see especially Chapter 6). But it is interesting to consider whether the theistic arguments of the most well known and widely discussed nonevidentialists, like the arguments of Anselm & Co., can be metamorphosed into support for another conclusion—the conclusion that *skeptical religion* is justified. It will be my claim, here in Part IV, that they can be. Thus in the present part of the book we begin a new phase of "generous appropriation," promoting *adaptations* of traditional arguments that will be more fitted to survive than the originals. As it happens, in these three chapters the needed alterations are considerably less radical than in the previous three. For no transition from an evidential (truth-supporting) to a non-evidential mode of thought will need to be undertaken: the arguments of Pascal & Co. are already operating at the nonevidential level. And the connection between the value—usually some pragmatic benefit—these writers tell us we ought to pursue and the possibility of support for skeptical religion will not be hard to see. We will therefore often be able to make use of the arguments themselves fairly directly instead of appealing only to the broader concerns that generated them, as in the previous chapters.

Having said that, precisely because the arguments of our nonevidentialists *are* fairly close to the arguments I shall finally endorse, questions of interpretation—about how their arguments have been, and might be, developed and, sometimes, how they are related to each other—will be more important here than in the previous three chapters, and will take up more of our time. I want to get straight about two matters in particular: in what form has their reasoning been most influential as alleged support for theistic belief? And how is it most *plausibly* thus taken? Then I will show that the moves being made, however plausible, do not in the end provide adequate support for theistic belief or for attitudes intended to lead thereto. (That they do not provide the individual newly divested of theistic belief adequate support for nonbelieving theistic *faith* either I will in most cases take as demonstrable by reference to the detailed discussion of Part I.)

Now the idea of nonevidential support for theistic belief, as earlier suggested, is already addressed and ruled out in *Skepticism*. But despite the relevance of that earlier book, somewhat as in Part III I want also, in each of the chapters in this part, to spend a little time showing how the argument discussed therein can be shown to fail as support for theistic belief on *independent grounds,* grounds pertaining to the details of the argumentation actually employed by the nonevidentialist in question. Having thus removed any illusions about their potential theistic usefulness, I will more effectively draw these nonevidential arguments into my case for skeptical religion.

I begin with the form of reasoning that has come to be known as Pascal's Wager.

Pascal's Wager

1. *The Form and Content of the Wager Discussion*

Blaise Pascal is often credited with having founded decision theory, and
the argument he gives for the prudential rationality of betting on God in
a fragment near the middle of his *Pensées* is often presented by commentators as though its author had at his fingertips all the concepts and symbols
from that area of study. Now there is no doubt that he had some of its concepts, such as those involved in the so-called Expectation rule (more on
this below), though as we'll observe in a moment, his peculiar emphasis
and aim in this fragment prevented him from applying these concepts in
quite the way a contemporary philosopher might wish he had, or suppose
he should have. To prepare for thinking about all this properly, I put before us a representative sample of Pascal's own words (the Wager fragment
is long and involved, so even this extract is less than brief).

> Let us now speak according to our natural lights.
> If there is a God, he is infinitely beyond our comprehension,
> since, being indivisible and without limits, he bears no relation to us.
> We are therefore incapable of knowing either what he is or whether
> he is....
> ...Let us then examine this point, and let us say: "Either God is or
> he is not." But to which view shall we be inclined? Reason cannot de-
> cide this question. Infinite chaos separates us. At the far end of this
> infinite distance a coin is being spun which will come down heads
> or tails. How will you wager? Reason cannot make you choose either,
> reason cannot prove either wrong....

...Let us weigh up the gain and the loss involved in calling heads that God exists. Let us assess the two cases: if you win you win everything, if you lose you lose nothing. Do not hesitate then; wager that he does exist. "That is wonderful. Yes, I must wager, but perhaps I am wagering too much."...

...Even though there were an infinite number of chances, of which only one were in your favour, you would still be right to wager one [life] in order to win two; and you would be acting wrongly, being obliged to play, in refusing to stake one life against three in a game, where out of an infinite number of chances there is one in your favour, if there were an infinity of infinitely happy life to be won. But here there is an infinity of infinitely happy life to be won.... That leaves no choice; wherever there is infinity, and where there are not infinite chances of losing against that of winning, there is no room for hesitation, you must give everything. And thus, since you are obliged to play, you must be renouncing reason if you hoard your life rather than risk it for an infinite gain, just as likely to occur as a loss amounting to nothing.... Thus our argument carries infinite weight, when the stakes are finite in a game where there are even chances of winning and losing and an infinite prize to be won....

"...I am being held fast and I am so made that I cannot believe..." "At least get it into your head that, if you are unable to believe, it is because of your passions, since reason impels you to believe and yet you cannot do so.... [Behave] just as if [you do] believe.... That will make you believe quite naturally, and will make you more docile." "But that is what I am afraid of."

"Now what harm will come to you from choosing this course? You will be faithful, honest, humble, grateful, full of good works, a sincere, true friend.... It is true you will not enjoy noxious pleasures, glory and good living, but will you not have others?

"I tell you that you will gain even in this life, and that at every step you take along this road you will see that your gain is so certain and your risk so negligible that in the end you will realize that you have wagered on something certain and infinite for which you have paid nothing."[1]

It is evident that Pascal here imagines an interlocutor, and also that he is appealing to the prudence or self-interest of his interlocutor: the

---

[1] Blaise Pascal, *Pensées*, trans. A. J. Krailscheimer (Harmondsworth, U.K.: Penguin, 1966), fragment 418, pp. 150–153. Further references to this work, in both text and notes, are made parenthetically.

Wager fundamentally claims that to be religious facilitates *self-interested* aims. Some will find this immediately problematic. Pascal's claim, it may be said, is crass or even self-disqualifying as support for faith because of its endorsement of selfishness. At the very least, he is neglecting the possibility that *other* important goods—say, the well-being of sufferers in a far country—may come into conflict with what is in our best interest, thus (rightly) deterring us from its pursuit.

Since there is not much incentive to examine closely the structure or content of an argument one assumes is a nonstarter, let us briefly deal with this issue. Notice first that the suggestion about other important goods itself neglects that the best life possible for us cannot, on any reasonable view of it, be one that overlooks important goods; and in this observation we can detect an answer to the objector's earlier suggestion as well: while a life of narrow ego-centered pursuits that ignored the needs of others might be selfish, it should be obvious to all that this is not the best sort of life, and so there need be no concern about the rational pursuit of what is really in our best interest amounting to selfishness. Since this is the case, why should we deny what in any event seems obvious—that we have good reason to seek what is in our best interest?

These are not just my responses on behalf of Pascal. As the final part of the passage quoted above (a part often neglected by commentators) makes clear, Pascal himself saw the "gain" to which he appealed as including an increase in virtue. And elsewhere he links "the Christian's hope of possessing an infinite good" with "holiness" and becoming "free from unrighteousness" (fragment 917, p. 312). Now it is true that in the Wager fragment Pascal refers to "an infinitely happy life" and an "infinite prize," but given the context for such remarks, it is not at all clear that they should be interpreted as involving some crass and narrow appeal to heavenly bliss.[2] In any case, in my own development of the Pascalian argument, this will certainly not be the emphasis.

Having got rid of the bugbear of narrow and unenlightened self-interest or selfishness, let us quickly also attend to two further questions about parameters before looking more closely at the nature of Pascal's case: how specific a conception of God is he working with, and just what is involved for him in wagering, in betting on God?

Pascal's conception of God might seem quite general and content-less; after all, he speaks of God as "infinitely beyond our comprehension." But

---

[2] There is a reference to bliss elsewhere (fragment 149, p. 76), but it is linked to "knowing and loving" God, which is itself linked to the holiness and freedom from unrighteousness mentioned in the text. And the infinite good of loving God is said to be a "universal good" that all may possess "without diminution or envy" (fragment 148, p. 75).

I am inclined to think that this point is heightened for rhetorical effect, to help him sharpen his contrasts between the earthly and the Divine (more on this below). In any case, that it should not be taken as allowing *no* knowledge of God's nature, even for the skeptic considering what he should do according to "natural lights," is suggested by how easily Pascal speaks in the Wager fragment of the infinite God representing infinite *good*, and elsewhere—though, significantly, not in the Wager fragment—of God as just and also as wrathful in the face of wickedness (see, for example, fragment 427, p. 158). Pretty clearly, we are here being offered the standard personalist conception of God that has dominated Western discussion of things religious, and also all subsequent discussion of Pascal's Wager. I, at any rate, will assume this to be so.

What about the wager itself? What does Pascal mean when he talks about a skeptic or agnostic betting on God? This is sometimes read in terms of choosing to believe in the existence of God, and criticized accordingly (for whether one believes or not does not seem to be a voluntary matter). But this is a crude and insensitive reading. To see that it is, consider only the fragments of the *Pensées* in which we find the skeptic represented as *unable* to believe, as suspended unwillingly between the options of belief and disbelief, not knowing what to do[3]—fragments including even the Wager fragment itself, in which, as we have seen, Pascal's interlocutor complains of having been "made" so that he "cannot believe." Having said that, it does appear that, according to Pascal, propositional theistic belief is at least part of the *goal* that one who wagers on God must set for himself, as part of thus wagering. For he advises the complaining agnostic to "act as if" he believes, which behavior, Pascal suggests, will diminish oppositional passions and *lead* the agnostic to believe "quite naturally."[4] Acting-as-if must presumably involve adopting a positive attitude toward theism (this we might read in terms of propositional faith) and acting thereupon (thus instantiating one form of theistic operational faith). And presumably the latter element of "acting on" is thought of as continuing when propositional belief is arrived at, with the latter simply providing a new base for it. So, in sum, we can say that betting on God involves, according to Pascal, a whole way of life—one built on something less than belief at first but evolving into a belief-filled religious practice and commitment later. This

---

[3] Here see especially fragment 429, pp. 162–163.

[4] Many passages of the *Pensées* suggest that the appropriate reorientation of one's passions will lead one to "hear" God through the "heart," thus affording a kind of experiential evidence and associated certainty that might seem to take one quite far past the gambling mentality—leaving the Wager a ladder that one can kick away given what one sees when one has climbed up it. Just how Pascal would have defined all these relations and connected all his dots is unclear, since in the *Pensées* we have only the dots.

picture blends nicely with what Pascal says about wagering one's *life,* and with the idea of giving oneself to God that so dominates the *Pensées.*[5]

Having identified some of his parameters, let us try to clarify the reasoning Pascal undertakes within them. There is a standard account of it among philosophers as containing two or more distinguishable arguments for the prudential rationality of wagering on theism.[6] A fairly representative and also very clear and concise exposition of this interpretation comes to us from Philip Quinn.

> Suppose one has to choose between betting on *a* and betting on *b.* Assume that the probability of *a* winning is *p* and the probability of *b* winning is *q.* Let the payoff if *a* wins be *u* and the payoff if *b* wins be *v,* and let the cost of betting on *a* be *x* and the cost of betting on *b* be *y.* On these assumptions, as long as $pu - x \geq qv - y$, it is rational to bet on *a.*

Quinn here shows one way of expressing what in decision theory is called the "Expectation rule." Deliberating thus, with estimates of relevant probabilities and utilities to plug into one's schema, is called making a "decision under risk," but it yields a perfectly rational decision nonetheless (or so decision theorists will argue). Now suppose we think of Quinn's *a* as theism and of his *b* as atheism, and—remembering the passages from the *Pensées* quoted above—interpret Pascal as saying that that the payoff of a bet on theism is infinite. Let us also suppose that the alternative payoff and all the associated costs are finite. According to Quinn,

> [Pascal] sometimes speaks of even chances of winning and losing, which suggests that theism should be assigned a probability of one half. On that assumption, the expected value of a bet on theism is

---

[5] Jeff Jordan has a useful discussion of the various ways in which one might understand the actions and dispositions involved in Pascalian wagering (see his *Pascal's Wager: Pragmatic Arguments and Belief in God* [Oxford: Clarendon Press, 2006], pp. 18–19). He settles on something close to what I have described, though phrased in terms of the notion of "acceptance," which he borrows from William Alston (and which Alston borrows from L. Jonathan Cohen). Acceptance includes both taking a proposition mentally on board and acting on it, in the absence of belief. I argue in my *Prolegomena*, chap. 6, that it is not appropriate to apply this notion of acceptance in any straightforward manner in an analysis of faith (as at least Alston is inclined to do): there is more to faith than acceptance, and talk of acceptance also obscures an important distinction between two forms of faith, the forms of faith I here call propositional and operational.

[6] Almost everyone finds at least two distinct arguments. Ian Hacking, in his well-known discussion ("The Logic of Pascal's Wager," *American Philosophical Quarterly* 9 [1972], 186–192), claims there are in fact three. Jeff Jordan says there are four.

infinite and the expected value of a bet against it is finite. Hence, it is rational to bet on theism.

But now Quinn comes to the crucial part of his exposition, to an apparently distinct Pascalian argument that philosophers have often thought to be the central one (in his recent book on Pascal's Wager, Jeff Jordan calls it the "Canonical version" of the Wager)[7]:

> Moreover, as long as the probability of theism is greater than zero, no matter how small it is, the expected value of a bet on theism remains infinite and the expected value of a bet against it remains finite. So even if the chances are not even and theism is a real long shot, it is still rational to bet on theism.[8]

What should we say about this standard interpretation of Pascal? I suggest that a fairly extensive reformulation of his reasoning can be observed in it. Notice in particular that Pascal himself makes no explicit reference to the bet *against* theism and its expected utilities and costs: all of his attention is focused on the way an infinite good makes the wager *for* God overwhelmingly attractive. There are some suggestions and possibly some implications of his positive claims that are relevant to the former bet, but that is all. For example, when he first considers wagering, as we have seen, he asks what will come of betting that God exists, and concludes that one stands to "win everything" if one is right and can "lose nothing" if one is wrong. His interlocutor then expresses a concern about wagering "too much." Given Pascal's subsequent reassurances on that score and the associated references to happiness and to what his interlocutor would be staking as being finite, we can probably infer that he thinks the best one could gain by betting against God would be a finite happiness.[9] And in

---

[7] See his *Pascal's Wager*, p. 23.

[8] See Philip L. Quinn, "Moral Objections to Pascalian Wagering," in *Gambling on God: Essays on Pascal's Wager*, ed. Jeff Jordan (Lanham, Md.: Rowman and Littlefield, 1994), p. 61.

[9] It may be wondered why a skeptic must bet against God instead of remaining neutral. To this Pascal briskly replies: "You must wager. There is no choice, you are already committed" (*Pensées*, fragment 418, p. 150). His commentators have generally taken him to mean that the practical consequences of remaining neutral are the same as those of wagering against. There are difficulties here, but I will ignore them and assume that not betting and betting against may be treated as practically equivalent. In any case, many of the arguments we will discuss could still be formulated even if we took the alternatives to be wagering for God and not doing so (reading the latter as a disjunction of possible attitudes including both a studied neutrality on the issue and actively wagering against God). In my later development of the most plausible argument to be drawn from Pascal, I take the alternatives in this way.

a part of the Wager fragment not included in the quotation above, one finds a somewhat obscure reference to "wretchedness" as being, along with "error," something it is in our nature to avoid, which *may* be an allusion to evil as opposed to good that he thinks will be incurred by betting against God and losing.[10]

So why this obliqueness and apparent one-sidedness from a mathematician capable of as much thoroughness and formalization as is found in any of his commentators? Perhaps it is because he sees in a flash the apparent implications for prudential rationality of infinite goodness on one side of the wager he is discussing and does not bother writing out all the details in these notes—leaving this for a later, fuller discussion. Then there are Pascal's literary proclivities. Anyone who reads him can see that he loved surprising contrasts and opposites. And there at the head of the Wager fragment we find this apparent title: *Infinity-nothing* (fragment 418, p. 149). At first this contrast is used to underline how distant we must be from the Divine, if it exists, and our exceedingly great incapacities in matters of religion. But then things are turned neatly around—through the contrast between an infinite good and the nothingness of earthly happiness that dominates the betting discussion—to show how religious progress can nonetheless be made and indeed how a clear decision in favor of God instead of the agnosticism suggested by God's infinite distance is indicated. The infinite qualities of God at once pose the problem and present the solution. If there is a Divine reality, it is infinitely distant from us. Listening only to this, reason might recommend settling down in agnosticism. But because of another infinite quality—God's infinite *goodness*—reason must, all things considered, recommend commitment to God instead.

I think these points about a hurried and sketchy beginning and those attractive contrasts and the allure of Divine goodness do contribute to an explanation of why Pascal's own procedure seems not to line up exactly with that of his commentators. But they are most forceful in conjunction with yet another point, concerning Pascal's main aim, which must be said to be religious conversion. In a passage reminiscent of Anselm, he ends the Wager fragment with these thoughts (which come almost immediately after the last passage from my long quotation above):

> If my words please you and seem cogent, you must know that they come from a man who went down upon his knees both before and after to pray this infinite and indivisible being, to whom he submits his own, that he might bring your being also to submit to him for

---

[10] See fragment 418, p. 150.

your good and for his glory: and that strength might thus be reconciled with lowliness.[11]

What we see here is that Pascal is not just aiming to produce some clever
reasoning, fat with symbols and decked out in the latest mathematical garb.
He is on a mission to help us start to close that great distance between
God and ourselves, to reconcile strength with lowliness, infinity with nothing, to lead us to the point where we can begin to fill an "infinite abyss"
with an "infinite and immutable object" (fragment 148, p. 75). This is a
very positive mission, which may explain why Pascal is not heavy-handedly
playing the hell-fire card in addressing the skeptic. In human beings, as
much of the *Pensées* (for example, fragments 105–122) attests, Pascal sees a
strange combination of greatness and wretchedness, and his prudential urg-
ings are in the last analysis a call for us to reclaim our greatness—which is
linked in his mind with virtue and holiness, and a deepened religiousness.

Putting all of this together, I suggest, yields an interpretation of the Wager
fragment somewhat different from the standard one. In this fragment we
do not have two or three or four relatively independent arguments aimed
at a dispassionate skeptic, but rather a continuing dialectical conversation
with a skeptic who *does not want* to commit religiously, designed to persuade him to let go of his life—to give it to God. In a first appeal, we have
the first subversion of the agnostic's appeal to infinite distance: you stand
to win *everything* (infinity) and what you lose, if you lose, is *nothing*. This
point about "nothing" it is natural to interpret as referring to the loss of at
most a finite good, which is as nothing by comparison with the infinite.

But it still seems to be the loss of a certain kind of good life. This is why
the skeptic can wonder whether he risks losing too much. What if he risks
the good of this life for nothing—there being no infinite reward? Perhaps
a life is too much to risk.

Pascal's first response to this is an abstract demonstration of the prudential rationality of risking one good life to win an infinity of goodness: the
infinite always trumps the finite in an expectations game. Infinity-nothing.
Here we find him expressing the assumption that there is as good a chance
of theism being true as of it being false. I submit that this is Pascal's own
view of the relevant probabilities, for it is underlined elsewhere in the
Pensées, where the skeptic's dilemma is invariably presented as involving
evidence on both sides, not the complete absence of evidence.[12] (It is true

---

[11] *Pensées*, fragment 418, p. 153.

[12] See *Pensées*, fragment 429, pp. 162–163. It is sometimes supposed that Pascal drops
this assumption halfway through the Wager fragment, but notice how it reappears several
times, and also near the end in a reference to "even chances of winning and losing."

that, according to Pascal, reason cannot decide the issue, but this is not—as some critics of Pascal's probability estimate have supposed[13]—because reason has nothing to go on at all but rather because, so he thinks, reason finds considerations giving weight to both sides.) Just to drive his point home, caught up in the enthusiasm generated by his infinity-nothing contrasts, Pascal points out that, in the abstract, even if theism has a much lower probability than atheism—he never imagines that it might be as low as zero—the infinite still represents the way to go. Infinity-nothing. This, he says, is prudentially decisive.

But abstract considerations like this, though they respond to the skeptic's allegedly rational basis for remaining purely skeptical, may not be enough to prevent the skeptic from allowing "this-life" considerations to deter him from making the needed commitment. And so Pascal as missionary has more to do. First the skeptic protests that he is psychologically incapable of believing. When Pascal responds with psychological devices for overcoming the psychological incapacity, the skeptic worries somewhat pathetically that they *could work:* indeed, that is just what he is afraid of! No matter how rational or possible the Wager may be, he simply does not want to risk any this-worldly good: he is still assuming that he will somehow be harmed or bereft of good in this life if he accepts the Wager and loses. Thus Pascal has to show him that this is not the case, and in a concrete way. There is nothing to be afraid of, he argues. For the religious life will bring concrete benefits also in the earthly life of those who take it up—it's not just a matter of some abstract infinite fulfillment in the hereafter. Indeed, he urges (again the enthusiastic demonstration of how overdetermined a positive decision is), the skeptic will be *better off* in this life by wagering!

Now it is tempting to interpret this part of the dialectic in terms of a whole new argument, an argument moving beyond the earlier talk about probabilities and claiming that one will be better off by wagering for God *whether God exists or not* (this, in decision theoretical terms, is a "dominance argument," applicable not to a "decision under risk," where the Expectation rule applies, but to a "decision under uncertainty," where probability estimates are unavailable but the utilities are all on one side). Jeff Jordan, for one, interprets it thus.[14] But I don't think this approach reflects what Pascal sees himself as doing here. The skeptic Pascal imagines here is deterred by passions, not by a calculating reason considering the alternatives, thinking first about what follows if God exists and then about how things must be if God does not exist. His skeptic needs persuasion that appeals to the passions. Pascal ends, therefore, not by saying "So whether

---

[13] For example, Hacking.
[14] See his *Pascal's Wager,* p. 24.

God exists or not..." but rather by drawing a dramatic picture of a path in which one gradually achieves the infinite good for which—as the *Pensées* taken as a whole show he supposes—we all dimly long, and which he hopes to entice the skeptic to follow. The seemingly abstract hereafter will only be a deepening of a wonderful concrete goodness already tasted in the here and now.

Perhaps to the disappointment of philosophers, then, a fair bit of what we have here is really more a matter of *preaching* from a God-intoxicated man who finds it difficult to imagine God's nonexistence or an agnostic's thoroughly honest doubt than a straightforward, non-question-begging philosophical argument of the sort that might be articulated in decision-theoretical terms (some of Pascal's later "premises," as we have just seen, verge on being ones that only a believer could accept). Pascal wants the skeptic to hear and respond positively to the transcendent yearnings within himself—which, when he is rightly provoked, will come back to him like echoes from an infinite abyss—and to realize the great goodness attainable right now and continuing in the hereafter which comes from striving for closeness to God. And with this "hearing," so he thinks, will come the final, fullest awareness that a supremely attractive and infinite good can be won by wagering and that the life "given up" to do so is really only a kind of snakeskin shed to put on garments appropriate to eternal life. *This* time the interlocutor will see that the cost of commitment, properly considered, is *literally* nothing. Infinity-nothing.

That is my interpretation of what is going on in the Wager fragment. As I have indicated, the latter seems to involve preaching as much as philosophical reasoning. But this needn't prevent us from asking what is the strongest argument for believing in God that one might extract from this somewhat rambling conversation. Indeed, one might imagine the *skeptic* asking this. Let us give the benefit of the doubt to Pascal's skeptic interlocutor. Suppose that he is not really the emotionally and morally handicapped individual Pascal imagines but rather represents our skeptic from the twenty-first century, here engaging with Pascal in the seventeenth: an individual passionate about *understanding* and willing to listen to reason. Which argument will he choose as developing Pascal's case for the inculcation of theistic belief most strongly?

I suggest that at this point Jordan becomes relevant once again. The "extra" argument he attributes to Pascal (though, if I am right, not utilized by Pascal himself) is what our twenty-first-century skeptic returned to the seventeenth should find most interesting and worthy of attention—at least when its claims about prudential good are given distinctively Pascalian content. This is because it tries to show an advantage for theism in every possible situation and for every possible time in which the skeptic might find himself. This argument appears to cover all the bases. And it does so without indulging in talk about infinite utilities that might be problematic (even if *God* is infinite, and knowing God means experiencing good unlimitedly, in the sense of unceasingly and always more deeply, should we think of *what is experienced* as ever literally an infinite good?). Nor does it chain itself to probabilistic commitments that are just as problematic (if there really is as much darkness concerning matters religious as Pascal supposes, and as an honest skeptic in the seventeenth century might well claim to find, could this extend even to assessments of probability?). This form of argument, in short, promises to do the most while requiring the least. In developing it, we can even preserve some of Pascal's background ideas about "transcendent" elements in our experience and the concrete nature of the good to be associated with an infinite God, which Jordan hardly touches. As it turns out, some of Pascal's preaching had a rational core.

So what are the details of this argument? Now that the stage has been set, it will not take long to identify them. What we face is uncertainty. We know that either theism is true or it is false, but reason cannot tell us which it is or even, clearly, what the relevant probabilities are. But, nonetheless, there are clear prudential reasons for becoming a theist and living accordingly. For suppose theism is true. Then one stands to gain unlimitedly by becoming a theist and wagering for God, through the ever-enlarging relationship with God that will ensue, and this is obviously much more than the limited good one might hope to achieve under that scenario even while not wagering for God. But now suppose theism is false. Even so one does better by wagering that it is *not* false and coming to believe this and fully committing oneself to God, than by not doing so. For through a commitment to God—through assiduously following up on the various signs of God in our experience—one can do the most to enlarge *oneself* and fulfill one's own nature in the present life. (Of course this will not be one's motive once one is a believer, in which situation one will consider oneself to be interacting with God and responding to God, but it can and should influence the skeptic considering whether to become a believer.)

A limited human life is still, in thought and imagination, oriented toward or "aimed at" the unlimited, always seeking to transcend itself. The signs of God, even if they are unable to lead us to a life with God beyond the grave and are in that sense misleading signs, must, if dedicatedly pursued, help us to develop this natural propensity most fully. Following them, one might even say, brings to human life a certain "infinite" quality. Any right-thinking, prudent human doubter wondering what to do in her situation of uncertainty must accordingly find such a life eminently desirable, much more desirable than a life full of shallow materialistic pursuits or even the life of a pure skeptic who is also morally pure but remains firmly seated on the fence, unwilling to explore seriously those possibilities of transcendence. Hence, *whether theism is true or whether it is false*, the most prudent and—other things being equal—rational thing for the skeptic to do is to wager on God.[15]

Call this the Pascalian Dominance Argument. According to the Pascalian theist as we shall understand her, it represents a trump card she can play in just any situation.[16]

2. *Evaluating the Pascalian Dominance Argument*

Suppose, then, that the Dominance Argument just adumbrated is the argument that our honest skeptic, traveling back to the seventeenth century for some interaction with Pascal, should extract from the conversation. Now our question is this: how should she *assess* it upon her return to the twenty-first? Even if we allow that the probability of theism is inscrutable and not zero (as many readers of *Skepticism*, Part III, might not be willing to do), should we accept each of the two moves made by that argument? I think not. Here is why.

(1) First, why should an appropriately reflective skeptic expect to gain an unlimited good, if God exists, *only* by wagering on God? Is it really so clear that God would be unavailable in the hereafter to those who, because of the ambiguity of the world, remain uncommitted to God in the here and

---

[15] I will have my own way of dealing with the "other things being equal" clause, when the time comes to do so, as indicated in previous chapters. How might a theistic Pascalian approach it? Perhaps this is the point where Pascal's talk of moral virtue would be reintroduced. Maybe the best a theistic Pascalian could say is that if a by-product of wagering theistically is that one becomes faithful, honest, humble, full of good works, and so on, the prudential goodness of wagering could hardly be overridden by other factors. (Won't any other claims on us be satisfied somewhere in a truly virtuous life?) Some reasons for denying that this argument goes through are suggested in the next section.

[16] Someone might wonder why I have focused on the good of pursuing transcendence instead of on the moral virtues Pascal himself brings to the fore—virtues I describe, in the previous note, as merely a "by-product" of wagering theistically. The answer is that I want to focus here on *distinctive* Pascalian points (points that are not already made by other of the nonevidentialists whose work I am exploiting in this part of the book), and, as it happens, the moral arguments are well covered elsewhere. One might think that the Pascalian point about transcendence is not distinctive because of its similarity to points about alignment with the ultimate and imaginative fulfillment drawn from Anselm in Chapter 6. But as we'll see more fully later on in the present chapter, the Pascalian point is prudential—about what is desirable for one's own life as opposed to simply admirable—in a way that the Anselmian points are not.

now? It is not. Pascal's austere Catholicism might imply such a thing, but if we turn on our "natural lights," we may see that it reflects only our own petty divisions (*nothingness*) rather than God's goodness (*infinity*). Perhaps the unlimited good of relationship with God would be enjoyed by all eventually, if there were a God, because all would at some point be allowed to see this good for what it was. With ignorance thus transformed into the knowledge of acquaintance, how could a choice in favor of God fail to be the result for an honest skeptic? And how could that fail to lead to unlimited good? (Here we see how an argument like the Pascalian's can be undermined not just by increased philosophical sophistication about infinity or probability but by clearer theological vision; it must be said that Pascal's contemporary critics in philosophy tend to ignore this.)

A similar point to the one just suggested is made by Terence Penelhum in his *Religion and Rationality*.[17] To this, Quinn responds by saying that salvation is an undeserved free gift, and that so long as the nonbeliever gets what he deserves, there is nothing wrong with God freely giving salvation to someone else.[18] But this picture strikes me as morally and theologically misconceived. By "salvation" the Pascalian must mean the good of relationship with God, a good for which, a theist will say, we have been created, and one that a perfectly loving God (and Pascal's God clearly is perfectly loving) would necessarily make available to all.[19] Salvation is not something we can imagine an emotionally healthy and even somewhat morally advanced Divine being treating in the casual and detached and arbitrary manner apparently envisaged by Quinn and, one might add, by centuries of immature theology.

But suppose that Quinn is right. Even so, this can afford no assurance to the skeptic that he will attain salvation only by wagering on God, for the traditional God may freely do good things that it is not wrong not to do. We anticipate supererogatory behavior even in finite, imperfect specimens of humanity—how much more so in an unsurpassably great Divine being? I conclude that our skeptic has no clear reason to think he will do *better* by wagering on God than by not doing so, given that God exists, and that belief of the first claim of the Pascalian Dominance Argument is accordingly unjustified.

(2) What about the argument's second claim? Suppose that God does not exist. Is it still better to wager on God than not to do so, as the Pascalian claims? Here it is forgotten that the denial of theism (i.e., atheism: "God

[17] (New York: Random House, 1971), p. 218.
[18] See Quinn, "Moral Objections," p. 77.
[19] For much more on related matters, see my *Skepticism*, chap. 9, esp. sec. 4.

does not exist") is equivalent to a vast *disjunction* of mutually exclusive alternative propositions. Some of these are known; some, no doubt, are unknown. The disjunction includes naturalism, whose truth might indeed seem compatible with less this-worldly good than the argument is able to associate with God. But it also includes, inter alia, a variety of other, nontheistic religious propositions, all of which, by definition, entail ultimism and so promise an unlimited good enabling transcendence of our limitations—and many of which, furthermore (especially the unknown ones!), contribute to the darkness and uncertainty that even a twenty-first-century skeptic must feel concerning religion. Now suppose that one of these alternative religious propositions is true. That is, suppose that the nonexistence of God is instantiated positively by the existence of some other religious reality, maybe one of the extant alternatives from religious traditions we know about, such as Buddhism; maybe one we humans, falling rather short of infinity and at an early stage of religious investigation, still know nothing about. This, surely, cannot be ruled out if the nonexistence of God cannot be ruled out. And suppose one's failing to wager on God is instantiated by one's wagering that there is some other such religious reality and forming a religious commitment in connection with it, pursuing transcendence in a religious practice flowing from that commitment (perhaps one's wager picks out the particular religious reality that happens to exist; perhaps only some ultimistic disjunction excluding God that is made true by it). Surely in that case one would not do better by wagering on God. Indeed, what the Pascalian Dominance Argument shows is that if God does not exist, the best way of ensuring contact with the genuine article, transcendentally speaking, may well require wagering *against* God.[20]

Pascal notoriously dismisses nontheistic religious possibilities, practices, and people, reserving for them the category of the "heathen." But in hindsight we can see that he should have been led by a version of the skepticism that so influenced him—that is, by the future-oriented, developmental skepticism I have defended—to withhold judgment on all such matters, since after his time many of his "ignorant heathen" have been shown to have rather sophisticated philosophical systems and salvific social structures all their own![21] And, of course, our twenty-first-century skeptic must leave open the possibility of many new discoveries about religious possibilities affecting us in *our* future. Thus it is, at best, not at all clear that in a scenario in which God does not exist, one must nonetheless do

---

[20] This is of course my version of the famous "many-gods" objection to Pascal.

[21] For an illuminating discussion of the skeptical influences on Pascal, see Terence Penelhum, *God and Skepticism: A Study in Skepticism and Fideism* (Dordrecht: Reidel, 1984).

better by wagering on theism than by not doing so. Which is to say that the second claim of the Pascalian Dominance Argument is in no better shape than the first.

In sum: the Pascalian Dominance Argument *over*estimates the positive religious benefits of wagering for God if God exists and *under*estimates the positive religious benefits that may flow from wagering against God if God does not exist. Perhaps in the seventeenth century, in a context shaped by narrower shared assumptions than could ever pass muster today, such an argument would have more force.[22] But not in the twenty-first.[23]

3. *The Skeptical Dominance Argument*

This is the point at which many inquirers are inclined to close the book on religion. The evidence does not support theism, and Pascal's Wager cannot be made to work either, so they complain. But such a conclusion to the religious quest betrays shortsightedness. For even if some such nonevidential move cannot justify theistic belief, we must still consider whether it might be adapted to support skeptical religion. When the distinctions between theism and ultimism and between belief and faith are introduced, and when we remember the vigorous form of religiousness to be associated with ultimistic faith, a whole new possibility appears on the religious landscape, calling for our careful consideration and scrutiny. In the rest

---

[22] Nicholas Rescher stresses this "local" character of much Pascalian reasoning in his *Pascal's Wager: A Study of Practical Reasoning in Philosophical Theology* (Notre Dame, Ind.: Notre Dame University Press, 1985).

[23] In his *Pascal's Wager*, Jordan tries to rehabilitate the theistic wager. He distinguishes, within the disjunction to which I have referred, between naturalism and the other, religious possibilities. Then he argues that if the "God does not exist" alternative were to be realized because of the truth of *naturalism*, theistic wagering would promise the greatest benefits to the deliberating skeptic, because we have reason to think that theistic belief enhances human flourishing *in this life* and lack such reason with respect to the other religious possibilities (the relevant studies not having been done). This, he argues, gives theism the advantage overall: since theism does at least as well as the other alternatives in other respects and in this respect does better, it is the option we should favor in a wagering situation. (See especially chap. 3, sec. 4, of his book.) In my view, Jordan takes the idea of turning ignorance into a virtue rather too far, but I will save argument on these matters for the chapter on William James, since in Jordan's hands the Wager argument is really a Jamesian argument (he even calls it the Jamesian Wager) and the relevant prudential benefits are Jamesian benefits. The "benefits" that my Pascalian has in mind are not such things as zest or emotional peace but rather the goods of transcendence I have emphasized. These, it seems to me, at least when prudentially construed and applied, are distinctively Pascalian.

of this chapter, I want to show how this possibility emerges in connection with Pascal, and how a variation on the Pascalian Dominance Argument does indeed strongly support skeptical religion.

The first thing to notice here is that even if the theistic bet is off, we must still consider the merits of a more general religious wager. Even if the disjunct from the big disjunction of religious propositions represented by traditional theism cannot be adequately supported in the Pascalian manner, how about the *disjunction itself* (which we have learned is equivalent to ultimism)? What sort of argument might be tried here?

I suggest we can argue as follows. Either ultimism is true or it is false. Reason cannot tell us which it is or even, clearly, what the relevant probabilities are. But, nonetheless, there are clear prudential reasons for wagering on ultimism. For suppose it is true. Then, by wagering, one has the opportunity to be aligned in one's own being with something ultimately real and valuable, the best attainable approximation to which prudence must surely dictate as an aim. To our twenty-first-century skeptic, who will want to realize for herself such an approximation to an alignment of the sort in question, this must appear very attractive. The point here is one we can relate to our earlier chapter on Anselm: alignment with the Divine, as there shown, is intrinsically valuable and worth pursuing on that account; but if realized, as we are presently assuming, such intrinsic value would also add greatly to the *richness of one's life,* and so the relation in question must furthermore be *prudentially* attractive. But also, if ultimism is true, one can by wagering be readying oneself for ever *deeper* discoveries in connection with the Ultimate. And for the prudent person, the good that pursuing such aims successfully would bring into one's possession must obviously be much more attractive than the good one might hope to achieve under the scenario in question even while not wagering on ultimism.

But now suppose ultimism is false. Even so, one does better by wagering that it is *not* false than otherwise, because through a *commitment* to the Ultimate—through assiduously following up on the various signs of ultimacy in our experience—one can do the most to enlarge *oneself* and fulfill one's own nature in the present life, which is another aim it is in our interest to pursue. (Here we are, inter alia, appropriating considerations from the Anselmian Imaginative Fulfillment Reason, which can be prudentially adapted in much the same way as the Anselmian Alignment Reason alluded to above.) A limited human life can still, in thought and imagination, be oriented toward or "aimed at" the unlimited, always seeking to transcend itself. The signs of ultimacy, even if they are unable to lead us to some great good beyond the grave and turn out to be in that sense misleading, must, if dedicatedly pursued, help us to develop this natural potential most fully. Following them, one might even say, brings to human life a certain "infinite" quality. Any right-thinking, prudent human doubter wondering what to do in her situation of uncertainty must accordingly find such a life eminently desirable, much more desirable than a life full of shallow materialistic pursuits or even the life of a pure skeptic who is also morally pure but remains firmly seated on the fence, unwilling to seriously explore those possibilities of transcendence. Hence, *whether ultimism is true or whether it is false,* the most prudent and rational thing for the skeptic to do is to wager on it being true.

This argument has some decided advantages over its theistic counterpart. But before getting to those, I need to deal with another issue, in connection with the nature of the wagering behavior to which my argument also refers. Earlier we saw that according to Pascal, wagering religiously is a matter of the inculcation of belief and an associated religious practice. It is important to clarify that—and why—for our skeptic of the twenty-first century (or even a circumspect skeptic from the seventeenth) this will never do, and also how an alternative emerges.

Imagine a brief continuation of Pascal's running dialogue which features the style of the original, from which I quoted at some length earlier. The skeptic begins. "I am made so that I cannot believe, and honesty prevents me from undertaking the self-deception required by the Wager as it has been presented to me (I am asked to take steps to see as *strong,* evidence I know to be weak). Now you think real experiential evidence will come to me if I do this—my heart will become attuned to the voice of God—at which time I will have a belief well grounded in evidence. But this is because you are a believer. I, as a nonbeliever, cannot factor in such a proposition; I cannot believe it right now even if you can and do! Hence wagering now must still do violence to my intellect and undermine my virtue."

Wait a minute—it is Pascal who thinks as you suggest! You are now back in the twenty-first century talking to someone several times removed from Pascal, who is a nonbeliever like you but nonetheless finds something to work with in Pascal's ideas. I even agree that the self-deception you have described is to be avoided. But I would want to finesse this point somewhat in connection with an alternative that Pascal overlooks—though he comes close to noticing it when he talks about how a religious practice can be begun through "acting as if."[24] Careful attention to the concept of faith shows that there is a distinctive propositional faith attitude (naturally

---

[24] Other Pascalians too have gestured in the direction of some nonbelieving religious attitude that might be more permanently sustained, but the unclarity of their accounts only underlines the urgent need for some "precisification" of the sort my thoroughly developed account of propositional and operational faith provides. See, for example, Rescher, who in

enough, I call it propositional faith) that is quite capable of grounding a religious life *on an ongoing basis*. It does not have to be turned into belief to do so, as Pascal assumes, and in fact all kinds of benefits, intellectual and religious, may flow from *not* conceiving it as some kind of temporary "stand-in" for believing. Furthermore, as we'll see more fully in a moment, the prudential benefits normally associated with religious belief can also be obtained by means of such nonbelieving religious faith. This leads me to the following principle (and here's the finessing I mentioned before):

> (P) It is all things considered irrational to take steps to self-deceptively induce religious belief on prudential grounds in circumstances of religious uncertainty when benefits at least as great as those one seeks to achieve thereby can be procured without self-deception by fostering a positive religious attitude that does not require belief.

It seems to me that a modern Pascalian should be led by this principle and by an awareness of propositional faith to understand the wagering behavior in a manner quite different from Pascal's own. I suggest that we think of wagering not as the inculcation of religious belief, whether theistic *or* ultimistic, but rather as the free adoption and indefinite continuation of a form of life grounded in propositional faith. No self-deception there!

I interrupt the dialogue at this point. Having shown how the idea of wagering can and should be developed without any reference to belief (though with a promissory note about comparability of benefits), and that it must at any rate be understood in a nonbelieving sense in my argument, let us return to a consideration of how much stronger the ultimistic argument is than the theistic. A first obvious point is this. Since at the higher level at which it is operating the only other realities needing to be considered are going to be, by definition, *nonreligious,* there is no possibility of responding to the ultimistic argument with an analogue of my criticism (2) above, which wonders why the falsity of the proposition in question (there, theism) might not be instantiated by the truth of some *other* religious proposition promising ultimate good. That issue cannot even arise at this level.

But what about a criticism analogous to my *(1)* above: if ultimism is true, might one eventually achieve an unlimited good in connection with it without now wagering on ultimism? If so, even a prudent skeptic might feel no inclination to make the ultimistic wager. The idea, I suppose, is

---

his *Pascal's Wager* vacillates among talk of "belief" (p. 65), a nonbelieving "endorsement" (pp. 52–53), and "hope" (p. 72).

that we have no more reason to expect that the value of the Ultimate, generically construed, will be communicated to us *only* if we become religiously committed in the present than we have to expect that a relationship with God in the hereafter depends on our becoming committed to God now. Perhaps religious benefits will at some point be available to us, should ultimism be true, whether we presently adopt a religious *life* or not. And thus there is no clear prudential reason to adopt such a life.

But this objection should only provoke us to recognize the need for some additional adjustments. We need to see that the usual identification of utilities in Pascalian reasoning as infinite or finite, limited or unlimited, is somewhat crass and misses something rather important, prudentially speaking—and that this mistaken way of looking at things also infects the criticism at issue here (though not the skeptical Pascalian argument, as I have developed it). According to this way of looking at things, if an infinite or unlimited good awaits me in the afterlife, then my life could not be improved, and as a rational and prudential person I could hardly ask for more. For what could be better for me than an infinite or unlimited good? But if that is all a prudent person could wish, then it seems to follow that a prudent person should be quite content with a *completely horrible life here and now* so long as she is sure of an unlimited good hereafter. Such a life and a life different only in the fact that it is also unceasingly blissful in the here and now would indeed have to come out equal on the prudential scales!

Clearly something has gone wrong here. And what has gone wrong is that we have focused purely on quantitative calculations, with an infinite or unlimited amount of value associated with a life than which there could not be a greater, instead of thinking about the full range of goods and the various levels of evaluation that must engage the attention of prudence. We need to think more unrestrictedly about what is *prudentially preferable* for the deliberating skeptic, allowing for qualitative and not just quantitative forms of measure. Clearly a horrible earthly life plus eternal bliss in some way add up to an unlimited good, but that doesn't mean that the alternative of bliss starting right now shouldn't seem preferable to anyone properly prudent. And perhaps alignment with the Ultimate in the here and now, together with an unlimited religious good in the afterlife, must similarly be deemed prudentially preferable to a life that features only the latter of these two goods. Since the criticism in question misses the point that would enable this possibility even seriously to be considered, it is, needless to say, somewhat less than impressive.

Having said that, the possibility just mentioned needs serious consideration, and needs to be shown to be realized before we are out of the woods on this issue. Following this through will permit us to clinch the case for skeptical Pascalianism and also confirm the suitability of faith (as opposed to belief) to the obtaining of the benefits I am recommending.

So hear again our skeptic and her interlocutor. The skeptic has been listening and is unsure about the merits of my proposal. "I'm putting out all my prudential feelers, as you recommend, but still finding the life of moral commitment and intellectual inquiry *without* religious commitment very attractive. Why not commit myself if and when the evidence is clearer? Let the Ultimate reveal itself to me if it wants my commitment! The goals of contributing in some small way to the positive evolution of the human species and to a great future good including peace and justice that perhaps only future humans will know are surely noble goals, whose pursuit enriches my life far more than the shallow materialistic pursuits of that imaginary skeptic you and Pascal keep talking about. And I don't need a religious commitment to profess these goals. I can be active in pursuing them while remaining solidly on the fence."

What you say about your goals is quite true. But notice that by taking on a religious commitment in my sense you do not lose any of this; you only add to it. And what is added you should also find prudentially attractive if your feelers are in good working order. (The fact that this commitment requires only faith, which is designed for when the evidence is *un*clear, and not the self-deception of self-instigated belief, only makes this more obvious.) For consider. Either the Ultimate is real or it isn't. If it *is,* then your lack of a religious commitment of some sort means that you are not fully working with the grain of the universe, and are unprepared to take full advantage of any more complete revelation of the Ultimate, and opportunity for self-enhancement in relation to it, that the future may bring. Then there is a gap between your life and the way things are which you need to step over if you are to be lined up in your thinking and behaving with objective reality—and notice that faith lines you up in this way as much as belief. If the Ultimate were real and if its reality were revealed to you, you would think that it made your life better to step over that gap. So why doesn't it make your life better *now,* on the assumption that ultimism is really true? And I haven't even mentioned the considerable number of virtues bound up with wanting to be thus aligned with the Ultimate, should it exist, and behaving accordingly. These virtues are ones a prudent person should certainly want to have, for they must make his life better. But you can't properly pursue them given only the nonreligious goals you profess.

"But what if the Ultimate *isn't* real? If it isn't, then I can be aligned with how things are only by *not* taking up a religious commitment! For this reason, and in light of my present goals, which you have affirmed as laudable, my present life must surely be about as good as I could make it under that scenario."

It might seem so. But look again. You could only really be aligned with the nonreality of the Ultimate, should that be a fact, by believing or having faith that there is no such thing, and I don't think this is something you can be contemplating as a pure skeptic. In any case, how important it is to be aligned with a certain set of facts (and the degree of value thus conferred on one's life) depends rather a lot on the nature of those facts. And here Pascal's old distinction between the infinite and the finite can once again be made to do some work. For the reality with which you are aligned if you are aligned with the Ultimate is infinite and unlimitedly good, whereas the reality with which you are aligned if ultimism is false and you are aligned with *that* fact is finite and limited. Notice that this disparity also shows up in the relative prudential value of those two states of alignment. Beyond this, I must emphasize that there are plenty of opportunities for the pursuit of what I have called "possibilities of transcendence" which you give up if you opt to remain a pure skeptic. Of course, if there is no Ultimate reality, these can never lead to one (though while practicing skeptical religion you would naturally always fail to be apprised of the fact that there isn't one, if indeed it were a fact). But *regardless* of what is the case, taking advantage of these opportunities will enlarge and enrich your life in all the ways I have described already. So, again, you keep all the goods you have mentioned and simply add more if you move from pure skepticism to skeptical faith—and this regardless of whether the Ultimate is real or isn't.

"But I am perfectly happy with my life as it is. And I feel no need to look forward to a life hereafter. I *might* want a continuation—in full strength—of *this* life with its customary connections. But the idea of another life for which I should ready myself, or of pursuing 'possibilities of transcendence,' just leaves me cold."

Indeed, another life may not seem that attractive, especially if we are finding comfort and happiness in this one. But you overlook several things. One is that aims it is objectively in our best interest to pursue may not be immediately attractive to us. Perhaps we need to learn to appreciate certain possibilities—including ones involving more than one life of toil and gradual achievement—more fully. But if so, then that such possibilities "leave us cold" may not be a reliable indicator of their prudential significance. Another point you overlook is that when I spoke of readying ourselves for deeper experiences of the Ultimate, I did not exclude that those might be occurring already in *this* life—either upon a fuller revelation of the existence and nature of the Ultimate or (perhaps more hopefully) through some of the ins and outs of skeptical religious practice, even before we are able to be sure that this is what they portend. And, of course, all of this was part of a discussion of how things would be, prudentially, if there *were* an Ultimate reality—and in that case one might be stuck with another life whether one wanted it or not!

As for how things are if ultimism is in fact *false*, and the pursuit of transcendence I spoke of in connection with that: perhaps here it would be helpful to think of those experiences all of us have had that, in the throes of the experience, we would be quite ready to label with that word "transcendent"—experiences that, as we might put it, invite us to turn our nothingness in the direction of infinity. Pascal of course says much about this, while giving it a specifically theistic interpretation. In our own time we have the sociologist Peter Berger speaking of "signals of transcendence," by which he means such things as our occasional sense of "trust in the order of reality" (our sense that "everything is all right"), or the experience of "joyful play," in which ordinary time seems suspended, or of invincible hope, or of "monstrous evil," or even of humor, which intimates redemption from the "imprisonment of the human spirit in the world."[25]

Though Berger's word "signals" might be too strong here, especially if we imagine that these experiences can occur without any ultimate transcendent reality being even dimly perceived in them, it is still true that he has identified certain very important sorts of human experience that might naturally lead one to consider the possibility of a religious dimension to life, and to think it worth pursuing. And, of course, I have not yet mentioned those common experiences we would more readily label experiences of the numinous or the sublime. I would wager that you have had experiences falling into at least one out of all these categories. *Now imagine an unlimited extension and deepening of the peculiar sense of significance to be found in them.* How could you fail to find this attractive?

What ultimistic religion means, one might say, is lending one's imagination and will to this possibility of a religious dimension to life. And if you do so, and if more transcendent experiences result, and if in them you are indeed objectively related to the Ultimate, then even if at the time you remain uncertain as to whether that's so (as you must if your state is one of faith instead of belief), the value of your life has surely been increased. You certainly want to understand that there is such a reality if indeed there is, and this is as close as, in all honesty, you can come to that. And even if you are *not* objectively related to the Divine in such experiences, the richness of your life has still been increased by them and by the larger horizons of imaginative and physical activity sponsored by them. You, of course, may never come to know that there is no such reality if there isn't (in taking up skeptical religion you are, inter alia, betting that there *is* in

---

[25] See Peter L. Berger, *A Rumor of Angels: Modern Society and the Rediscovery of the Supernatural* (New York: Doubleday, 1990), pp. 61–79.

order to realize what can be achieved thereby, in case it is procurable—and this may very well remain your condition). It is in the nature of the case that, while practicing skeptical religion, you will not be thinking of these as benefits you are achieving despite the falsity of ultimism. But they are nevertheless benefits you must *now* take into account, and think about in that light, as a reflective skeptic considering whether there is a good prudential argument for *taking up* the religious life. And I suggest that if you think about the matter carefully, you will see that the Skeptical Dominance Argument is indeed a good prudential argument, quite capable of handling such objections as you have raised.

So much for the dialogue, which was getting somewhat one-sided anyway. Suffice it to say, if our skeptic really is a skeptic, and a prudent skeptic, the ultimate possibility must gnaw away ever more irritatingly (that is to say, convincingly). Our Skeptical Dominance Argument, with its three aims of Prudential Alignment, Readiness, and Transcendence, is only designed to give it real bite. I close with a parable:

A certain man awoke, as from a dream, to find himself unable to move or speak, with his eyes, ears, and nose covered so that all he could sense were faint shapes and dim sounds and vague smells. From the content of the dream he inferred, and thereupon found himself invincibly believing, that he was in one of two conditions: either he was in a beautiful river valley, with flowing streams and blossoming trees, which he would one day soon be released to explore and experience more fully, or he had been placed in a vast and complex machine, hideously impressive in the efficiency of all its works, in whose gear wheels he would shortly be crushed. But his dream did not tell him which condition he was in. Nevertheless he imagined that the shapes he faintly saw were distant hills and that the sounds he dimly heard were those of water rushing by. He imagined himself touching a tree's rough bark upon his release and looking up to see it soaring to the sky. He pictured tasting fruit from nearby branches, and when he caught a vague smell, drifting, so it seemed, upon the wind, he imagined that it came to him from blossoms carried along by the river. For he reasoned to himself: "Either I am in the beautiful valley and will soon be released, or I am not. If I *am*, then my behavior is perfectly aligned with how things are—I am in a good state of affairs and thinking and acting accordingly—and this is better than being at odds with how things are, better than being evilly or neutrally disposed when in fact things are very good. So I should behave as I do. But even if I am *not* in that most happy state, my behavior still enables me to rise above the limitations of my circumstances and to 'touch' those trees and 'taste' that fruit and 'see' the hills and 'hear' the rushing stream and 'smell' the blossoms in the only way that will ever be available to me, and this, too, is better for me than being evilly or neutrally disposed, sinking deeper into the limitations that have been thrust on me. So I should behave as I do. And, therefore, whether I am in that happy state or not, I should behave as I do."

CHAPTER 10

Kant's Postulate

Pascal's famous dominance argument, which appeals to self-interest, is only one of many nonevidential maneuvers in which theists have indulged over the centuries, hoping to replace the multiply-punctured proofs of theism. Another comes to us from Immanuel Kant, who declared that in denying knowledge he was making room for faith. Kant seeks to persuade human religious thought to stay off the theoretical path that leads to punctured proofs and tries to guide it instead to the promised land of *morality*, where, he thinks, we will find a proper justification for belief in God. His basic idea is that we must believe in the existence of God in order to properly accommodate our unavoidable moral duty. Belief in the existence of God is therefore justified by practical reason—concerned with how we ought to live—even if not (as Kant thought he had shown) by theoretical reason. Precisely because it is practical reason that justifies theistic belief, no further speculation concerning, say, the nature of God is allowed: such speculation trespasses on territory that Kant's critical philosophy seeks to place out of bounds for us. It is enough for us to see how belief in God is intertwined with our practical commitments. It arises out of and is justified by them.

In this chapter I want to get as clear as possible on what Kant's moral maneuvers portend for theism, and then to show that, although they cannot help theistic belief to survive, quite similar maneuvers do provide aid and sustenance to skeptical religion.

1. *Morality and God in Kant*

The usual interpretation of Kant in philosophy of religion is based on what he says in the second *Critique*,[1] where the main relevant passages are these:

> By a postulate of pure practical reason I understand a theoretical proposition which is not as such demonstrable, but which is an inseparable corollary of an a priori unconditionally valid practical law. (226)

> We *should* seek to further the highest good (which therefore must be at least possible). Therefore also the existence is postulated of a cause of the whole of nature...which contains the ground of the exact coincidence of happiness with morality....Now it was our duty to promote the highest good; and it is a...necessity connected with duty as a requisite to presuppose the possibility of this highest good. This presupposition is made only under the condition of the existence of God, and this condition inseparably connects this supposition with duty. Therefore, it is morally necessary to assume the existence of God. (228)

> All that here belongs to duty is the endeavor to produce and to further the highest good in the world, the existence of which may thus be postulated though our reason cannot conceive it except by presupposing a higher intelligence. (229)

> The righteous man may say: I will that there be a God...I stand by this and will not give up this belief. (245)

> It is a duty to realize the highest good as far as it lies within our power to do so; therefore, it must be possible to do so. Consequently, it is unavoidable for every rational being in the world to assume whatever is necessary to its objective possibility. The assumption is as necessary as the moral law, in relation to which alone it is valid. (245n)

Kant's notorious obscurity, in part involving a tendency to qualify or alter thoughts expressed in one place when he returns to them in another, makes his work on moral arguments for theism, like his other work,

---

[1] See Immanuel Kant, *Critique of Practical Reason and Other Writings in Moral Philosophy,* ed. and trans. Lewis White Beck (Chicago: University of Chicago Press, 1949). Page references in the text are to this work.

something of an interpretational quagmire. But on the face of it, he is in these passages saying that it is our duty to further or promote[2] the highest good, which he sees as a perfect proportioning of happiness and virtue; that our having this duty implies that the highest good is possible;[3] and that *that* implies that God exists, because nature on its own cannot be expected to deliver the neat and tidy result that we look for when we look for the highest good.

One issue here, as Robert M. Adams has remarked, is that this argument certainly appears to be an attempted *proof* of the *truth* of the claim that God exists from (mostly) moral premises, contrary to what Kant suggests when he says his conclusion is not demonstrable.[4] But leave that issue aside for the moment; it will be resolved below. Another apparent problem—one fastened on by J. L. Mackie, among others—is that even if we have a duty to promote the highest good and Kant is right in his famous and widely accepted dictum that "ought" implies "can," all that immediately follows is that our *promoting* the highest good is possible, not that the highest good itself is possible.[5] Well, yes, one wants to say, this may be all that *immediately* follows, but perhaps another premise—that our promoting the highest good is possible only if the highest good is possible—is assumed but suppressed by Kant and is to be taken in conjunction with the conclusion Mackie grants to yield the obvious further conclusion.[6] If that premise is assumed by Kant, then that the highest good is possible follows mediately even if not immediately and he is off to the races.

Or is he? Why should we suppose that the suppressed premise is true? And even if it is true, how does it follow from the conclusion it permits (that the highest good is possible) that God exists? Doesn't that conclusion imply at most that God, a reality ensuring the moral order of the universe, *possibly* exists?[7]

One way of sorting all this out emerges if we think of promoting the highest good as *helping to bring it about,* which according to a perfectly natural interpretation of those words cannot occur unless it will come about,

---

[2] In one passage he says "produce," but that can't be literally true if the highest good is grounded in a supernatural causality. (Perhaps, however, a link could be forged here to what William James says about—in my phrase—alethically faith-contingent goods. See Chapter 11 for more on this notion.)

[3] Once he says that its actual *existence* is postulated. A way of dealing with this is suggested a little further on.

[4] See Robert M. Adams, "Moral Arguments for Theistic Belief," in *Rationality and Religious Belief,* ed. C. F. Delaney (Notre Dame, Ind.: University of Notre Dame Press, 1979), p. 124.

[5] See J. L. Mackie, *The Miracle of Theism* (Oxford: Clarendon Press, 1982), p. 109.

[6] Adams comes close to saying this. See his "Moral Arguments," p. 124.

[7] Mackie also makes the latter point. See *Miracle of Theism,* p. 109.

and if we think of its possibly coming-to-be in terms of *practical realizability,* which requires that conditions for it be in place even if it itself does not yet exist and so cannot in that sense be called actual. This would, for example, render what Kant says about possibility in the third passage quoted above consistent with what he says—almost in the same breath—about the existence of the highest good, which of course now means the *future* existence of that good (if the highest good is practically realizable then it will come to be). It would also allow us to make plausible the premise I have invited us to think of as a suppressed premise. Mackie criticizes the point it is making by saying that we can "improve the condition of human life" and that this is all it takes to promote the highest good. Apparently Mackie is taking "promote the highest good" in the fairly weak sense of "do something that must be done for the highest good to exist." In this sense one could promote the highest good even if it has no chance of ever coming about—even if to entertain the idea that it will come about would be, in Mackie's words, to entertain "vain hopes."[8] But if "promote" is, more strongly, interpreted to mean "help to bring about," then if promoting the highest good is possible, so must be the highest good. Furthermore, if the highest good is possible in the sense of practically realizable, then (assuming that nature without God cannot ensure the "exact coincidence of happiness with morality") it follows that God actually exists.

This interpretation, the careful reader will have noted, still leaves us with the question whether Kant's God is really the omnipotent, omniscient, and perfectly good being of traditional theism as opposed to some we-know-not-what sufficient to ensure that the universe is morally ordered. I will return to this. Right now I want to point out that the argument has been rendered logically valid at a significant cost: precisely because "promote" has been given such a strong interpretation, the claim that we are obligated to promote the highest good must now seem implausible. As Adams says in response to a reconstruction of Kant's reasoning in the relevant respects similar to mine, "in any reasonable morality we will be obligated to promote only the *best attainable approximation* of the highest good" (my emphasis), not the highest good itself.[9] If we accept Adams's point, then we must say of Kant's argument, all things considered, that it falls prey to that classic dilemma of reasoning: on one reading it is invalid, and when we make adjustments to our reading to ensure its validity, it has at least one false premise. Either way, then, it appears that Kant's argument fails.

But with a little imagination, so I suggest, we can find another way of reading the critical passages above which will generate a more interesting

[8] See ibid.
[9] Adams, "Moral Arguments," p. 124.

argument. To do so, I recommend attention to the following details from those passages: Kant's reference to our duty as one of *seeking* or *endeavoring* to further the highest good; and his reference not, as the Adams interpretation would lead us to expect, directly to the existence of God as following from his reasoning, but rather to our need to *postulate* or *assume* or *presuppose* or *stand by* the claim that there is a God. These details should prompt us in the direction of a "subjectivized" or nonevidential version of the argument initially stated above. That is, Kant can be read as saying that it is our duty to *seek* to further or promote (help bring about) the highest good and that this seeking by its very nature involves *thinking* (or "postulating") the highest good as possible in the sense of practically realizable; and that thus thinking—because, as he says, we cannot otherwise "conceive" the highest good as realizable—implies thinking that God exists. It is very easy to confuse this subjectivized version of the argument with the more "objective" one (which makes no reference to seeking or thinking), or somehow to run the two types of argument together. It is clear that interpreters of Kant have sometimes done so.[10] Perhaps Kant himself did so.[11] In that case, we should disentangle the two approaches and try them both. Now we have already tried the objective one and found it wanting. So it is reasonable to pursue the other, as I am here doing.

The new argument seems much cleaner—no need to introduce "suppressed" propositions into it—and more plausible than the old. But is it still too much for Kant to expect that we seek to help bring about the highest good? If Mackie were right, then we could in a reasonable sense seek to further or promote the highest good even if we only tried to do something the highest good would require while thinking the highest good itself, in its full glory, a vain hope. But anyone who has read Kant must know that he would regard this as a thin and anemic and quite unsatisfactory

---

[10] Take, for example, Peter Byrne, who in his formulation of the Kantian argument gives it the following premise: "Moral order and causality are only possible if we postulate a God as their source" (*The Moral Interpretation of Religion* [Grand Rapids, Mich.: Eerdmans, 1998], p. 56). Notice the slide from objective possibility to subjective postulation. These things are quite independent but run together in this formulation.

[11] Though it must be said that the subjective thrust of Kant's reasoning is made quite clear in other of his writings; what we need, therefore, is not just (as I have said) imagination but attentiveness to what else he says on the topic. At the end of the third *Critique*, for example, Kant returns to the moral reasoning of the second and makes its subjective nature quite clear. In a note added to the second edition, he even says that the "moral argument does not supply any *objectively valid* proof of the Being of God" but merely proves to the skeptic that "if he wishes to think in a way consonant with morality, he must admit the *assumption* of this proposition under the maxims of his practical reason." What we have here is "a *subjective* argument sufficient for moral beings." (See Kant's *Critique of Judgment*, trans. J. H. Bernard [New York: Hafner Press, 1951], p. 301 n. 15.)

substitute for his more robust notion. According to Kant expert Michel Despland, "Kant maintains a broad, generous view of possible human well-being, even at times kissing the hem of utopia."[12] Of course we don't want anything *so* utopian that we must revert to the Adams criticism already aired above. But I don't think this will be the result of accepting the new Kantian understanding of our duty. If I endeavor to help bring about the highest good, I *aim* at doing so and do actions expressing this aim, and it does not seem unduly demanding to expect this much from us. Later I defend this assessment more fully in connection with a version of Kant's argument that has been adapted to serve my own purposes. For now, let me simply register my judgment that the subjectivized argument we are considering is the most plausible argument to be distilled from the second *Critique* passages that have guided our discussion so far.

There is more to be said in assessment of the argument we have found, but it will be useful to postpone this discussion until we have out in the open the other strands of Kant's moral reasoning on behalf of theistic belief. The point from the second *Critique* we might call "presuppositional." It is the one most commonly focused on by commentators. The other strands, with a little oversimplification, might be united under the label "motivational." (These labels will, at any rate, provide simple and convenient means of reference in later parts of this discussion.) This latter sort of reasoning is prominent in Kant's *Lectures on the Philosophical Doctrine of Religion,* where he says that "our morality has need of the idea of God to give it emphasis." This idea, he continues, should make us "better, wiser and more upright. For if there is a supreme being who can and will make us happy, then our moral dispositions will thereby receive more strength and nourishment, and our moral conduct will be made firmer."[13] As my earlier word "strands" suggests, there are several distinct points here, which we will be able to identify if we spread our net a bit more widely over various of Kant's writings.[14]

---

[12] See the foreword he wrote for *Kant and the New Philosophy of Religion,* ed. Chris L. Firestone and Stephen R. Palmquist (Bloomington: Indiana University Press, 2006), p. xii.

[13] *Lectures on the Philosophical Doctrine of Religion,* in *Immanuel Kant: Religion and Rational Theology,* trans. and ed. Allen W. Wood and George di Giovanni (Cambridge: Cambridge University Press, 1996), p. 342. The fact that Kant can make such points shows that commentators like Nicholas Rescher are wrong when they say that Kant *only* looked "backward to presuppositions" and *never* "forward to consequences." (See Nicholas Rescher, *Pascal's Wager: A Study of Practical Reasoning in Philosophical Theology* [Notre Dame, Ind.: Notre Dame University Press, 1985], p. 42.)

[14] Though some of my formulations of Kant's points are somewhat different, I am much indebted in this part of the discussion to John E. Hare, "Kant on the Rational Instability of Atheism," in *Kant and the New Philosophy of Religion,* pp. 64–68, 72–73.

(1) Theistic belief—and not just belief but also practice, as his *Religion within the Boundaries of Mere Reason* clearly reveals—is thought desirable by Kant because it affords a continual reminder of the moral law and its contents as well as their signal importance. God is construed by theists as a mighty and majestic moral law-giver and moral laws are taken as expressing Divine commands, so in religion one will be sure to hear about morality regularly, and what is heard will be expressed in an authoritative tone of voice.[15] Aimed at here, one might say, is moral alertness and respect, as opposed to moral forgetfulness and apathy.

(2) Theistic belief and practice, further, will nourish in us the needed belief that, despite appearances, we can form and maintain a good will. We need, and such religious practice can provide, a certain "courage and firmness of attitude" with respect to our own personal prospects, as opposed to personal pessimism and inconstancy.[16]

(3) Theistic belief and practice will also nourish the belief that my efforts and those of others will be appropriately coordinated by a "higher moral being through whose universal organization the forces of single individuals, insufficient on their own, are united for a common effect."[17] So: confidence in corporate moral strength, as opposed to fear of moral conflict or disunity.

(4) With theistic belief and practice, furthermore, comes a belief in reward and punishment with the associated incentives[18]—this presumably is seen as beneficial because it provides a kind of motivational boost, and helps to ward off moral indolence.

(5) Finally, we can say, according to Kant, that theistic belief and practice make it more likely that I will be able to maintain the belief that my moral goals and the goals of other good persons will be fully realized in the end, when the highest good fully comes to be. What is provided here some

---

[15] See *Religion within the Boundaries of Mere Reason,* in *Immanuel Kant: Religion and Rational Theology,* pp. 59–60, 177–178, and also *Lectures,* p. 348.

[16] Kant writes: "How it is possible that a naturally evil human being should make himself into a good human being surpasses every concept of ours.... In spite of that fall, the command that we *ought* to become better human beings still resounds unabated in our souls; consequently, we must also be capable of it, even if what we can do is of itself insufficient and, by virtue of it, we only make ourselves receptive to a higher assistance inscrutable to us" (*Religion,* p. 90). And again: "[Only by] faith in this supplement for his deficiencies [can one] lay hold of the courage and firmness of attitude he needs to live a life pleasing to God" (*The Conflict of the Faculties,* in *Immanuel Kant: Religion and Rational Theology,* p. 268).

[17] *Religion,* p. 133.

[18] In the *Lectures* Kant records his opinion that it is "highly necessary," after taking an interest in morals, to "take an interest also in the existence of God, a being who can reward our good conduct; and then we obtain strong incentives which determine us to observe moral laws" (349). Divine punishment is mentioned here as well.

writers have called moral hope, as opposed to moral despair or a sense of futility or demoralization.[19] But perhaps it would be better to speak of confidence or optimism—a very general optimism to distinguish it from the similar attitude already discussed under (2), which is restricted to one's own personal prospects.[20]

Taking these points together with the presuppositional point from the second *Critique,* we can summarize Kant's overall view as I am construing it by saying that, according to him, we cannot even *try* to fulfill our moral duty with respect to the highest good (the harmony of virtue and deserved happiness) without postulating that God exists, and that we are not nearly as likely to *persist* in trying to fulfill it if we do not both postulate the existence of God and take on the form of religious life with which such a mental attitude is customarily associated.

This view raises many questions. In addition to the question about the content of "God" left over from earlier discussion, we have at least the following: Does Kant have a correct picture of the highest good? Are the "benefits" put forward by his motivational reasoning all properly regarded as such? What exactly does it mean to "postulate" God's existence? Does this entail forming the propositional *belief that* God exists? And how is one to go about doing so rationally in the absence of even the appearance of evidence? The question about the highest good I address later, when I come to develop my own view. But we can address the other questions now, and I suggest that by doing so we will already be able to see that Kant's fullest, most plausible case must still fail to provide adequate support for traditional theistic religion.

Let us begin with the questions about postulation, evidence, and motivational benefits. Kant uses the term "postulate" to distinguish what's going on here from theoretical cognition (knowledge) and also opinion (which, as he understands it, necessarily lacks an adequate basis). When we postulate the possibility of the highest good and also God to support

---

[19] For the reference to hope, see John E. Hare, *The Moral Gap: Kantian Ethics, Human Limits, and God's Assistance* (Oxford: Clarendon Press, 1996), p. 272 n. 73. This expression is a little misleading in Hare's case because he clearly thinks it is a *belief* that is generated. For the reference to demoralization, which is somewhat undiscriminatingly made the focus of what Kant has to say in the distinguishable "strands" of reasoning we are presently exploring, see Adams, "Moral Arguments," p. 125. The present emphasis is also central in Allen Wood, *Kant's Moral Religion* (Ithaca: Cornell University Press, 1970).

[20] The need for something to make such optimism possible and ward off the despair here mentioned is a constant theme of Kant's *Religion,* which places a very heavy emphasis on the radical evil in human nature. It is interesting to note the role Kant sees for religious community in dealing with all this. See especially *Religion,* pp. 130–134, 179–181.

it, what we do is grounded in reason but—Kant hastens to add—"only in respect of its practical employment."[21] Postulation involves a kind of "holding true," and sometimes this is said to be "not inferior in degree to knowing, even though it is completely different from it in kind."[22] Indeed, the moral theist is sometimes described as absolutely convinced.[23]

But at other times something less than belief as I am understanding it appears to be involved. (Indeed, in one place we read, intriguingly, that "a skeptic can still have religion.")[24] In Kant's *Critique of Judgment* this view is especially obvious. Here we find that the propositions involved in postulating the possibility of the highest good and the existence of God are called "things of faith" and their postulation "is a mere assumption in a reference which is practical and commanded for the moral use of our reason." Again, postulating or having faith is said to be "the permanent principle of the mind to assume as true…that which is necessary to presuppose as condition of the possibility of the highest moral final purpose." It is "trust in the attainment of a design." It can even be a "doubtful faith."[25]

Although Kant continues to use the language of belief, and is unclear in what he says on matters related to it, for example whether the belief involved in moral faith requires conviction or not, it may therefore be said that he is working his way toward something much more adequately accommodated by the concept of beliefless faith I have developed than by any full-blooded notion of belief. (As the second to last passage with which we began has it, "I *will* that there be a God" [my emphasis].) In any case, that the most attractive rendering of Kant's view will need to *take* him in this way is strongly supported by at least the following considerations: (1) that it is in the very nature of his reasoning that he has presented no evidence for theistic belief, and so, given the involuntariness of belief and the psychological impossibility of believing what one sees as evidentially unsupported (on this see *Prolegomena*, pp. 65–67, 213–214), if he wants the genuine article belief-wise, he will have to countenance self-deception (as most assuredly he would not—and we should not—want to do); and (2) that his reasoning cannot show that *more* than beliefless faith is required for the nonevidential goods he mentions, namely engaging our moral duty and persisting in our attempts to fulfill it.

---

[21] See *Critique of Judgment*, p. 324.

[22] See *What Does It Mean to Orient Oneself in Thinking?* in *Immanuel Kant: Religion and Rational Theology*, p. 14.

[23] See *Lectures*, pp. 355–356.

[24] Ibid., p. 355.

[25] See *Critique of Judgment*, pp. 322–325.

The first of these points should be clear enough already. But it may be worthwhile to fill out the second. It is evident that to think the highest good as possible and God as existing we do not need to *think that* (i.e., believe that) the highest good is attainable and that God exists. We need do no more than imaginatively project the states of affairs referred to and give our mental assent to them in the manner of the beliefless propositional faith thoroughly discussed in *Prolegomena*. If we do the latter, we will be quite able to pursue the duty of promoting the highest good, regarding this as our duty. Thus full-blooded theistic belief is not required for the latter state to exist, and is not justified by Kant's "presuppositional" argument.[26] Furthermore, if we adopt theistic propositional faith and also seriously, committedly act on it, generating a theistic faith practice in community with others of like mind, we will realize all the "motivational" benefits that might, within a theistic frame of reference, have a serious claim to be regarded as such. Such a faith community would unleash the relevant psychological and social factors as effectively as a belief community. (Remember here how we saw that Kant himself says that "a skeptic can still have religion.") In it we would still have the desired resources to ward off moral apathy and forgetfulness, personal pessimism and inconstancy, fear of moral conflict or disunity, moral laziness, and moral despair.[27] The upshot is this: Kant's moral arguments are not at all plausible when taken as arguments for theistic *belief*. By looking now at the remaining question about the content of "God," we will be able to show that they do not, in the relevant sense, support a *theistic* frame of mind either.

First let's observe that Kant himself seems to have been less than sure about this. As he puts it in one surprisingly clear passage: "For determining our ideas of the supersensible we have no material whatever, and we must derive this latter from things in the world of sense, which is absolutely inadequate for such an object. Thus, in the absence of all determination of it, nothing remains but the concept of a nonsensible something which contains the ultimate ground of the world of sense, but which does not furnish any knowledge (any amplification of the concept) of its inner constitution."[28] Now it is true that even in the same context, Kant muddies the waters by speaking of an "intelligent Being" and a "moral Being"

---

[26] A similar point is made in such terms as "assent," "acceptance," and "commitment" but not filled out in Allen W. Wood, *Kant* (Oxford: Blackwell, 2005), p. 182, and also in Byrne, *Moral Interpretation*, pp. 67–68.

[27] I have approached these benefits negatively, in part because in that way we avoid the question whether Divine reward and punishment represent appropriate moral motives. Arguably they do not, but even if that is so, we can all agree that moral *laziness* is to be avoided!

[28] *Critique of Judgment*, p. 318.

and an "author and governor of the world." Apparently this is because he thinks we find such concepts unavoidable when considering how the great final purpose embedded in the highest good might be realized.[29] But if we look closely we will also find the point that intelligence, purposiveness, and causality might be completely different in the Divine from what it is in us,[30] and the suggestion that detailed talk of God as omnipotent, omniscient, and so on should be accepted, if at all, because of its "popular usefulness."[31] As this last quotation indicates, perhaps Kant sometimes vacillates on the nature of the Divine because of the specific notions embedded in the popular religion of his time, which—as his "motivational" reasoning shows—he would dearly love to enlist in the service of morality.

Whatever Kant's own view may have been, we clearly must say that the specifically theistic conception of the Ultimate is not *needed* for the moral purposes he is seeking to advance. As Peter Byrne remarks, "there are other religious metaphysics which will fit the bill."[32] Byrne further explains that Kant saw theology as an anthropomorphic imaginative exercise that made religious ideas *usable* for morality, in response to which he comments that "many different symbol systems can be used to relate value to ontology in the manner required."[33] And our own exploration of ultimism has informed us that every religious view, by definition, sees unlimited value in the Divine and an unlimitedly great good as our potential inheritance. Thus, it seems, just *any* religious view should be capable of playing the roles reflection on which brings theism to mind for Kant.

All of this is radically deflationary with respect to any Kantian attempt to prop up specifically theistic belief by moral means. Indeed, by thinking about Kant's most plausible arguments we have arrived at a dead end for theism. But as I want now to show, this theistic dead end is just the gateway to an argument strongly supporting skeptical religion.

2. *The Kantian Contribution to Skeptical Religion—Stage 1*

To get through the gateway just mentioned, we need only take one step beyond the point to which we are brought by our discussion of Byrne's comment concerning other "symbol systems." We need only appreciate that

[29] See ibid., pp. 306–307.
[30] Ibid., p. 306.
[31] Ibid., p. 313.
[32] Byrne, *Moral Interpretation*, p. 39.
[33] Ibid., pp. 62, 91.

a proper use of the imagination renders *any* particular and detailed religious symbol system unnecessary: simple ultimism is enough. If we bring ultimism into focus, and think carefully about what acting on it would involve (as we have done in Chapters 2 and 3), then we can see that a commitment to it of the sort that skeptical religion represents can procure for us every moral benefit that a Kantian could want. Then, also, we can see that the *importance* of those moral benefits generates a strong Kantian *argument* for skeptical religion—call it the Moral Commitment Argument for skeptical religion—as well as a corresponding aim, which I call the Moral Commitment Aim. I will be developing this point in my own terms, but its Kantian pedigree should be readily apparent.

The commitment I have in mind is a commitment to what I shall call the *human good,* which I shall understand in a strong sense entailing universal justice and the opportunity, for everyone, of achieving full potential. I will not linger over questions about the merits of Kant's conception of the "highest good" or the relation between his notion and my own—though it will no doubt be uncontroversial that achieving our full potential entails realizing virtue and happiness in one form or another. The more focused notion of human good that I plan to utilize will, I think, allow me to realize the full potential of a Kantian form of reasoning more easily, and is all that is required to do so.

In its most compressed form, the Kantian argument I commend to twenty-first-century skeptics runs as follows: We ought all to adopt a commitment to the human good, that is, the aim to carry out such a commitment is rationally required. Now a commitment to the human good that is genuine and morally commendable must be sincere and conscientious, leading one to make use of whatever resources are available and not independently ruled out for the carrying out of this difficult moral task. (Call such a commitment a *wholehearted* commitment.) But none of us can display a commitment to the human good fitting this description in the absence of a parallel commitment to skeptical religion. Thus we should all adopt skeptical religion.

That is the short version of the argument. But it certainly can be, and needs to be, more fully developed. I suggest that we can do so in two stages (stages corresponding roughly to Kant's presuppositional and motivational reasoning). The first stage, which is my concern in this section, gets us to the conclusion that ultimistic propositional faith is rationally required and runs as follows. (1) We ought all to be wholeheartedly committed to the human good. But (2) such a commitment involves faith that the human good will be realized—call this *moral* faith. It follows that (3) moral faith is rationally required. But (4) the human good will be realized only if there is a transcendent reality on the side of the good capable of ensuring its realization. Hence (5) faith that there is such a reality—call this *transcendent* faith—is also rationally required. Now (6) the rational version of transcendent faith, given that one is wholeheartedly committed to the human good, is one in which the transcendent reality on the side of the good is thought of not just as transcendent but as fully ultimate and salvific. Hence (7) faith that the transcendent reality in question is of this sort—which is to say *ultimistic propositional faith*—is rationally required as well.

Does this reasoning succeed? Let us consider how its various moves can be defended and made convincing.

Take the first premise. Here it may be objected that, given what I mean by "the human good," I have placed too heavy a burden onto our shoulders. To speak of perfect justice and fulfillment of potential for all is not just unrealistic, in this context it is also unkind! The most we have reason to do is to take on a commitment to leave the world better than we found it, and this we can do even if we do not think of ourselves as seeking to achieve such extravagant moral goals.

But this objection can be answered. To be committed to the human good is to profoundly *value* such states of affairs as are here mentioned and to aspire to be part of their realization, to seek to contribute to that cause—a cause one sees as shared with many others. Perhaps, for example, one becomes a doctor and volunteers in Appalachia, intending in this way to lessen suffering and set processes in motion that will contribute to general well-being. Obviously one who is committed to the human good does not think of its realization as depending entirely on her. Her commitment and its differences from alternatives are to be understood more in terms of the sort of *orientation* it involves than in terms of the amount of good she herself expects to achieve in a single lifetime. Though she may be said to be *pursuing* the human good, this is only because she, unlike someone lacking her commitment, sees her more immediate pursuits within the context of that larger goal.[34] Thus there is no reason why the degree of difficulty involved in such a commitment should be seen as unacceptably onerous.

Is the commitment nevertheless unrealistic? Well, it might be if there were good reason to believe that the human good will not be realized, but that is not so. Here I would be inclined to argue on the basis of my case, defended in *Skepticism,* for religious skepticism: the human good is realizable if ultimism is true, and nothing rules out that it is true: religious

---

[34] An analogy: I may build a table intending simply to build a table, but I may also build a table intending my doing so to be a contribution to the larger goal of furnishing someone's house—a goal that I and others share. Just in saying we share it I already admit that there is a sense in which it is a goal we may all claim as our own.

disbelief, just like religious belief, is unjustified. The commitment in question might also be unrealistic if it couldn't rationally be taken on without good reason to believe that the human good *will* be realized. Sometimes it has seemed to people, because of the very great value it represents, that such a goal must be such as will be realized. But this conclusion evidently does not follow. As F. R. Tennant memorably puts it, "The 'thinking reed' may face the world as a judge rather than as a suppliant; but so far as moral ideals alone can inform us, the world may expunge both him and them, however intolerable the thought may be."[35] And if, again, religious belief and a generalized religious disbelief are alike unjustified, there is no *independent* support for a positive belief here either. Happily, a commitment to the human good can be perfectly rational without the belief that it will be realized. And though (as we will see in a moment) faith that it will be realized *is* required, the skeptic about the realization of the human good who is thinking about whether to adopt such faith is unable rationally to say that it is unrealistic. For to do so would be either to confuse faith with belief or to slip once more into the view that what one who is committed to the human good seeks to further will not or probably will not be realized—a view that by virtue of her very skepticism a skeptic about the realization of the human good is not in a position to endorse.

Suppose, then, that the commitment in question cannot be said to be unacceptably onerous or unrealistic. This, as the objector will point out, does not yet show that reason supports it more strongly than alternative commitments such as the one mentioned by her objection—in some way to leave the world better than one found it. How can this additional claim be defended? As follows.

(i) If, activating the relevant dispositions of empathy and respect, we take seriously how good even some significant movement toward the relevant goal would be and how extremely far we have yet to go to arrive even at that (how poor things are at this early stage of our development, in what is only the twenty-first century), we will see that we have good reason to seek to do more than just leave the world a little better than we found it. Suppose so. Does that mean we should aspire to human perfection instead? Well, we should aspire to *contribute* to it, holding the goal to which we wish to contribute before our minds, if, as seems to be the case, doing so will make progress toward that goal more likely. The point here is that if we are committed to the human good, it is more likely that some significant part of what is required to achieve it will be realized; and *this* is good and can, especially given our current condition as a species, be seen to be good as well as worthy of encouragement by anyone, even the objector.

[35] F. R. Tennant, *Philosophical Theology*, vol. 2 (Cambridge: Cambridge University Press, 1930), p. 95.

(ii) If, activating the same dispositions of empathy and respect, we were truly to ascribe to the lives and deepest needs and aspirations of others, of all times and places, the importance we detect in our own, we would be literally overwhelmed by the force of what we saw. Reason is not partial and so may be expected to support just such a judgment. Since, given the value we associate with them, we take our own deepest needs and aspirations as supporting pursuit of their fulfillment, the judgment in question must supply a powerful reason indeed to aim in whatever way we can at the fulfillment of the deepest needs and aspirations of all.

(iii) Finally, we may note that respect and empathy will also lead us, more particularly, to consider the weight of all the unredeemed suffering that is entailed by such goals as are here in question not ever being achieved, and for *this* reason move us to adopt the orientation in question. There is an interesting problem of evil for a pure skeptic uncommitted to a truly universal justice and the good of all. Moral impulses may have led her to doubt or deny that there is a perfectly good God (and may also contribute to her doubt about ultimism). Surely a God at all like us in moral respects would seek to ensure perfect justice and the realization of the full potential of all. But precisely here, in realizing that her moral impulses are of this sort, the pure skeptic must also realize the claim on *her* of a commitment to the goods in question.

Given these points, it seems that being properly "on the side of morality" means seeing oneself as working toward states of affairs associated with the human good even when there is no justification for assurance that it will obtain. What we have here can be compared to the situation one is in if, recognizing the importance of what one is about, one seeks to make progress toward being a good parent even though it seems that, genetically and environmentally, almost everything is against it. Or—another analogy—you might think of doing something you hope will help someone, perhaps someone trapped in an overturned automobile, when you know that your best efforts may well not be enough without the assistance of some person or force you have no reason to believe will appear. In these circumstances, the value of human life is such that you have excellent reason at least to try. In sum: the human good is so important and so bound up with what it is to be moral that one who is only a skeptic with regard to its realization could not possibly be rationally excused from becoming committed to its realization.[36]

---

[36] We may indeed be kissing the hem of utopia, as Despland said in that earlier quote, but as the same writer says of the Kantian view, "faith is the free and personal act of affirmation which struggles against the split (inside the self and outside of it) between what is and what ought to be." (Michel Despland, *Kant on History and Religion* [Montreal: McGill-Queen's

That takes care of the first premise of our argument. What about the second, which claims that a wholehearted commitment of this sort will be seen to involve faith that the goals in question will be realized (moral faith)? It is hard to imagine how one could actually display such a commitment to the human good without picturing the world as one in which it is realized. And, clearly, one will give to this imagined state of affairs a positive evaluation. Furthermore, belief that it will obtain, as we have seen, is unavailable. So it appears that already three of the conditions of propositional faith are present.

What about the remaining condition, mental assent to the imagined picture of things? Well, how else is one with the commitment in question going to respond to it? Surely not with rejection or indifference. Here the nature of the commitment—and, in particular, its difficulty (which was made a basis for objection before)—can be called upon as support: we must draw on whatever resources are available and not otherwise ruled out as illegitimate to help us. And the full attitude of faith, not just some weaker attitude of the sort that might be represented by hope alone, is both available and must represent a powerful resource in the pursuit of the human good. It follows that in taking on the commitment in question we commit ourselves as well to having moral faith. But why, it may be asked, is hope on its own not perfectly satisfactory—at least as good an attitude to take toward the proposition in question as faith? Why shouldn't we act in hope and so just on the possibility that the proposition is true instead of more extravagantly postulating its actuality? The answer, already suggested, is that hope is not appropriate to a commitment and purpose of the sort in question. I might hope that I will win the lottery, and be motivated by my hope to purchase a lottery ticket, but I could hardly form the (probably foolish) *commitment* to winning the lottery or to seriously advancing my chances of doing so without going beyond hope at least to faith. Even if I could, I would not be likely to prosecute my purpose very enthusiastically or effectively if all I had in mind was hope and a possibility. Hope is, as we might say, intellectually bittersweet. What it offers with one hand it is constantly taking away with the other. In propositional faith there is an extra element of definiteness and constancy—assent to a certain picture of the world, voluntarily assumed—that makes all the difference.

Some might disagree, suggesting that whether hope is sufficient in the case I have described depends on the odds and the values at stake. If my ultimate goal in entering the lottery is to save my grandson's life by securing a ransom (a case analogous in its seriousness to the serious moral

---

University Press, 1973], p. 145.) Surely we could not struggle better than to become committed to the human good, as here construed.

commitment here discussed), and my only real chance of doing so involves winning the lottery, hope may be a sufficient *motivation,* and the possibility of winning a sufficient *justification,* for betting. Moreover, if my chances of winning, while low, are not non-negligible (they are one in ten, say, or one in one hundred), my motivation for betting, given hope, is even stronger, and my justification even more obvious.[37]

But the issue here is not just about betting. It is about becoming *committed to winning.* (I have granted that hope might be sufficient for merely buying the ticket.) Perhaps the reply will be that, in the grandson case, hope is sufficient also for such a commitment. But notice that in making such a commitment, forming such a purpose, one must imaginatively project success: I have to think to myself "I will win" to form the purpose to win, just as I have to think to myself "I will save my grandson" to form the purpose to save my grandson. "Mights" and "coulds" and "possiblys" aren't going to cut it here. And, in any case, would any grandfather committed to saving his grandson rest content with them? By moving beyond such tentativeness to imaginative definiteness, one makes available to oneself possibly critical psychological resources that are otherwise unavailable, and any wholehearted would-be rescuer, recognizing both the importance of the commitment and its difficulty, will avail himself of them. (One can easily imagine an interview with grandpa after the child is rescued in which the former says the following: "I just stubbornly kept before my mind the picture of his being saved and refused to let it go, and kept affirming to myself that that's how things would turn out, even though I knew it might very well not be so. That's what kept me going.")

Applying all this now to the case at hand: it is hard to see how we are even *able* to form or in any disciplined manner to pursue a purpose to contribute to the achievement of the human good without moral faith. But even those who (psychologically speaking) needn't assent to the relevant moral proposition in this way to manifest some sort of commitment (if such there be) *should* do so, in order to make their seeking more wholehearted, and to provide for themselves the extra psychological resources such faith brings with it. Thinking again of our earlier analogies: it is proper for me to have faith that I will become a good parent (and not just hope), if much seems to be arrayed against it. With such faith I manifest the depth of my commitment and am more likely to be able to make progress toward my goal. Similarly for the case of the overturned automobile: bewildered and anxious and yet wishing to help, it is a sign of strength and good sense for me to concentrate my mind and have faith that I will find some way to do

[37] For this objection I am grateful to William Wainwright, who developed it in response to a paper of mine at the 2006 meeting of the Society for Philosophy of Religion.

so—to represent the world to myself as one in which I make the right efforts and they are assisted in whatever way is required, mentally affirming the content of this picture. The application of all this to the justification of moral faith is obvious. To be on the side of morality in the way that we are discussing requires having faith that reality is on its side too. And so the second premise of the argument and also the interim conclusion that follows are shown to be fully defensible.

Let's look now at the next premise of our argument, which says that what moral faith envisages will obtain only if there is a transcendent reality on the side of the good capable of ensuring that it does; and its next conclusion, that if we see this and are behaving rationally, we will also have faith that there is such a reality (transcendent faith). The support for the premise comes from the fact that if all we are given is this life, and there is nothing more than the physical universe and no transcendent reality on the side of the good, then the tragedy of such things as undeveloped potential and lives cut short is irremediable. Perhaps with much time and effort, the world could evolve toward a much better quality of justice and much greater well-being. But even then it would not be the case that every human being realizes her full potential, because many tragedies are such as are likely to be forever beyond our control, and because the horrific suffering of the past and the many lives already cut short cannot even possibly be healed by our efforts. (Maybe it is because of this that some secularists are inclined to suggest—mistakenly, as we saw—that reason is content with moral goals falling short of the one here emphasized.) The *conclusion* seems to follow, since if one really has rational faith with respect to the content of a proposition *p*, one must also have faith with respect to any (less than clearly evidenced) proposition *q* one considers to be entailed by *p*. Thus if the proposition that the human good will be realized entails the proposition that there is a transcendent reality capable of ensuring that it does, then any rational person who has faith with respect to the former proposition and sees the connection will have faith with respect to the latter as well.

And so we arrive at the last and crucial premise of our present piece of reasoning. According to this claim, the rational *version* of transcendent faith, from the perspective of a commitment to the human good, must be one in which the transcendent reality on the side of the good is thought of as not just transcendent but as fully ultimate and salvific. What can be said on behalf of this claim? Why—to raise a possible objection—isn't it enough for the person of transcendent faith to rest content with the (admittedly vague) proposition that *something* transcendent suffices to protect the deepest moral values? Why is the more specifically religious version of the proposition rationally better?

It is better for several reasons. (i) Just thinking about the vaguer proposition's entailments already forces us to move beyond it and some distance toward the religious one. For example, there could be no transcendent reality on the side of the good and capable of ensuring its realization unless what is metaphysically ultimate were also at the very least not opposed to the good. For if what is metaphysically ultimate is opposed to the good, then *nothing* will suffice to support it. But if our faith must be enlarged to embrace such additional parts of ultimism, why not go all the way with it?

This first point is most persuasive when taken together with certain others, which I now elaborate. (ii) The state of affairs involving a transcendent reality on the side of the good that is morally most to be preferred is clearly one in which ultimism is true: reality is more deeply and more richly responsive to our moral striving if it includes the truth of ultimism than it is on any other conceivable scenario. Indeed, if there is a transcendent reality that is metaphysically ultimate, and also salvific, then the very deepest truths about reality are on morality's side; and if this reality is also ultimate in value, then the possibilities for the production of good in human life must be literally unlimited in depth and richness. But anyone committed to the human good will certainly find the idea of unlimited human potential more attractive than limited. Thus in thinking about how the vaguer proposition should be filled out we have an excellent reason to take it in an explicitly religious direction.

(iii) It is natural for the human mind to *seek* such a "filling out" or "closure." If all we assent to is the claim that *something* transcendent can take care of things, we will naturally think about how it is able to do so, how it should be seen as related to other realities, and so on. This will be distracting at the very least, and disconcerting if such reflection renders one (however irrationally) unsure as to whether the reality one has envisaged is really up to the job. Saying that the reality in question is not just transcendent but also ultimate and salvific in our senses fills in all the blanks and gives one an object of contemplation truly worthy of such attention.

(iv) Finally, it may be noted that certain other goods associated with faith, discussed in other chapters of this book, are best served, if we have faith at all, by a fuller religious faith. Since our decisions about how to relate to such goods should not be compartmentalized but rather made part of an overall approach to life, if we have a decision to make about one (as here), we should take guidance from the others. And this means that we have a reason, in the present case, to give an explicitly religious content to the claim about transcendent realities with respect to which we have faith.

It seems, then, that there is no reason to stop short of ultimism here, and plenty of reason not to. And that is why the rational version of transcendent faith, from the perspective of a commitment to the human good, must be one in which the transcendent reality on the side of the good is thought of as not just transcendent but as fully ultimate and salvific as well. It follows immediately that the final conclusion of the argument we have been assessing is true: ultimistic propositional faith is rationally required.

3. *The Kantian Contribution—Stage 2*

But ultimistic propositional faith is only one part of the story where skeptical religion is concerned. What about the *operational* faith that, as it were, puts feet on the propositional attitude? Is there a Kantian justification for this? (Notice that if there is, we will have another justification for the propositional faith that it presupposes.)

Yes, indeed. For, in addition to the counterpart to Kant's presuppositional reasoning which we have developed, there is a counterpart to his motivational reasoning, which generates several more propositions for our argument, as follows: (8) Given (at least present) human limitations, our success in moral matters is constantly threatened by temptations toward forgetfulness, apathy, fragmentation of effort, and indolence, by personal pessimism and inconstancy, by social pessimism, and also by a general despair about the human good ever being achieved, among other things. (9) A wholehearted commitment to the human good by definition requires helping ourselves to the best resources available for the cultivation and maintenance of attitudes contrary to these (call such attitudes *commitment* attitudes). Now (10) skeptical religion provides the best, most effective way of cultivating commitment attitudes; and as the first stage of this reasoning has shown, we are already rationally committed to its propositional core. Hence (11) we should cultivate commitment attitudes by adding religious operational faith to propositional—which is to say that the totality of skeptical religion is rationally required.

Does *this* stage of our Kantian reasoning succeed? I think it clearly does. Very little could be more obvious than (8), and (9) is made true by our earlier definition of the relevant terms. The only other premise is (10), so let us focus on that—and on whether (11) follows from the preceding premises.

That the second half of (10) is true follows straightforwardly from (7), which was established by earlier reasoning. This is significant, for if we have already arrived at a commitment to skeptical religion at the propositional level, and are casting about for a framework for living, a way of life, that will support a commitment to the human good, *and* see the usefulness, in this regard, of operationalizing our propositional commitment, won't it make the most sense to do so—wouldn't it be a waste of time to look *elsewhere* for those vital resources for moral living?

This might be true—and so (11) might follow—even if skeptical religion were not clearly the best framework for moral living available to our skeptic. Let us now consider just how good it is. How does it ward against such things as moral forgetfulness, apathy, fragmentation of effort, and indolence, against personal pessimism and inconstancy, social pessimism, and a general despair about the human good ever being achieved? Well, by being set upon a religious path, with one form or another of community support, aimed at something imagined to be ultimate in reality and in value and the source of our true good, we are the beneficiaries of a *unifying framework for living* of the most all-embracing variety, with the strongest and most positive forms of social and psychological reinforcement, in which realization of the human good is truly central. And notice that whatever independently identifiable forms of moral support there may be can be woven into such a form of life, where they are subsumed within the broadest possible frame of reference and unifying focus.

How could this be improved upon? Even in the absence of belief, assenting to ultimism and holding the possibility of its truth before our minds, taking it *as* true in the manner of faith, will help to work against despair over the prospects of morality and that fragmentation of personality and diffusion of efforts to which the challenges of life and the many winds of cultural influence make us vulnerable: it will help to integrate our motives and to intensify our moral focus. Of course this itself can operate successfully on an ongoing basis only if there is support for its continuation. And that is where participation in the full stream of religious life comes in. (Think here of religious practices like meditation, and of participation in a mature religious community.) Acting *on* our assent in the ways described in earlier chapters, uniting our energies with those of others similarly motivated, allowing our dispositions to be shaped by the religious life—all of this will support and also further the effects already mentioned, providing a structure within which intellectual and moral development of the relevant sorts can take place.

Everyone, surely, is familiar with the role of religious community in providing social and psychological support for living as well as avenues of disciplined service. Where religious community in the actual world has failed to live up to its potential in this regard it has been on account of the narrow intellectual commitments and ideological loyalties that in skeptical religion are entirely absent. These are constraints under which Kant's original argument—especially as developed in his *Religion*—also labored. It is certainly less than obvious that a conservative Lutheran form of religiousness provides the best forum within which to advance toward the human good, with the latter's universalist and inclusivist dimensions. But skeptical religion can take the wheat and leave the chaff. Altering the metaphor, it prunes back the tree of religiousness to the point where vigorous new growth is possible—of the sort described in Chapters 2 and 3. And this makes all the difference, permitting unrivaled support for moral living without the encumbrances thereof that have weighed down religiousness in its short journey through the actual world thus far.

Now it should be noted that nothing in these points about the psychological value of religious faith implies that we need faith to prompt us to action in pursuit of moral ideals. It is not as though we need some incentive or inducement to moral activity which religion provides, perhaps in the form of distinctively religious sanctions (rewards and punishments). God forbid! The creatures, especially persons, which moral precepts are about, and also (derivatively) morality itself and its ideals, have *inherent* dignity and are *inherently* worthy of a very deep respect, and a proper recognition of this should give one ample motivation to get going morally quite apart from religious inducements (indeed, it should lead one to reject the latter because of their obvious connection to unworthy prudential considerations). But while this is the case, we may yet benefit from religious support if it helps us to *keep* going, and to face the enormity of the moral task with a clear focus, and also boldness and good cheer. What we are talking about here is in the end not so much motivation as *fortification* and *structure*. Religious faith, properly implemented, can provide these instrumental benefits.

It seems clear, then, that (11) does follow from previous reasoning—which is to say that our Kantian argument for skeptical religion goes through. Kant's moral reasoning is powerful, but not as support for theistic belief: it needs to be redirected to the task of supporting skeptical faith. We have, in other words, found it necessary to deny Kant's substitute for true faith to make room for the genuine article.

CHAPTER 11

James's Will

The American psychologist, philosopher, and onetime artist, William James, was a passionate pluralist rather than a monist, more interested in the many than in any One, fascinated with diversity and—living as he did on the cusp of the twentieth century—with change of all kinds. In his work on religion he was quite prepared to accept the possibility of both a religious and a nonreligious layer of reality and of plurality within each. He never really believed in the truth of materialism. But, as we will see, he didn't clearly believe in the truth of any of its contraries either. He always experienced at least some of the tension between these various possibilities. This has endeared him to many similarly ambivalent readers. As a recent interpreter has it, "in explicating what it is like to stand in that open space and feel the winds pulling you now here, now there, James describes a crucial site of modernity and articulates the decisive drama enacted there."[1]

And yet, at the same time, James was an ardent defender of religious commitment, a religious commitment he presumably thought compatible with both his uncertainties and his ecumenical and pluralist leanings. His defense of such commitment is more unambiguously practical in its orientation than either Pascal's or Kant's. Indeed, so focused was he on the practical results of beliefs formed by inquiry that he used the word "pragmatist" to identify his most general intellectual stance. All of this serves to bring him quite close to the skeptical religiousness defended in this book—closer, perhaps, than any other historical figure I have discussed.

---

[1] Charles Taylor, *Varieties of Religion Today: William James Revisited* (Cambridge, Mass.: Harvard University Press, 2002), p. 59.

Now such an assessment may seem optimistic. For in James, along with ambivalence and terminological vagueness that leave his true view hard to read, there are clear positive references to a personal and limited Deity and also evident dalliances with talk of belief and probability. Given all this, a reader of James may think his views rather more distant from my own than I have suggested. For example, here is James on how faith operates: "Considering a view of the world: 'It is *fit* to be true,' she feels; 'it would be well if it *were* true; it *might* be true; it *may* be true; it *ought* to be true,' she says; 'it *must* be true,' she continues; 'it *shall* be true,' she concludes, '*for me;* that is, I will treat it as if it *were* true so far as my advocacy and actions are concerned.'"[2] This "faith-ladder," as he calls it, can certainly put one in mind of what I have called skeptical faith. And yet James uses various words, not just the word "faith," in relation to the attitude here described. Perhaps most commonly he uses the word "believe," and especially because he also uses this word in the title of one of his most famous essays, James is known far and wide as an advocate—not just in the religious realm but certainly there—of the "will to believe." This makes it seem that he must countenance just the sort of self-deception against which I have already several times inveighed (the self-deception involved in talking oneself into a belief one initially sees as poorly evidenced), and that his basic position is therefore a believing one that I must resist.

I will argue, however, that the apparent differences here are misleading. The religious version of James's will to believe, when carefully examined, seems to involve something quite different from propositional religious belief as ordinarily construed, and his talk of a specific God or gods is often erased within a much more generally framed "religious hypothesis," which James appears to realize we will be experimenting with for a long time to come.

But can we do more than show that James is not going to have much to say in criticism of the position staked out here? Can it also be shown that he has distinctive *arguments* we can use to support skeptical religion, arguments that may be added to those derived from other thinkers? At first it seems the answer must be no. Though not many of the goods introduced by or capable of being developed from the work of previous nonevidentialist thinkers have eluded his gaze, James does not appear to offer many new goods of his own. But perhaps his *mode* of argument is interestingly distinctive? This does seem to be the case: I will argue that James's writings at least suggest two forceful new ways of reasoning in support of our conclusion. The first is derived from his famous essay "The Will to Believe."

---

[2] William James, "Reason and Faith," in *Essays in Religion and Morality* (Cambridge, Mass.: Harvard University Press, 1982), p. 125.

The second is based on James's "faith-ladder." In these arguments we will often hear the echoes of themes discussed in previous chapters, but as I have said, the ways of proceeding with these themes suggested by his work are distinctive—and James does also, as we will see, have some new themes of his own.

But before getting to these arguments, let us consider whether James is really as close to being an advocate of skeptical religion as I have claimed.

1. *The Many Faces of Jamesian Belief*

James often said that he should have called his famous essay "The *Right* to Believe" instead of "The Will to Believe," but I think he may have been mistaken about which word needed changing. James recognizes that "believe" as commonly used denotes a natural, spontaneous, and (in itself) quite involuntary mental response involving the thought or feeling that some state of affairs is realized or obtains. He often uses the word that way himself. In a chapter on belief in his *Principles of Psychology* he even calls belief "the sense of reality" and says of it that it is "a sort of feeling more allied to the emotions than to anything else."[3] Religious belief, then, should presumably be an involuntary sense that some religious state of affairs obtains. And a will to believe, in the religious realm, should presumably involve something like the voluntary production or maintenance of such an attitude. But in the Jamesian writings that most directly address the will to believe, this is not what we find.

It takes a bit of looking to find James's true views on this matter. While developing his many insights, James is often more concerned to associate than to disambiguate,[4] and this is no more evident than in "The Will to Believe." At the beginning of that long essay he seems to admit the oddness of speaking about belief as though it were voluntary: "Does it not seem preposterous on the very face of it to talk of our opinions being modifiable at will?"[5] But this sense of oddness, it turns out, comes from

---

[3] William James, *The Principles of Psychology*, vol. 2 (Cambridge, Mass.: Harvard University Press, 1981), p. 913. As Richard Gale shows, however, James waffles even here: see his *The Philosophy of William James: An Introduction* (Cambridge: Cambridge University Press, 2005), pp. 49–50. For an account that preserves the connection to reality and the emphasis on involuntariness but disputes the correctness of any reference to feeling, see my *Prolegomena*, chap. 2.

[4] This nice (and kind!) way of describing James's freewheeling approach I picked up from Lad Sessions.

[5] William James, *The Will to Believe, and Other Essays in Popular Philosophy* (New York: Dover, 1957), p. 4.

focusing too narrowly on such beliefs as are obviously and overwhelmingly supported by evidence—for example, belief that Abraham Lincoln's existence is not a myth. "It is only our already dead hypotheses that our willing nature is unable to bring to life again."[6] (James here muddies the waters by suggesting—in overeager anticipation of his later strategy against the evidentialists—that the reason they're dead is usually our *willing antagonism*. I doubt this covers the proposal that Abraham Lincoln never existed, or indeed very many similar proposals all of us reject.)

Our willing nature, James says, means not just "deliberate volitions" but "all such factors of belief as fear and hope [these will be central to his essay's argument], prejudice and passion, imitation and partisanship, the circumpressure of our caste and set. As a matter of fact we find ourselves believing, we hardly know how or why."[7] Stretching the notion of "willing" to the point where willing can occur even as we simply find ourselves in a certain state without knowing how or why may seem to be twisting that notion all out of recognition. But we can understand what is going on here if we proceed carefully.

First notice what is, for James, an important distinction between beliefs evidentially or intellectually determined and ones *otherwise* determined. Those otherwise determined flow from our "passional tendencies" (notice that the idea of passion is here being used much more generally than in the previous quotation; indeed, it now covers all the factors there mentioned).[8] And passional tendencies often involve *going along with* prejudices and pressures of various sorts (and with desires and emotions—passions more narrowly construed), or *seeking to retain* such things as partisan loyalties, when beliefs are formed. Here "willing" as any of us might understand it is more obviously in play. Thus when we simply find ourselves with a certain view not knowing how or why, it can still be because of the will! For example, take our belief that truth can be known. This, says James, is nothing "but a passionate *affirmation* of desire." And immediately he also says that, in relation to the radical skeptic who goes another way, "it is just one *volition* against another—we *willing to go in for life* upon a trust or *assumption* which he, for his part, does not care to make" (my emphasis).[9]

Already several things have been conflated or are in danger of being conflated. As J. C. S. Wernham puts it, in relation to a list of possibilities similar to the one I shall provide, "unhelpfully, James did not choose

[6] Ibid., p. 8.
[7] Ibid., p. 9.
[8] Ibid., p. 11. Cf. p. 9.
[9] Ibid., pp. 9–10.

between these different things: he chose all of them."[10] We start with a basically legitimate distinction between beliefs as involuntary tendencies to sense reality as thus-and-so formed by the evidence having its way with us and beliefs—involuntary tendencies of the same sort—more directly due to non-intellectual causes. Then we very broadly call the latter passional though noticing that the will may be involved when passions (broadly or narrowly construed) are doxastically influential. Now we slide back and forth between speaking of passions and speaking of the will as causally active in the formation or maintenance of beliefs. At this stage both are still distinguished from involuntary belief, as cause from effect. But then— perhaps because the will still has too weak a role here, a role weaker than James really has in mind?—we move from speaking of the will or of volition as a cause of belief to speaking of *belief itself* as more directly volitional, as a voluntary "affirmation of desire."

This might seem again to be simply a way of speaking about how our wants are allowed to dictate beliefs, in the ordinary sense of "beliefs." But it also suggests something stronger—something like a voluntary *endorsement* of a proposition we desire to be true. Notice that, if this is so, then the original effect, the involuntary "sense of reality," has disappeared and been replaced by something like a reworked version of the cause: a determination to *treat* as true a proposition whose truth we find approvable, to regard a state of affairs *as if* it were real. That it is so is confirmed when a moment later the word "assumption" appears (there would be no need to be willing to plump for an assumption if we really believed).[11] And, as if that weren't enough, the notion of believing is then broadened from a voluntary mental endorsement (the idea of which is retained in the notion of an assumption) to the more thoroughgoing endorsement represented by a total approach to living: being willing to behave in a certain way throughout one's life; to "go in for life" *on* the aforementioned endorsement or assumption. By this last stage, it is evident that we have something corresponding quite closely to both propositional and operational faith *instead* of belief (though with those two treated more or less as one).

If this interpretation seems mistaken, the product, perhaps, of my passional need to make James a precursor of Schellenberg, consider the evidence elsewhere in this essay. The latter's central thesis, of course, is that

---

[10] James C. S. Wernham, *James's Will-to-Believe Doctrine: A Heretical View* (Montreal: McGill-Queen's University Press, 1987), p. 101. Wernham thinks that, in the end, James is recommending "gambling on God," a nonbelieving state similar to the one I will find in him, which Wernham intriguingly links (though without full commitment or discussion) to the idea of faith (pp. 101–105).

[11] Cf. this comment by James: "Faith is synonymous with working hypothesis" (*Will to Believe*, p. 79).

"our passional nature" may in certain circumstances be allowed to "*decide* an option between propositions" (my emphasis). When it comes to our personal relationship, for example, I may need to be "*willing to assume* that you must like me, and *show* you trust and expectation" (my emphasis). Interestingly, this is called "faith on my part in your liking's existence." It is also called "faith based on desire." James further speaks of how we may "*yield* to our hope" that the religious hypothesis may be true and our "passional need of *taking* the world religiously," thus "*backing* the religious hypothesis against the field" and "*obstinately* believing," contrasting this with "remaining skeptical" by "*waiting* for more light," in which condition we must lose a certain good just as we would if we "*chose* to disbelieve" (my emphasis). Most important, we have this in a note: "Since belief is measured by *action*, he who forbids us to believe religion to be true, necessarily also forbids us to act as we should if we did believe it to be true" (my emphasis).[12] A careful look at the content of these quotations, especially the last one, in which the original, involuntarist understanding of belief as well as the distinction between the propositional and operational levels have, again, completely disappeared, will confirm the shifts documented above. No doubt James was influenced in all this by his pragmatism. (The note just mentioned goes on to make that clear.) But the point is that in the essay of that title, the will to believe is, after the smoke has cleared, not at all a will to get or maintain that original involuntary propositional "sense of reality," which would require self-deception, but really a will to *replace* it by voluntarily adopting a certain attitude and also living thereby.

In "The Will to Believe" James speaks of "the appeal of religion" to "our own active good-will."[13] When this reference to good will appears again in the Appendix to his final, unfinished work, *Some Problems of Philosophy*, we have a chance to see his last word on the subject of religion. It differs somewhat from what we found in "The Will to Believe," but still my general points about James on religious belief are confirmed.

As background, let me quote some words from a Jamesian letter that appears in the introduction to *Some Problems*, a letter concerning the "will" referred to in its Appendix: "This is essentially a will of complacence, assent, encouragement, towards a belief already there—not, of course, an *absolute* belief, but such beliefs as any of us have, strong inclinations to believe, but threatened."[14] Here the activity of the will is once again distinguished from belief: we seem to be talking about a will to *go on* believing (this might

[12] *Will to Believe*, pp. 11, 23, 25, 27, 26, 28, 26, 29n1.
[13] Ibid., p. 28.
[14] See Peter H. Hare's introduction to *Some Problems of Philosophy*, by William James (Cambridge, Mass.: Harvard University Press, 1979).

seem related to what was said above about the maintenance of belief). Also, it appears that nothing rules out the involuntarist understanding of belief—isn't this represented by that word "inclinations," which suggests being drawn into a certain view of things? Perhaps. But I submit that "inclinations" may here better be interpreted in terms of preference and approval—being drawn *toward* a certain view by desire and positive evaluative beliefs as opposed to being drawn *into* it by its seeming reality.

This interpretation is confirmed in the Appendix itself. Here the "strong inclinations to believe" of the letter are replaced by "faith-tendencies," and "will of complacence, etc.," by "our not-resisting our faith-tendencies, or [by] our sustaining them in spite of 'evidence' being incomplete."[15] And now note what James says about the faith-tendencies:

> These faith-tendencies in turn are but expressions of our good-will towards certain forms of result. [They are] extremely active psychological forces, constantly outstripping evidence. The following steps may be called the "faith-ladder":
> 1. There is nothing absurd in a certain view of the world being true, nothing self-contradictory;
> 2. It *might* have been true under certain conditions;
> 3. It *may* be true, even now;
> 4. It is *fit* to be true;
> 5. It *ought* to be true;
> 6. It *must* be true;
> 7. It *shall* be true, at any rate true for *me*.[16]

This "faith-ladder" is evidently a movement of positive evaluation, approval, desire, . . . all culminating in the determination to stick by a certain view of things—as the other, earlier version of the faith-ladder has it, to "treat it as if it *were* true so far as my advocacy and actions are concerned." And since this mounting pressure of good will toward a religious picture of the world is said to be identical to the faith tendencies which are said to be identical to the inclinations to believe which are said to be identical to the "belief already there" of the Jamesian letter, it follows that, according to James, it is precisely this mounting pressure of good will that our will sustains and encourages and enacts over time when we exercise the "will to believe."[17]

---

[15] *Some Problems*, p. 112.

[16] Ibid., p. 113.

[17] A couple of sentences after the passage just quoted, James seems to *identify* good will and the will to believe: "Intellectualism's proclamation that our good-will, our 'will to believe,'

Notice that nowhere among the steps of the faith-ladder describing what James here calls faith or belief tendencies do we find the sense, in respect of the view in question, that it *is* true.[18] No, ordinary belief—belief as James himself understands it in his chapter on that subject in the *Principles*—has here been subtly but radically transformed into a sort of pro-attitude to which we may respond by voluntarily assenting to and acting upon the view in question. So once again, though in a somewhat different way, we find that James is not endorsing the production or maintenance, in the face of nonsupportive evidence, of religious belief as normally understood, but rather has a position quite close to that of this book. Certainly, if one wants to create a coherent view here, one will succeed much more naturally by moving in the direction of propositional and operational faith and the understanding of the relations between them and the concepts surrounding them that I have articulated than in the direction of a "sense of reality" (of necessity) self-deceptively induced.[19]

An objection to this account should now be considered, which will lead me to qualify it slightly. In both the Appendix to his last book and the earlier essay "Reason and Faith," in which the faith-ladder also appears, James

---

is a pure disturber of the truth, is itself an act of faith of the most arbitrary kind." This is puzzling, for in the first passage quoted from the Appendix (interpreted in light of the mentioned letter), these two are clearly distinguished. Perhaps James's sense of style could not resist in this manner adding "will to believe" to another expression including the word "will" instead of saying "good-will *and* will to believe," or perhaps "good-will" is here meant to *include* the ongoing affirmation or endorsement of the ladder's seven steps.

[18] Unless 6 be taken as entailing as much, which seems implausible, since then the presence of 7 in the list would be hard to explain. Note also that 6's "must" is supposed to be an expression of "good-will," and so is best read as a response involving strong desire and approval rather than an expression of conviction in reaction to apparent proof and/or logical necessity, neither of which could possibly be relevant here.

[19] Here, and precisely given the explanation I have provided in *Prolegomena*, chap. 2, of the distinctions among relevant concepts, another intriguing interpretational possibility presents itself: perhaps James is systematically conflating belief-that and belief-in, propositional religious belief and (what I have called) *affective* religious belief—often referring to the former but meaning the latter. That this is a live possibility emerges early in "The Will to Believe," when James gives examples of passionally formed beliefs (p. 9). Here he clearly does conflate belief-that and the affective belief-in. For believing in molecules and believing in democracy (two of his examples) are rather different! (To begin to see how, notice only that believing in democracy does not mean believing *that there is such a thing as democracy*.) Especially given what we have since learned about the "faith-ladder" in *Some Problems*, the slip here must now be regarded as possibly illuminating. If James *is* thinking in terms of the concept of (affective) belief-in, that would certainly explain why so often he appears to have in mind not believing that God exists but *thinking well* of God's existing and experiencing corresponding emotions. And notice that by adding to this positive attitude of belief-in a determination to treat the relevant proposition as true (though without the belief that it is) and to live accordingly, you generate precisely what I have been calling the faith response, which combines propositional and operational faith.

adverts at a certain point to talk of probabilities. For example, in "Reason and Faith" he says this: "In no complex matter can our conclusions be more than *probable*. We use our feelings, our good-will, in judging where the greater probability lies, and when our judgment is made we practically turn our back on the lesser probabilities as if they were not there."[20] This suggests that the tentativeness and uncertainty that seem to be expressed in the faith-ladder, and that seem such a large part of the background to the argument in "The Will to Believe," at least as I have understood it, ought not to be taken at face value. Moreover, the passions that in our discussion have so far been made to appear as something like "motivators" for a leap in the dark are here presented as more like "discerners" of where probability lies. Thus they really function as additional *evidence* that in "willing to believe" we will ourselves to attend to—thus sustaining real believing tendencies (in the original sense of the *Principles*)—in circumstances where traditional reason, which looks down on such "soft" evidence and is in any case inclined to wait for certainty, will only disapprove. The upshot is a picture rather different from the one I have associated with James—and very different from the skeptical religion of this book.

Larger themes from James the pragmatist are involved here, and the objector can make use of them to support her objection. Most important, there is James's idea—influential, for example, in another essay on religion, "Reflex Action and Theism"—that our mental life, including all aspects of our passional and volitional nature, has arisen as it has because it is well adapted to the world. Thus if we find in human beings a persistent propensity for religious desires and experiences, and if these are involved in human flourishing, then perhaps we can infer that they *tell us something about how things are*. James's comments about the passions discerning probabilities fits nicely within this larger Jamesian theme, and that it does so should, it may seem, give me pause in attributing either of the views reconstructed above to James.

This is an interesting objection. Some parts of it have recently been developed in detail by William J. Wainwright in his *Reasons of the Heart*.[21] But Wainwright is somewhat tentative in what he attributes to James—and rightly so, for James is also tentative (moments of ambivalence appear even in "Reflex Action and Theism," as Wainwright notes).[22] It is not at all obvious that James thinks the religious view probable or our passions capable of discerning that probability. Consider, for example, that a view

[20] "Reason and Faith," p. 125.
[21] *Reasons of the Heart: A Prolegomenon to a Critique of Passional Reason* (Ithaca: Cornell University Press, 1995).
[22] Ibid., p. 102 n. 32.

may seem to represent the "greater probability" (James's expression) even when we are unsure whether it is probable *overall*, and also that we may use our passions to judge probabilities because we feel some judgment has to be made and nothing else—no solid evidence—tells us which way to go. James is, indeed, commonly interpreted as saying that we may let our passions decide when there are no intellectual grounds for deciding, perhaps because he explicitly says this in "The Will to Believe." But it doesn't follow that our passions represent an additional source for discerning truth. It may rather be more along the lines of "go with what you *want* to be true or what *should* be true when no grounds for judging what *is* true are available." Certainly everything James says about good will is in accord with this.

Notice also that there is no mention of probabilities discerned by our passions in "The Will to Believe": at the end of that essay, indeed, we are told (by means of a quotation from Fitz James Stephen) that we face a "riddle" and a "leap in the dark" in the midst of "whirling snow and blinding mist through which we get a glimpse now and then of paths that may be deceptive."[23] This doesn't sound much like an awareness of probability or confident belief. James himself, in that essay, speaks of how "my passional need of taking the world religiously might be prophetic and right," but he never takes this as generating more than the possibility that the religious hypothesis "*may* be true" (my emphasis).[24]

Having said that, the objection does show that just how we should take James on these matters is not perfectly clear. The paths I have found through the whirling snow and blinding mist of his prose may be deceptive. And I have not even touched the subject of James on religious experience, which can be taken as an extension of religious passion or treated as independent of it, but either way raises the question whether James would have a different view of the evidence if such experience were admitted as evidence. His famous work *The Varieties of Religious Experience* certainly suggests as much at times. According to his biographer, Ralph Barton Perry, James once said "I myself believe that the evidence for God lies primarily in inner personal experience."[25]

So what to do? My own central aim in these chapters does not require me to arrive at definitive solutions to interpretational problems that arise. Indeed, here it is quite sufficient for our purposes to have cast as much doubt as we have on certain popular readings of James which connect his

---

[23] *Will to Believe*, p. 31.

[24] Ibid., p. 27.

[25] R. B. Perry, *The Thought and Character of William James* (Boston: Little, Brown, 1935), p. 323.

work to belief as usually understood. My inclination at this stage, all things considered, is to proceed as follows. Either James in his heart of hearts *did* think that what we experience in our heart of hearts—in the form of deep religious desires or else deep apparent perceptions of the Divine— suffices to justify a judgment that religious claims are probable and also acquiescence in a real preexisting belief created by such inner events or he *did not*. If—as I myself suspect—he did not, then I would claim that my exposition above brings us closer to his real views and shows that he was quite close in his own thinking to some of the central themes of this book. If, on the other hand, he *did*, then, as shown in *Skepticism*, an extra dose of doubt about the ability of passions and religious experiences to serve as indicators of religious truth at this early stage of our development is in order for James, and then also, should the added skepticism take hold, the natural direction for any revision or adjustment of James's thinking to take is one that leads right into this book. So, regardless of what we say in response to the objection adumbrated above, it still follows that we can feel free to take James's thinking as, all things considered, most naturally and appropriately adapted to support the will to *imagine* rather than as supporting—in any ordinary sense—the will to believe.

2. How Generic Is James's Religion?

I have spent some time trying to unravel knots in the interpretation of James on "the will to believe"—this because of the intrinsic interest of the discussion, its obvious relevance to this book's conclusions, and also the central status accorded to James in the literature on nonevidentialism. But now we need to consider the *object* of the attitude defended by James. And here, because the terrain is less difficult, I can be somewhat briefer. James is usually viewed as a nonevidentialist defender of theistic belief. Is this proper? Or is he really, as I have suggested, gesturing toward something more general like ultimism?

It is evident that—artist and pluralist and forward-thinking pragmatist that he is—James in his religious thought is much less confined within conventional conceptual parameters than other historical figures we have discussed. These other thinkers, in varying degrees, seemed to find it difficult to think beyond theism. James is willing to speak much more vaguely of "the religious hypothesis," meaning by this in "The Will to Believe" the dual claim (1) that "the best things are the more eternal things, the overlapping things, the things in the universe that throw the last stone, so to speak, and say the final word" (this first affirmation James summarizes as "perfection is eternal"); and (2) "that we are better off even now if we believe [religion's] first affirmation to be true."[26] And in *The Varieties of Religious Experience* James finds it important to identify "in the broadest possible way" the claims one finds in religion. These are "1. That the visible world is part of a more spiritual universe from which it draws its chief significance; 2. That union or harmonious relation with that higher universe is our true end; 3. That prayer or inner communion with the spirit thereof—be that spirit 'God' or 'law'—is a process wherein work is really done, and spiritual energy flows in and produces effects, psychological or material, within the phenomenal world."[27] A Taoist could sign on to these broad formulations as well as a Christian, and although none of them is identical to ultimism, clearly they are closer thereto than to any of the details of the various extant *qualified versions* of ultimism, like traditional Christian theism.

Now some writers have found such broadness and vagueness uncomfortable or irritating, viewing it as one more instance of James's inability to pin down clearly what he really means or stick with a single idea or avoid conflating ideas, as in the discussion we have already canvassed. The "single idea" many have wanted him to stick with is of course traditional theism, which gives a personal face to the generic religious hypothesis. Some would even claim to find this in James, noting that in "The Will to Believe," for example, he says that for most of us, if we are religious, "the universe is no longer a mere *It*...but a *Thou*."[28] However, we should remember that "inner communion" with the "spirit" of the universe (surely sufficient for an I-Thou relation) is, in the passage just quoted from the *Varieties*, said to be possible whether that spirit be God or law.

To this the response may be that in "The Will to Believe" James speaks of the higher universe as taking a "personal form," and of the I-Thou relation as effected "person to person."[29] On the basis of these references, Jordan, for one, quickly infers that "monotheism, in other words, is established, and not polytheism."[30] But this inference is overquick, for even in the same paragraph James merrily speaks in a pluralistic vein of "making the gods' acquaintance" and "believing that there are gods," showing—whether he be taken literally or metaphorically—that the category of personalist religion is far from being exclusively taken up by monotheism.[31]

---

[26] *Will to Believe*, pp. 25–26. Notice here that (2) would be absurdly narrow and quite unrepresentative of James's pragmatist stance if we took "believe" only in the "sense of reality" way instead of broadening our interpretation of it as suggested in the previous section.

[27] *The Varieties of Religious Experience* (New York: Penguin Books, 1982), p. 485.

[28] *Will to Believe*, p. 27.

[29] Ibid.

[30] Jeff Jordan, *Pascal's Wager: Pragmatic Arguments and Belief in God* (Oxford: Clarendon Press, 2006), p. 178.

[31] It might be thought that James is only being poetic when speaking of "the gods," but the *Varieties* shows otherwise: James is there quite prepared to allow that "the universe

Wherever we want to prescribe a limit or assign definite content, James says "Wait a minute, things might be like *this* instead." And when in the *Varieties* he tells us what is included in his own religious "over-belief" (the more detailed conception of the Divine to which he is drawn), he remains vague—hardly going beyond his earlier formulation when he speaks of "something ideal, which in one sense is part of ourselves and in another sense is not ourselves, [and] actually exerts an influence, raises our center of personal energy, and produces regenerative effects unattainable in other ways"—admitting that his over-belief will seem like a "sorry under-belief" to many.[32]

As these latter comments already suggest, James's vagueness, his frequently quite generic statements of what, intellectually, a religious commitment might involve or does involve in his own case, is not simply carelessness—it is quite deliberate and purposeful. And in detecting the reason in his book on *Pragmatism,* we cannot help but notice the similarity to another emphasis of the present book—namely, our emphasis on the open future: "You see that pragmatism can be called religious, if you allow that religion can be pluralistic.... But whether you will finally put up with that type of religion or not is a question that only you yourself can decide. Pragmatism has to postpone dogmatic answer, *for we do not yet know certainly which type of religion is going to work best in the long run*" (my emphasis).[33]

Indeed, James is *so* open that his religion could be said to be *more* generic than any ultimistic one! In the slogan "Perfection is eternal" from "The Will to Believe" and in certain other comments, James suggests ultimistic leanings, but, especially when developing his own belief at the end of *Varieties,* he demurs. What the facts require is only the idea of something "other and larger than our conscious selves" with which we can experience peaceful union. "It need not be infinite, it need not be solitary."[34] Is this a problem for one, like me, who wants to win Jamesian approval for commitment to something as strong as ultimism?

Well, it is not quite right to say that I am looking for such approval: there may on a number of points be a gap between us and James which we can only urge Jamesians to cross, on grounds suggested in James or on independent grounds. Such is the case here. The grounds for preferring ultimism as a focus of commitment are principally two. First, the result of doing so, as James himself suggests in talking about what *religion* says, is more authentically religious than the Jamesian alternative: this claim is

---

might conceivably be a collection of [godlike] selves, of different degrees of inclusiveness, with no absolute unity realized in it at all" (p. 525).

[32] See *Varieties,* pp. 515, 523.

[33] William James, *Pragmatism and other Writings* (New York: Penguin, 2000), p. 131.

[34] *Varieties,* p. 525.

developed in detail in my *Prolegomena*, Chapter 1. But second, what reasoning supports in the way of religious commitment is often something *depending* on an explicitly ultimistic commitment. There may be some goods that can be realized with only a finitist development of the "something more," but others eminently worth realizing—as earlier chapters in this part and in the previous part of this book reveal—require a full-blown ultimistic framework for the religious life.

Suppose, then, that in James there is a generic approach agreeably similar to or assimilable to the approach of this book. At this stage we must still notice that James seems at loggerheads with me on a central point I have defended in this connection: that *only* generic religiousness is justified. Whatever James says about his own predilections, he clearly expects actual religious life to be in many cases cashed out quite specifically—and he has no objections to this and indeed seems to endorse it. In the *Varieties* he says this: "The spiritual excitement in which the gift [of living in the higher union] appears a real one will often fail to be aroused in an individual until certain particular intellectual beliefs or ideas which, as we say, come home to him, are touched.... [Thus] over-beliefs in various directions are absolutely indispensable, and...we should treat them with tenderness and tolerance so long as they are not intolerant themselves."[35] And right after the passage I quoted before from *Pragmatism* on "the long run" we find these words: "The various over-beliefs of men, their several faith-ventures, are in fact what are needed to bring the evidence [of what works best] in."[36]

Although in the latter case James's "several faith-ventures" are, as the context shows, actually only two, namely his own pluralist, finitist approach and absolutistic religious monism (a distressingly incomplete disjunction of possibilities), we might charitably take him to be arguing as follows: in order to see which specific elaboration of religion from the many available works best, both intellectually and otherwise, we need people instantiating the various possibilities. And the earlier argument we may summarize thus: specific forms of religion corresponding to the various possibilities are indispensable if we are to have religion—real, live religion—at all, for bland generalities must fail to excite serious human attention. We have, then, these two Jamesian arguments for rejecting my idea that only generic religion is justified.

I would reply as follows. The second argument is sufficiently answered in Part I of this book. It has long been an unthinking prejudice that generic religion must be either unclear, unfeasible, or insubstantial—or else the option represented by such religion has not even been entertained to

---

[35] Ibid., pp. 514–515.
[36] *Pragmatism*, p. 131.

the point where a prejudice against it has become possible. But by getting specific about such generic religion in this book, we have been able both to bring this option into clear focus and to reveal its considerable merits in all relevant respects.

What about the first argument? Here we are asked to imagine as an ideal (when appropriate ultimistic adjustments to Jamesian thinking are made) a *community* of religious faith practices, each focused on a different elaboration of ultimism, with new ones added as new elaborations of ultimism come to light. But already, with this last clause, a problem is revealed. For just how are those "new elaborations" to be brought to light? Perhaps the answer will come in terms of the "science of religions" James imagines, in distinction from various practices of religion.[37] But are religious scientists—who, as James himself admits, may find it "hardest to be personally devout"[38]—to produce the new conceptions from scratch? Surely it may only be *through* religious life that they will be uncovered. But what sort of religious life is conducive to such discovery? Surely not a religious life focused on some *other*, competing idea. That, precisely, is what has prevented new discoveries so far. Rather we need to imagine a religious life that is not restricted to any single option but opens out to more, always more, indeed making that *part* of its own religious practice—thus also doing fuller justice to the notion of a truly ultimate reality than is otherwise possible. In other words, we need to imagine skeptical religion.

The point James makes about the future is helpful here. Like most of us, he doesn't see its true force. But having just started to get used to the idea of millions of years in the human past, he may perhaps be forgiven for not yet having adjusted to the idea of millions of years in the human future. The true force of this point is such as to require us to look askance at the well-worked and well-worn extant elaborations of ultimism (or attempts at such elaboration), to expect that what the world has so far seen in the way of religious ideas, or is likely to come up with anytime soon, may be completely inadequate to a truly ultimate reality, at least when those ideas are taken individually as opposed to disjunctively. Perhaps in the distant future we will be able to afford the luxury of having individuals and groups live by elaborations of ultimism that, after all the preceding investigation, seem most probable and inviting to them, but for the foreseeable future, any such indulgence must only stand in the way of the complete shift of orientation required to make human progress in religious matters more likely, and must occur under the threat of simply *slowing* our progress toward religious enlightenment instead of revealing vital new evidence.

[37] See esp. *Varieties*, pp. 433, 455, 456, 488–490.
[38] Ibid., p. 489.

Since there are in any case, as we saw in Chapter 1, so many goods associated with a more generous and inclusive openness, I conclude that a pragmatic consequentialist like James must, on balance, favor skeptical religion focused on simple ultimism as the option best suited for all.

3. *The Competing Duties Argument*

In the previous two sections I have argued that James's will to believe should really be construed as a will to imagine, and that the proposition James recommends we imagine as true and live by has much in common with ultimism—and should have even more in common with it than it does. Thus any informed and circumspect Jamesian turns out to be an advocate of skeptical religion. But by what distinctive arguments will she *defend* skeptical religion? The first of two arguments I want to develop is derived from "The Will to Believe," filled out with one or two ideas gleaned from other Jamesian writings. I will state and defend what seems to me the strongest reasoning suggested by this essay, simply sidestepping all the structural and other flaws to be found in its argument, most of them well known from decades of commentary.[39] And I will assume the results of the previous two sections in my statement of it, speaking of skeptical religion and ultimism instead of James's "belief" and "religious hypothesis."

Here is how the reasoning might go. As twenty-first-century skeptics presented with the option of skeptical religion, we must choose whether we will adopt such religion, thus siding with ultimism in nonbelieving faith, or stick with *pure* skepticism—a choice that the available evidence is not, by relieving us of our skepticism about ultimism, able to remove for us. Now at this point we will be sure to hear a voice counseling us to hold back because siding with ultimism may turn out to be siding with a falsehood, and it is our duty, as responsible inquirers and concerned citizens, wishing to know how things are and also to improve how things are, to have as little to do with falsehoods as we can. Furthermore, it is not pleasant to find out that one has staked one's life on an error.[40] Moreover, the voice will say, if only we wait, we may uncover *more* evidence, including such

---

[39] For example, given the way James sets things up at the start, we should be talking about a choice between his "religious hypothesis" and its denial, but it is very hard to make sense of his later discussion in those terms. And the notion of a live, forced, momentous, and thus "genuine" option is at points vague and also inconsistently applied, and furthermore not clearly needed. Moreover, James's idea that those who do not go along with the religious hypothesis are invariably determined in their response by fear of being wrong is not very persuasive.

[40] James (over)emphasizes this point in *Will to Believe*, pp. 18, 19, 27, though he also mentions the others (pp. 17, 19–20).

crucial evidence as will allow us to turn our skepticism into a rational, well-grounded belief that ultimism is true, or that it is false, and thus deepen our understanding of the world. So all things considered (things intellectual, moral, and prudential), we really ought to remain pure skeptics.

But there is another voice we should hear as well. It reminds us that we have a *dual* duty: a responsibility not only to avoid commerce with falsehood and error as best we can, but also to do what we can to discover and live by *truths*—especially important truths. It reminds us, further, that it may be rather optimistic to suppose that convincing evidence as to the truth about religion will soon become available, and so a method of discovering this truth, should it exist, which consists in simply waiting may well be less than effective. It would not be pleasant either to discover that we have wasted a lifetime of opportunities for interaction with a Divine reality that was really there.[41]

Moreover, so this voice tells us, it may be that ultimism is true but that convincing evidence of its truth and the intellectual understanding this would bring can come only if many of us make precisely the sort of commitment that is at issue here. There are propositions—call them "epistemically faith-contingent propositions"—that are true but the discovery of whose evidence is contingent on having faith that they are true and living thereby. Take, for example, the proposition that your new acquaintance is trustworthy. It may only be by actually having faith that he is and acting thereupon—that is, by trusting him—that you will get the evidence that proves it. Holding back, even a hopeful holding back, may be a recipe for learning and gaining nothing from this relationship. It would not be surprising if ultimism were such a proposition; if because of its difficulty and subtlety, it were such that convincing evidence of its truth becomes available only with the toil and enlarged experience and conceptions of many whose ultimate commitment is in its cause. Furthermore, there are propositions—call them "alethically faith-contingent propositions"—whose very *truth* depends on a prior faith that they are true and commitment to a corresponding form of life. Take, for example, the proposition that a terrorist's plan to crash a plane into the Capitol will be foiled. It may only be because many passengers have faith that this proposition is true and act accordingly, in the face of imposing counterevidence, that the proposition *becomes* true. Ultimism could also be such a proposition, the truth of that part of its claim which refers to the attainability of an ultimate good depending on many of us joining together in its name, even before convincing evidence of its truth (in other respects) has been won,

---

[41] For similar points, see *Will to Believe*, pp. 18–19, 28.

to make the world a better place and realize whatever transcendent value may be available to beings such as we are.[42] Considering, then, these facts about epistemically and alethically faith-contingent propositions, the second voice tells us, we really ought to go *beyond* pure skepticism to faith.

These two voices seem to lead at least to a stalemate, with no easy solution pointing to the exclusive influence of wishful thinking or fear of embarrassment or, for that matter, high-minded intellectualism, on either side. Passion will necessarily have a role in whatever one does here, perhaps—if the goal is understanding—even the same passion! And responsibility, whether intellectual or moral or prudential or some amalgam thereof, can be taken as pointing in either direction. Thus it seems that one must simply choose, following the passion alive in one's own heart. At the very least, the religious choice is in every relevant sense permissible.

But when we consider more fully how our skeptic is *only* a twenty-first-century skeptic, we can go beyond this as well to argue that the religious choice is in fact the best choice she can make.[43] In a world as messy and undeveloped as ours, in which we have not yet taught any bell of absolute evidence to toll wherever truth exists, we must expect to be duped sometimes and to make risky choices in favor of a proposition if we want to be on the side of the most important truths, should they obtain, and thus avoid living as though they do *not* obtain when they do—which latter form of life (should it be the result of our not risking error for truth) would make its own concession to falsehood. In our situation of immaturity, it would be even less surprising than it would otherwise be if the needed evidence were unavailable because ultimism is epistemically faith-contingent. At this early stage of the game, some lightness of heart and willingness to act beyond the evidence must therefore be intellectually preferable to the heaviness and severe caution of those who order us always to wait for stronger evidence (evidence that may just for that reason never come) before committing ourselves in faith.[44]

---

[42] James makes similar points to those here developed in terms of the two odd kinds of proposition (using similar secular examples) in *Will to Believe*, pp. 24–25, 28. (The distinction between the two kinds, unclear in James, is nicely brought out—though with different labels than I am using—by Jordan in his *Pascal's Wager*, pp. 175, 179.) The striking point about helping salvation along is made very clearly by James in *Pragmatism:* "Does our act then *create* the world's salvation so far as it makes room for itself....Does it create, not the whole world's salvation of course, but just so much of this as itself covers of the world's extent?...I ask *why not?*" (p. 125).

[43] Not many think of James himself as wishing to take the extra step to "best." But some do. See, for example, Wernham, *James's Will-to-Believe Doctrine*, chap. 4. Wernham distinguishes between a "not-immoral-to-believe" doctrine and a "foolish-not-to-believe" one, finding both in James.

[44] James makes points very similar to the last two mentioned, using the idea of "lightness of heart" and also the bell-tolling metaphor, in *Will to Believe*, pp. 19, 30.

And this is especially the case where religion is concerned. For surely it would be good to be on the side of ultimism, if it were true. For one thing, and quite apart from any purely intellectual benefits, in that case one would be working together with higher forces for the salvation of the world.[45] In our chaotic situation full of suffering, the possibility that ultimism is *alethically* faith-contingent must be regarded as even more important than it would otherwise be (and perhaps that result would also be less surprising in our situation, since there appears to be no presently effective *Divine* initiative to stem the tide of horrors). Even if ultimism is—for reasons independent of our efforts or the absence thereof—in fact false, by making a religious commitment in the face of doubt one can *imagine* oneself as interacting with higher and ultimate things for the good of the world and thus live a more strenuous and useful life than is otherwise possible. And the emotions released thereby and by experiences of apparent union with higher forces (experiences compatible even with skeptical religion) can be greatly invigorating, a positive tipping point when debilitating melancholy strikes and, more than that, a source of zest for living.[46] All things considered, then, twenty-first-century skeptics—with "twenty-first" taken as signaling our immaturity rather than humanity come of age—should see themselves as called, intellectually, prudentially, morally, to what one might term a Divine experiment, which may at the same time provide the most satisfying result in the *human* experiment, both in the short term for those who participate in it thus and in the much longer term, for the world.

That, then, is the argument that emerges from "The Will to Believe" when one views that essay with a charitable eye, and when certain

---

[45] A comment to this effect, in terms of "doing the universe the deepest service we can," appears out of nowhere in *Will to Believe,* p. 28, in a context where the benefits mentioned are mostly prudential, not moral. But there are plenty of other places where James emphasizes the moral benefits of faith and speaks about helping the higher powers (or, even if not them, humanity) in the upward march to a better world. For example: "[The best among the religious] are impregnators of the world, vivifiers and animaters of potentialities of goodness which but for them would lie forever dormant." And also: "Who knows whether the faithfulness of individuals here below to their own poor over-beliefs may not actually help God in turn to be more effectively faithful to his own greater tasks?" (*Varieties,* pp. 358, 519).

[46] The benefits mentioned in this sentence are often noted by James. In the *Varieties,* for example, he says that one of the characteristics of the religious life is "a preponderance of loving affections" (p. 486), and that in religion one finds "an excitement of the cheerful, expansive, 'dynamogenic' order, which...freshens our vital powers...overcomes temperamental melancholy and imparts endurance to the Subject, or a zest, or a meaning, or an enchantment and glory to the common objects of life" (p. 505). For relevant discussion, see Ruth Anna Putnam, "Varieties of Experience and Pluralities of Perspective," in *William James and the Varieties of Religious Experience* (London: Routledge, 2005). Putnam questions the force of some of what James says on this score, but the force of her own comments is limited by their being restricted mostly to traditional religion.

adjustments based on earlier investigation in this chapter and on the situation of our twenty-first-century skeptic have been made. In light of even earlier investigation, it will be clear that its reasoning is not entirely original; strands of what we have heard from other writers can be found woven through it (of course the idea of combining all these things can itself be seen as original). But the idea of faith-contingent propositions, whether epistemic or alethic, and of competing duties in the intellectual realm have a distinctively Jamesian ring. We could call the argument by various names but I call it the Competing Duties Argument. Emerging from it we have an aim that (naturally enough) I call the Competing Duties Aim: the aim of mediating and reconciling the demands made on us by our competing duties to avoid commerce with falsehood and error, but also to do what we can to discover and live by truths—especially important truths. By structuring the argument in the way we have, we find that Jamesian thinking about the "will to believe," so long embroiled in controversy but now transformed into the soul of plausibility, makes its own contribution to the defense of skeptical religion.

The critic, however, may not yet be prepared to regard this thinking as quite the *soul* of plausibility, so let us consider the reasons for hesitation that may arise. Granted, with the adjustments we have made, no accusation of self-deception can any longer get a grip on the Jamesian argument, and given the overlap with earlier discussions, some complaints may already have been dealt with elsewhere in the book. But there are others. (1) *The emotional implausibility objection.* "Your argument refers to emotional benefits for the one who has faith. But here, backing off from the more robust idea of belief must come back to bite one in the heel. For it is precisely such belief that is needed for those benefits! That is, unless one spontaneously, involuntarily experiences the existence of the Ultimate as reality, as do the subjects of James's study in the *Varieties*, one will not find in oneself the emotions he finds in them." (2) *The unwarranted implication objection.* "Presumably the idea behind the notion of 'helping to make ultimism true' is that if some or many of us have faith, the world—in particular, the human situation—will reach a level of improvement or desirability in the nearer term that is otherwise unobtainable. This implies that such a good state is not achievable through the concerted efforts of those who, completely undistracted by religious commitment, simply love the world. Why should anyone believe this?" (3) *The one-sidedness objection.* "Faith may indeed be a way of looking for evidence, and it may even be a way of finding it, if ultimism is true. But what if ultimism is false instead? Aren't we diminishing our chances of finding out that it is false, if it is, by having faith? And yet shouldn't those two intellectual discoveries commend themselves equally to the true inquirer?"

Let us take these objections in turn.

(1) We can deal swiftly with the emotional implausibility objection by simply pointing back to earlier discussion. We have already seen, especially in Chapter 5, how imagination is sufficient to cause emotions of the relevant type. No doubt the feelings of the true believer will be in a way more fervent, but there are clear counterbalancing deficits that may be set against the benefits apparently associated with such fervency. Here we may add that James himself, who was never a true believer, testifies to the emotional power of "faithfulness" to a religious world-picture in his own life.[47]

(2) The unwarranted implication objection asks why anyone should believe what the argument implies: namely, that a good world-state of the relevant sort is not achievable through the concerted efforts of those who simply love the world. But the Jamesian argument does not require that this be *believed.* We need only regard it as an epistemic possibility. And that it is at least this much is shown by our discussion of the morality of faith in Chapter 10. Religious faith of the sort defended here does not distract one from moral endeavor or seek to substitute something else for it but rather *magnifies* what can be achieved in this domain.

(3) In response to the one-sidedness objection, three points need to be made. First we need to see that—as shown by the Jamesian argument— one apparently has to choose between devotedness to investigation and intellectual results on one side and devotedness to investigation and intellectual results on the other. The two voices, it seems, cannot win our equal attention: if we listen to one, we will hang back and look out, with attempted impartiality, for more evidence on both sides (thus possibly missing evidence for ultimism that can come only from religiously committing oneself); if we listen to the other, we will move forward in religious commitment, opening ourselves to evidence for ultimism that might become visible only that way (thus possibly missing the evidence against it that might be easier to see if we tried to remain completely impartial). *Either way*, then, there appears to be an intellectual drawback.

Let us provisionally accept the "forced choice" assumption lurking here. The second point can then be made as follows: if we have to choose, we should choose the side favoring the truth of ultimism—and this for quite general intellectual reasons. The point is that one who loves understanding will tend to find positive general truths (truths of great scope

---

[47] See *Varieties,* p. 519. As can be detected here and elsewhere, James had his struggles with "soul sickness" and found the "poetry" of religion to be uplifting.

about what exists) more attractive than purely negative truths (truths about what does not exist) or positive truths of lesser scope. It is not hard to see why. If I can learn what makes the universe tick by discovering some very general positive truth about it of the sort represented by the most fundamental scientific theories or by ultimism, I will learn something of much broader ramifications, and thus something more capable of putting me in touch with a host of other truths as well, than can be vouchsafed to me by any proposition telling me that even a very general claim such as the claim of some scientific theory or of ultimism is false or by discovering the truth of a particular claim, such as a claim about the number of pebbles in my driveway.

And now follows the third point, which tells us that the forced-choice assumption previously accepted on a provisional basis is in fact false. Ironically, because of how a commitment to ultimism (as we saw in Chapters 2 and 3) pushes us toward an even wider and deeper and more fine-grained understanding of our experience and of the world than we might otherwise be motivated to take up, it can do justice not only to one side of the debate *but to the other as well.* If we think about it, we will see that by plunging ahead into a faith commitment to ultimism, and living it out, we are, if anything, more likely to discover any facts counting against ultimism that there may be than we are if we hold back. Certainly we cannot be put in a poorer position in this respect. And the one who holds back has nothing similar to say in respect of facts potentially *supporting* ultimism. But then anyone who seeks to act on impartiality of concern here must be driven toward ultimistic commitment rather than away from it.

I conclude that the objections to our Competing Duties Argument do nothing to diminish its force. Indeed, by allowing us to see more clearly just how faith does the best job of mediating and reconciling the competing demands at issue here, they add to its force.

4. *The Ought-to-Be-True Argument*

But there is also a second argument that a Jamesian defender of skeptical religion might develop. I call it the Ought-to-Be-True argument. This can be built by reference to James's notion of a faith-ladder, with faith regarded as a "responsive gesture" that enables us to see various possibilities and ideals as they deserve to be seen, as in some sense they *ought* to be, if they have the unrivaled importance our experience and commitments drive us to ascribe to them. A related point appears in Chapter 8, where it is made in respect of beauty. In a moment I will return to this point, integrating it into the structure suggested by James. But what I want to emphasize here is how many *new* points can be added given the structure James offers us, and how powerful is the form of reasoning that results.

Let us look at this structure more closely. What James's faith-ladder suggests is that there are epistemically possible propositions that ought to be true even if they might not be true. What is it for a proposition to have this status? At least part of the answer is that it would be good for the proposition to be true and bad for it to be false. But I suggest that in the most relevant cases we can say something more too: that it would be *sad and appropriately felt sad* were the proposition to turn out false. In such cases, relatedly, we may speak of the presence of strong *desire* in any well-formed human being directed toward the state of affairs in which the proposition in question is true. And what James can be seen as suggesting is that, in these cases, it is highly appropriate for us to follow our desire into the responsive gesture of not just hope, which still timidly holds back, but the full imaginative commitment of faith that the proposition *is* true and also the operationalizing of such a commitment ("it *shall* be true *for me*").

Let us consider and assess this idea of a responsive gesture in a general way first, without tying it to the religious case. What we are talking about is a powerful, teeth-gritting determination to imagine and assent to and live by what ought to be the case and what that in turn makes desirable, even if in fact it may *not* be the case—whenever the truth of what ought to be so is not independently ruled out by reason. The latter qualification is important. Suppose the state of affairs consisting in certain children surviving a terrible flood, even though in the relevant sense it ought to obtain, obviously does not obtain; given the Jamesian qualification, no one following the policy suggested here will in such circumstances have faith that it does, and so be prevented from doing whatever is appropriate to do. But in situations where the relevant state of affairs is *not* so obviously a lost cause, the attitude in question is often appropriate. Suppose we have no reason either way to draw a conclusion on whether the children swept away by that flood can be saved. Isn't it obvious that concerned individuals should have faith that they can be saved—perhaps also allowing this to motivate and sustain their participation in a rescue operation? Or imagine a situation where (in similar circumstances of doubt) it ought to be the case that one finds one's way through a snowstorm, or that one's child navigates safely through to the other side of a depression, or that the party in power will be ousted, or that democracy spreads throughout the world, or that war can be made to cease.... Indeed, it is hard to imagine a case of the relevant sort in which faith is *not* called for, as a responsive gesture to the value one sees as sadly threatened. In all such cases, it seems clear that the best response—the response making the best whole of one's emotional and intellectual and other dispositions—will involve faith.

Notice also that if the only or best way for some such proposition to be made true involves the truth of a further proposition, the imperative of faith will extend to the latter as well. Consider, for example, a case where the only or best way one's child can defeat depression is by taking full advantage of the counseling she is presently receiving. Then the imperative to adopt faith with respect to her defeating depression extends also to her taking full advantage of that counseling.

Apply this now to religion. Obviously what we want to arrive at in the Ought-to-Be-True argument is the realization that ultimism ought to be true. But I suggest that this will emerge indirectly, as in the example just given. We will find a number of propositions which clearly ought to be true, but which are such that the only or best way for them to be made true involves the truth of ultimism. One example, adverting to our discussion in Chapter 8, is the proposition that worldly beauty is but the nearer side of Beauty. A way of reconstruing or reformulating some of what we said there is this: it would be sad, given all that naturally and appropriately rises up within us when in the presence of great worldly beauty, were it not the case that worldly beauty is but the nearer side of Beauty. And it is appropriate for us to desire that it be so. But the only, or at least the best, way for it to be so is if ultimism is true. Thus ultimism achieves the same status: now we can say that it would be sad were *ultimism* not to be true, and that it is appropriate for us to strongly desire that it be true.

James suggests a number of new ways of developing this sort of reasoning. In particular, we can add points about morality and the lives of others, our own lives, our religious experiences (if we have any), the human species, and even the universe. It is clear, from the many quotations given above and many other well-known Jamesian texts, that James thinks we should take our own lives and the development of our own consciousness seriously; that he thinks our religious experiences may be important clues to the existence and nature of a higher reality; that it is important for us to advance the well-being of our species over the long run and to respect the claims of morality; and that the universe is a strange and puzzling and wonderful thing. We can surely say on his authority—recognizing also the independent plausibility of what we say—that it would be *sad* were powerfully evocative religious experiences not to point beyond themselves to anything real; *sad* were the species, the whole project of human consciousness, to flicker out with a bang or a whimper instead of flourishing ever more fully over the longest of runs; *sad* were the strangeness and wonder of the universe not fulfilled in the infinite strangeness and wonder of ultimate things; *sad* were the wonder of our own individual conscious experience simply to cease just when we are starting to realize its benefits; *sad* were morality shallow instead of deep in the nature of things.

Looking upon these propositions carefully, with our emotional and other dispositions functioning properly, we will conclude that their truth, if known to us, would indeed be an occasion for sadness, and that their falsity is eminently desirable. In other words, it ought to be true not only that

(1) worldly beauty is but the nearer side of Ultimate Beauty

but also that

(2) religious experiences point beyond themselves to something real;

(3) the human species flourishes ever more fully over the longest of runs;

(4) the strangeness and wonder of the universe is fulfilled in the strangeness and wonder of ultimate things;

(5) conscious experience persists beyond the grave;

and

(6) morality is deep in the nature of things, reaching to the heart of reality.

We will also conclude that the truth of ultimism is the best (and in some cases the only) guarantee that such propositions are true. And, seeing that all of them call for the truth of ultimism, we are brought by a chorus of passionate reasons to our own religious faith-ladder, only slightly different from James's: Considering ultimism: "It is *fit* to be true; it would be well if it *were* true; it *might* be true; it *may* be true; it *ought* to be true; thus it *will* be true *for me;* that is, I will treat it as if it *were* true so far as my advocacy and actions are concerned."

Here the passions are obviously again relevant. What do they say? That there is a Divine reality? No, hardly (and here we see one way of answering Wainwright)—but they can tell us that there *ought* to be! And that makes all the difference, opening up a pathway of reasoning in support of religious commitment that must remain hard to see so long as we remain preoccupied with the left-hand side of the is/ought contrast. The idea here is not that desire and emotion are somehow an indication that things *are* as one wants them to be, but that they provide sufficient motivation and justification as well for the imaginative commitment of religious faith ("it *shall* be true...*for me*..."), which is required to do justice to the value discerned when we see that propositions like (1)–(6) ought to be true.

There are many ways of developing more fully the argument that such propositions as (1)–(6) ought to be true, and that the responsive gesture of religious faith is called for in relation to them. Let me pursue just a bit further the case for viewing thus the last two of those propositions: (5) and (6), respectively.

Taking up a life of religious faith in response to how one views a proposition like (5), with its reference to life after death, can be something one does for those loved and lost, as an appropriately serious gesture of love and respect. Paying this tribute is a way—the deepest way—of showing that some departed loved one *matters* to you, matters so much that even though you cannot be sure reality guarantees it, you will in your *imagination* live in a world suited to her needs: a world that will somehow bring her the continuing joy and the fulfillment she was on earth denied.

And it is not only for those whom we have intimately known that such a response is appropriately made. All of us either have loved ones like this or else know of individuals like this who were loved by others or individuals like this who were *bereft* of love but deserved to be loved. For any of them or for all of them, the responsive gesture of faith is warranted. Clearly a neglected but morally powerful argument for faith involving the idea of life after death is made available here.[48]

Consider also (6). Religious faith gives greater *solemnity* to morality than it could otherwise enjoy. This does not mean that somehow we now

---

[48] Here again the imagination is useful to us. It is interesting to find this recognized, after a fashion, in a recent book by the Christian philosopher and psychologist Robert C. Roberts: *Spiritual Emotions: A Psychology of Christian Virtues* (Grand Rapids, Mich.: Eerdmans, 2007). He speaks of us as beings with a "surveying imagination" (p. 61) who therefore can become aware of the severe limitations, relative to what is possible, of conscious existence—whose developed state may be the result of serious moral endeavor—being simply snuffed out. Roberts even recognizes in this connection the sadness, and the ought-to-be-ness, to which I have referred: "But if absolute death is not only my destiny but also the destiny of those people who are the object of my virtue, is there not something deeply sad about virtue itself? I am not pointing to anything like a logical contradiction here, but rather to a contradiction of how, in our heart of hearts, we must feel that things ought to be. Something is offensive, fundamentally shocking, about a universe that allows a being capable of love to be annihilated" (p. 75). But from this recognition he tends to veer in the wrong direction, viewing it as the "voice of God" (p. 56) calling one to Christian belief! The idea that contact with a personal God is mediated by such experiences is, upon proper reflection, quickly mired in skepticism and in any event distracts us from the human persons who should be the focus of our attention. One cannot get from this "ought" to an "is," and one certainly cannot get to anything as specific as the "is" of Christianity. But what one *can* do—and this is the new recognition and radical religious alteration that we need—is to make the gesture of a more general faith in virtuous response to the finite voices of *human beings*.

have more reason to follow its demands—no, those are independently grounded. But religious faith does allow us to picture morality as having a deeper place in the total scheme of things. Indeed, if ultimism is true, then an unlimited good and the possibility of an unlimited fulfillment lie at the heart of reality. One could not pay morality a bigger compliment—show it any more respect—than by picturing it thus and living accordingly.

These ideas about morality receive some support from an interesting work by George Mavrodes. Mavrodes speaks of how moral demands would be "superficial" in a naturalistic world. As he says: "Something that reaches close to the heart of my own life, perhaps even demanding the sacrifice of that life, is not deep at all in the world in which [on a naturalistic view] that life is lived." What is deep in a naturalistic world must, instead, be such things as "matter and energy, or perhaps natural law, chance, or chaos."[49]

What Mavrodes describes as entailed by the naturalistic view may indeed be odd, though this of course does not show that it is false. But what I am more inclined to emphasize is that someone with a deep and sensitive respect for morality will think it somehow *sad*—most contrary to what would be *fitting*—for facts about value not to be deep in the nature of things. Now this does not any more than Mavrodes' oddness show or tend to show that value *is* deep in the nature of things, but it does not have to show this in order to show what may serve to motivate faith, and what may be a good associated with having it. In picturing the world according to the ultimistic claim and living by that picture, we can do justice to the importance of morality and moral goals in our lives. It is a gesture we make *with* our lives.

And this permits an interesting realization in connection with the venerable old problem of evil. Indeed, there are horrible events. They arguably show there to be no personal God, and also might lead one to question whether there is an ultimate religious reality of *any* kind. But the idea here is that the very religious notion that is called into question by such events may serve, at another level, to do justice to the moral impulses that led us to call it into question in the first place. Thus similar moral considerations to those that may have led us to *abandon* religious faith (misunderstood as entailing theistic belief) may now be instrumental in our *regaining* it (properly understood).

All things considered, then, we have a ring of related propositions, (1)–(6), calling for faith in a manner leading us to see that religious faith is also in order, as the circle's center. Put otherwise, we have the realization that we ought to pursue—what I call—the Ought-to-Be-True Aim (the aim

---

[49] George I. Mavrodes, "Religion and the Queerness of Morality," in *Rationality, Religious Belief, and Moral Commitment,* ed. Robert Audi and William J. Wainwright (Ithaca: Cornell University Press, 1986), pp. 224–225.

of making an appropriate responsive gesture to what *ought* to be true in respect of our own lives, morality, our religious experiences, the human species, and the universe, even if in fact it is not), and that to do so in the best way calls for religious faith.

What can be said against this argument that has not already been dealt with, either here or in earlier discussion of the Competing Duties Argument? Perhaps this. Faith as a responsive gesture has true substance and moral significance only when we are dealing with alethically faith-contingent propositions—ones that by our faith we may hope to make true—like the proposition that I will make it through the snowstorm and the other propositions I have offered that intuitively seem to offer the most to my case. For here the value sadly threatened can be *saved* by our faith-effort. But the religious proposition of ultimism (and the other propositions I have connected to it) is *not like* those other propositions in this crucial respect. Hence we do not have anything of true substance and moral significance in the latter case.

I reply as follows. If we want to follow intuition, we will surely say that alethic faith-contingency is only one of the properties that may give the needed status to a proposition. Take, for example, the proposition that my child will come through her depression, which we may assume is doubtful. Surely faith is called for in this case, even when my child is far away and there is nothing (else) I can do. In such cases, we have, again, the opportunity to pay tribute through faith to the significance of ones loved, important causes, and so on. It is part of a morally deep life to pay appropriate tribute to the things that matter the most to us. And for a skeptic, *precisely because she is in doubt*, the tribute of *faith* is possible: it is her unique gift to the world. And the more we are skeptics, and the more we feel the sadness that would properly attend certain imagined outcomes presently in doubt, the more we are called to give of this gift.

Then, also, it must be pointed out that ultimism *may* be alethically faith-contingent. (This we saw earlier, in the context of the Competing Duties Argument.) For it may, at least for the foreseeable future, be through our own faith-nourished activities alone that the goodness of human life can be increased. What *from this time* belongs to salvation, in other words, may be up to us to achieve, and thus ultimism—which refers to an ultimate good—may be made fully true (on the correct interpretation of "ultimate good") only with our help. Indeed, it is one of James's signal contributions to have brought the notion of alethically faith-contingent propositions to our attention, and to have suggested this intriguing linkage with religion.

All things considered, then, the present objection appears to be without force. And so the Ought-to-Be-True Argument, like the Competing Duties

Argument, can be entered into our list of reasons for adopting skeptical religion. Each argument, in its own way, ought to remind us of James's faith-ladder, which (unlike the very different ladder of his admirer, Wittgenstein) we should *not* throw away once we have climbed up it, but rather keep ready to hand for whenever we fall away from a clear vision of things religious and sense the need to, once again, see the world of faith aright.

5. *General Conclusion to Part IV*

We have, then, a variety of new arguments for skeptical religion heralded in history by the most significant and frequently noted nonevidentialist writers. Pascal appeals to prudence; Kant to morality; James to both—though in his own way, distinctive in form and (to some extent) content. My discussion here and in the previous two chapters has been intended to elucidate the arguments of these thinkers, and also, thereby, to develop a sustained case for a certain way of viewing the thinkers, namely as precursors of a new understanding of religion and its relation to reason—an understanding more fitted to achieve success than the theistic understanding still so commonly associated with them. It is especially important that we see how each of these figures, in his own way, is vaguely indicating the possibility of a religious attitude other than belief, and how the clear concept of faith we have been utilizing helps to precisify and unify their efforts and bring that vague indication to fruition. When we further notice how in each case, with the goal thus construed, weak arguments are swiftly turned into strong, we should be able to hear the nonevidentialists, like the evidentialists, calling us to abandon the fragmented and so often futile efforts of the past and together pursue philosophy of religion in this new, much more promising, direction.

Looking back over the arguments of the last two parts of the book, we may wonder whether there is anything more that can be done with them. This question brings us to the borders of the promised land. But here we must remain outside. It will suffice if, by this question, our appetites are whetted for Part V, which concludes not the discussion of any particular part but that of the book as a whole.

KEEPING FAITH
Skeptical Religion as Reason's Demand

MUCH EARLIER ON, I said that by the end of the book we would see that not only is it possible to be true to reason while adopting faith, it is impossible to do so without it. Not only can faith satisfy reason's demands, faith is itself a demand of reason. Or, in my terms: faith is both negatively and positively justified. The time has come to make good on this claim.

That is what I do in this last part of the book. Here I bring the principles from Chapter 4—in particular P9, P12, and P16—back into play in order to prove, by reference to the various aims gathered along the way in Parts III and IV, that faith is both negatively and positively justified. Now, as I noted in Part II, the various arguments for faith I have developed in conversation with the figures discussed in Parts III and IV may, each of them, especially in the context of the others, already be taken as providing positive justification for faith—and this without recourse to our principles. So in a way the job I set out to do is already finished. (I will have a word or two more to say about this side of the book's results in section 1 of Chapter 12.) But by teasing out of those arguments the various aims to which our principles can be applied, we have put ourselves in a position to support the conclusion about positive justification with even greater precision and clarity and visible force. Furthermore, there are still some interesting twists in the tale left for us to experience, in connection with those aims. Hence Part V.

235

After some initial moves, we will see in Chapter 12 that *any one* of the aims we have extracted in our journey from Anselm to James can be used to make the clinching argument. But, after showing as much, I want also to formalize the results from Parts III and IV in several new ways. I begin by dividing the aims we have defended in the previous nine chapters into four categories, representing four distinct modes of reasoning on behalf of faith: personal, moral, aesthetic, and intellectual. Each of these categories, as I have said, represents its own additional mode of reasoning on behalf of skeptical religion. But, as we will see, the categories involved here can also work together in several ways—three, to be exact—generating new aims and (in connection with them) several additional modes of reasoning on behalf of faith. Multiple modes of reasoning involving our principles can thus be generated, and with them they bring multiple ways of fulfilling the promise of this book.

Faith Is Positively Justified: The Many Modes of Religious Vision

1. *Our Fundamental Results: Ten Modes of Skeptical Religion*

Let's begin by listing the various arguments for faith we found in Parts III and IV, in the order in which we harvested them:

Anselm: The Alignment Argument
The Imaginative Fulfillment Argument
Leibniz: The Understanding Argument
Paley: The Respect for Beauty Argument
Pascal: The Skeptical Dominance Argument
Kant: The Moral Commitment Argument
James: The Competing Duties Argument
The Ought-to-Be-True Argument

One thing the large plurality of arguments here immediately permits us to do is to cancel the ceteris paribus clause that (as I said in Chapter 6) should tacitly be seen as attaching to each of them. Any one of these arguments, by itself, even after the various defenses against objections I have provided, can say no more than that other things being equal, or so long as countervailing considerations are not forthcoming, it succeeds in providing sufficient support for skeptical religion. But, for each of the eight arguments, the other seven, spanning, as they do, every other area of human life, must surely represent among them every relevant competing consideration we should be prepared to encounter. And so, since the other seven clearly are *not* competing, the ceteris paribus clause can be removed. If, for example, considerations associated with the imagination and understanding and beauty and transcendence and moral commitment, and so on do not count against seeking to be aligned with what is ultimately real and valuable (I have of course argued, more strongly, that they count for it, but that point is not strictly necessary here), then we have grounds to conclude that the intrinsic appropriateness of seeking such an alignment, emphasized by the Anselmian Alignment Argument, provides us with a sufficient reason for adopting skeptical religion, full stop. And similarly for the other arguments. Seeing this, we have attained the final insight needed to complete each of the arguments.

This is what I had in mind when I earlier said that without recourse to our principles, the various arguments may, each of them, *especially in the context of the others,* already be taken as providing positive justification for faith, and, furthermore, that there is therefore a sense in which our task in this book is already completed. Let us take a moment to absorb this result. But then let us turn to the real focus of attention in this chapter: the various aims of human life those arguments support, which I have been setting out along the way, by means of which the case for skeptical religion can most clearly and precisely be made. Here they are:

A1. *The Alignment Aim* (p. 114): the aim of approaching as fully as possible a state in which one is aligned in one's own being with that of anything ultimately real and valuable.

A2. *The Imaginative Fulfillment Aim* (p. 114): the aim of realizing an expanded imagination capable of embracing more fully the idea of something ultimately real and valuable.

A3. *The Understanding Aim* (p. 123): the aim of promoting the conjunction of our various understanding-related interests (including cosmological ones) in the best available way.

A4. *The Respect for Beauty Aim* (p. 147): the aim of doing the conjunction of the following four things as well as we can: paying tribute to the world's beauty, doing justice to intense experiences of beauty, extending appreciation of the world's beauty, and contributing to the cultivation of concern for the preservation of the world's beauty.

A5. *The Prudential Alignment Aim* (p. 181): this is A1 pursued for prudential reasons instead of for its own sake.

A6. *The Readiness Aim* (p. 181): the aim of readying oneself for ever *deeper* discoveries in connection with the Ultimate.

A7. *The Transcendence Aim* (p. 181): the aim of continually enlarging and enriching one's life, of continually transcending previously attained heights in every area of human experience.

A8. *The Moral Commitment Aim* (p. 194): the aim of carrying out a wholehearted commitment to the human good.

A9. *The Competing Duties Aim* (p. 224): the aim of mediating and reconciling the demands made on us by our competing duties to avoid commerce with falsehood and error, but also to do whatever we can to discover and live by *truths*—especially important truths.

A10. *The Ought-to-Be-True Aim* (p. 231): the aim of making a fully appropriate responsive gesture to what *ought to be* in respect of our own lives, our religious experiences, the human species, and the universe, even when it *may not* be.

Notice that we have not needed to endorse any particular controversial ethical theory or theory of human nature to accept each of the aims in question as ones we should pursue—which is a good thing given human intellectual immaturity and the absence of clearly true theories of human nature or morality by which we may be guided. These are aims for beings at an earlier stage of evolution than would be presupposed by such attainments. But having in the preceding chapters defended these aims as ones we should adopt by means of arguments as simple and clear and convincing as we could muster, we may now draw some threads together.

A first point is mostly a reminder: each of these aims, as we have seen, is the better pursued by means of faith than in any alternative manner—for example, with the help of purely philosophical dispositions or some attitude of hope or by acting "as if."[1] Detailed arguments on this score appear at various points along the way in Parts III and IV. Here I pause only to note their effect and its relevance to principle P9, which bids us worry

---

[1] Some may wish me to comment further on the alternative of beliefless "acceptance," a notion associated with the work of L. Jonathan Cohen and, more recently, William Alston. I have several reasons for regarding faith-talk (understood propositionally and operationally) as preferable to acceptance-talk. These reasons are discussed in detail in *Prolegomena*, pp. 144–147 (see esp. 146–147), so I refer the reader to that source. Here I will say only that my concept of faith, as it seems to me, is more naturally integrated into the overall network of religious language and language about religion than the concept of acceptance (while preserving everything that is attractive about the latter), and is also capable of performing more religiously meaningful functions—precisely because of the distinction it forces us to make between the cognitive and the conative, a way of seeing and a way of acting, faith-that and faith-in.

about whether "some other disposition or action is more appropriate to the aim apparently sanctioning faith" than faith itself. We need worry no more. In each case, P9 has been shown to be inapplicable. Indeed, P9 is inapplicable and this threat to negative justification is thus defanged so long as neither hope nor any of the other alternatives is *superior* to faith in the relevant circumstances. And this weaker result is a fortiori provided for in the arguments I have developed.

A second point is this. Given the large number of aims we have supported and their representativeness in relation to all of life, we can rule out, for each aim, the idea that there might be important alternative pursuits that require or benefit from the absence of faith (and remember that we need not show that all those alternative pursuits themselves support faith to rule this out; the weaker point that they do not oppose it is all that is strictly required here). But that is to say, for each such aim, that our principle P12, which asks us to consider whether there might be "some aim (independent of the aim apparently calling for faith) that should all things considered be pursued" by anyone in the circumstances in question but "can only or best be pursued by not having faith," is also shown to be inapplicable. In Chapter 5 we took up a P12-type challenge formulated in terms of loyalty to reason. Results in the six chapters since, especially the results from Chapter 7, overwhelmingly confirm my conclusion in Chapter 5, that no betrayal of reason is properly associated with skeptical faith. But they also show that no other, similar challenge can be successful. Considering, in turn, the circumstances highlighted in each of the previous six chapters, in which, so we argued, some aim calls for faith, we may now conclude, by reference to results in the others, that there is no competing aim of the sort here referred to for anyone in those circumstances to be concerned about.

Our first two points bring us to an important milestone. Together with the points independently established in Chapter 4 concerning P10 and P11, they prove that in any of the circumstances of the past six chapters and for any of the aims that were said to be sanctioned therein, our twenty-first-century skeptic must conclude that a faith response to ultimism is at least negatively justified. And the final goal of our inquiry is not far distant. Recall principle P16:

> P16. A faith response is *positively* justified if (1) it is negatively justified and (2) some aim that should all things considered be pursued by us can only or best be pursued by making such a response.

Given what we have just seen concerning the negative justification of faith, it follows immediately that P16(1) is satisfied for each of aims A1–A10. And now a critical point, similar to our first result above: if what we said about P12 a moment ago is indeed true, then the ceteris paribus clause tacitly attaching to each of aims A1–A10 may also be canceled. If, for each such aim, the presence of the others shows that there is no significant competing aim, then—always assuming the supportive argumentation of the relevant chapter is sound—we can say of that aim that it should *all things considered* be pursued by us. But, if so, then P16(2) is also satisfied with respect to that aim. Which is to say, for each such aim, that P16 as a whole is satisfied with respect to it. It follows immediately that any one of aims A1–A10 will suffice to show our twenty-first-century skeptic that a faith response to ultimism is not just negatively but also *positively* justified.

We have, then, ten ways of arguing that twenty-first-century skeptics should, all things considered, come down from their fences and take up skeptical religion. Which is to say that we already have ten "modes" of faith before us (or behind us).

2. *The Modes Combined: Personal, Moral, Aesthetic, and Intellectual*

It would be gratifying if readers found all these modes convincing. But the case for skeptical religion certainly doesn't depend on all ten being successful. Indeed, we might at this stage proceed disjunctively, putting forward as a central claim that at least one of these is sound; our twenty-first-century skeptic can have her pick. (That, I suppose, would be an eleventh mode.) So much is all our case, thus far, *depends* on.

But there are other discoveries we can make if we think a bit further about how the modes together—more broadly, the ten aims and the arguments supporting them and the interests of the historical figures whose work we have appropriated in developing those arguments—can support skeptical religion. More than just their shared conclusion unifies these modes.

What is this "more"? I suggest that two related themes can be found stretched through all the modes, from beginning to end: (1) that skeptical faith, even if it has no evidential facts to appeal to in support of itself, is an eminently appropriate response to *value*, and (2) that such faith is needed to do justice to the *complexity and depth* in a human life and in the evolving life of the species. Religious faith, though it requires imagining the facts to have a certain character and though it would be undermined if they were shown to have a contrary one, is in the end a response not to fact but to value, and our thinkers have helped us to see just how wide is the range of values to which faith may respond—from alignment with the unsurpassable idea, complete understanding, and the expression and extension of beauty to transcendence, commitment to the human good, and what ought-to-be. Here we see not any one-sided wishful thinking but rather a multi-sided appreciation of value reflecting the complexity of a well-rounded human life and developing human community.

Which brings us to the second point: in responding to value in this way, the one who takes up skeptical religion is able, with unparalleled effectiveness, to express and celebrate and also further develop the unique complexity and depth of the human animal, which features such elements as imagination, intellect, and aesthetic sensibilities, as well as transcendent experience, prudential choice, and the capacity for virtue. Faith in connection with all the values I have listed engages and enlarges such human characteristics and capacities, and promises to take us further in the journey toward ourselves. This is what the arguments of Parts III and IV tell us when they are allowed to speak with one voice.

Having heard what they have to say, we are in a position to develop some more specific results on the basis of it. Observe first that we do have here a multi-sided complexity. And we can take those "sides" one at a time or together. Let's start by taking them one at a time. This step involves noticing that our ten aims can be grouped into four categories, reflecting four important areas or compartments or dimensions of human life: personal, moral, aesthetic, and intellectual. The groupings look like this:

Personal

A5. The Prudential Alignment Aim

A6. The Readiness Aim

A7. The Transcendence Aim

Moral

A1. The Alignment Aim

A8. The Moral Commitment Aim

A10. The Ought-to-Be-True Aim

Aesthetic

A2. The Imaginative Fulfillment Aim

A4. The Respect for Beauty Aim

Intellectual

A3. The Understanding Aim

A9. The Competing Duties Aim

In slotting aims into this category or that, I have observed the following rule: to belong in a category, an aim must be such as someone might have for the reasons appropriate to that category even if he or she did not form, for reasons appropriate to any of the other categories, the aims falling into those categories. (Some aims could no doubt appear in more than one category because the motives with which one should approach them are not unidimensional.)

Each category has corresponding to it a basic human drive or propensity. For the personal category it is the drive of self-preservation and self-fulfillment. (A more humdrum characterization would refer to prudence.) For the moral it is disinterested love of others and of the good. In the case of the aesthetic mode, I suggest that the basic human drive or propensity with which we are dealing is delight or wonder or, perhaps, fascination, commonly with things called beautiful but not only with them—which broad characterization may be needed to highlight concern with the aesthetic in all its varied forms, something we were not concerned to do in Chapter 8, where our focus was on natural beauty. Finally, for the intellectual category, the basic human drive or propensity is curiosity or the love of understanding or theoretically making sense of things.

Now it may seem odd that I have separated the moral category from the other three: isn't *any* aim that "should" be pursued—especially all things considered—going to fall into the moral category by definition? My answer is this: only if moral concepts are used loosely enough to make anything representing what reasons concerning action most strongly support a moral requirement, for by "what should be done" I mean precisely "what reasons concerning action most strongly support." And perhaps it should not be used that broadly. Perhaps a moral requirement represents one way a rational requirement may arise, but not the only way. To use an example from *Prolegomena* (p. 181): "perhaps I am not morally obligated to go out and make something of myself instead of lying about the house, but I may nonetheless clearly see that I have more reason to do so than to do any contrary action; thus making something of myself, though perhaps not *morally* required, is *rationally* required." Intuitively, some of the things we are talking about here concern moral commitment or moral virtue or moral value and others do not, yet are such as reason requires. Acting on this intuition, I continue with my four categories of aims. (Having said that, I also note that by the end of this chapter we will see how ultimately *all* of our four categories, including the moral, may be highly integrated with the others.)

What can we do with these groupings? Well, the first thing we can do is to turn them into new modes. For the aims in each grouping, though overlapping here and there, fit together quite neatly and are mutually enriching in a variety of ways, and fairly swiftly one can see how someone might take some such *enlarged result* as a basis for skeptical religion. For example, in the personal category we enlarge alignment with ultimate things at a time with readiness for *future* experience presently unimaginable.[2] To arrive at new modes here, one might, I suppose, seek to develop, for each category, a single compendious aim statement that incorporates and harmonizes the distinctive elements of each aim in that category. But one might also put forward a new aim statement for each, which the conjunction of arguments in each category links in the desired manner to skeptical religion. This is the approach I will follow. With this approach one has, inter alia, the advantage of being able to open things up to new arguments, as yet undeveloped: perhaps, for example, the aesthetic mode of reasoning (now broadened to include, among other things, beauty of every sort, whether beauty as instantiated by patterns of sunlight on the ocean or by van Gogh's *Irises* or by Mozart's *Ave verum corpus*) will in the future be much further enriched by ways of linking the aesthetic domain with the Divine that we have not had room to consider. (There are possible research programs here.)

So what might such additional aim statements look like? I suggest the following (where "doing justice" is in each case short for something like "realizing the full potential of"):

A11. *The Personal Aim:* the aim of doing justice to the personal dimension of human life.

A12. *The Moral Aim:* the aim of doing justice to the moral dimension of human life.

A13. *The Aesthetic Aim:* the aim of doing justice to the aesthetic dimension of human life.

A14. *The Intellectual Aim:* the aim of doing justice to the intellectual dimension of human life.

It is evident that each of these is an aim human beings ought to pursue. And the conjunction of arguments we have developed within each category must certainly strongly support the idea that the aim corresponding to

---

[2] It may be thought that the first of these goals entails the second, and here we have an example of what I have called "overlap": the dispositions appropriate right now for the alignment in question arguably *include* that readiness for future interaction with the Divine. Nonetheless, the second point is not one we would necessarily think of simply by contemplating the first: it brings out an element easy to overlook and so it too can enlarge our overall conception of how things are prudentially.

that category can only or best be pursued by adopting skeptical religion—
more strongly, indeed, than any single one of those arguments supports
the narrower aim associated with it in that category. So we have some new
modes of skeptical religion: the Personal Mode, the Moral Mode, the Aesthetic Mode, and the Intellectual Mode.[3] And each of them is, for the reason just given, more forceful than any mode we have seen so far.[4]

3. *The Completeness Mode*

But that is only the beginning. Taking all that we saw in the last section
together, the points from Part III together with those of Part IV, united
under the idea of faith as fulfilling the unique value-appreciating complexity of the human animal, now understood in terms of the personal,
moral, aesthetic, and intellectual dimensions of life, we can already see
how the possibility of a new and larger argument for skeptical religion is
dawning. I call it the Completeness Mode. It presents to us, once more, the
unique value-appreciating complexity of the human animal and human
species—but now in the more precise terms made possible by our four
categories. Human beings, so it tells us, can achieve the well-roundedness
and completeness they ought to seek only by making serious progress with
aims in *all* of the categories that have been mentioned. We ought, that is,
to pursue the following *meta*-aim:

A15. *The Completeness Aim:* the aim of living a complete, well-rounded
      life—vigorously avoiding narrowness and one-sidedness by
      pursuing the ensemble of personal, moral, aesthetic, and in-
      tellectual aims that best permits us to accommodate all aspects
      of the unique complexity of human life.

This aim certainly appears attractive. If any aim is worth pursuing,
surely this one is. (How could a wonderfully complex being such as we are

---

[3] Here there is no possibility of affirming that the aims involved are such as could be
formed without forming aims mentioned by the other modes. The aims to which these latter modes correspond, however, remain distinct precisely because in them, though not in
the former modes, results are combined, and combined in distinct ways.

[4] Note that the idea of increasing forcefulness among the modes is here interpreted according to the model of *Skepticism*, chap. 5, where two things are highlighted: the capacity
of the new reasoning to generate "a more plausible premise (or premise-set) from which a
shared conclusion can be inferred" (p. 110) and its being "capable of convincing a wider
range of responsible inquirers, and thus of doing more to contribute to a consensus about
the worth of responses to religious claims" (p. 111).

exercise that complexity by deliberating over what to do and find no better reason for preserving and furthering her complex nature—and thus for acting on the reasons for action the various aspects of her nature will suggest to her—than for permitting it to be weakened and broken down? Reason would thus be found inconsistent with itself.) And how are we most likely to pursue this aim successfully? Well, if even one of the subsidiary aims it is seen as including appears in the previous sections and has successfully been defended as providing positive justification for skeptical religion, then it can only be by adopting skeptical religion. And when we look at the fourteen aims so far identified and the arguments associated with them, it is hard to conceive that the aim of human completeness should not call for any of them to be fulfilled—and even harder to conceive this than it is to conceive lack of success for any one of those previous aims taken on its own (or for the disjunctive possibility earlier flagged). Thus with the Completeness Mode we arrive at an even more forceful mode of reasoning than any so far canvassed.

4. *The Unity Mode*

But the Completeness Mode is not the only one taking advantage of our combinatorial results. There is also the Unity Mode. What it points out is that one might be well rounded and complete in the sense of successfully pursuing aims in every area of human life but without having achieved harmony or *unity* between one's pursuits in these various areas of life. The personal aims one pursues might be in tension with the intellectual, the moral aims with the aesthetic, and so on. And even if one has harmonized all one's deliberate active pursuits, one might still find within oneself impulses and dispositions not contributing to those pursuits which are at war with the latter or with each other. Surely this is an undesirable state to be in. If there is anything that reason, as we know it, is bound to seek, it is unity in diversity. (And this holds not just for reason in what we might call its theoretical aspect, but, as a little reflection will show, also for aesthetic reason, moral reason, and prudential reason.) It follows that reason must have us seek a unified human life. This obviously generates the following aim:

A16. *The Unity Aim:* the aim of living a unified human life.

So how can the twenty-first-century skeptic best pursue this aim? Well, one needs again to find an aim under which various aims can be subsumed, but this time one will want to see the subsumption occurring in a manner that allows for the unification of all the various aims involved.

That is to say, one needs a larger aim that all the other aims can serve (and be served by) without falling into conflict with each other. And, more than this, one wants a larger aim that, when accepted as providing one's most general frame of reference, can lead to the harmonizing of many and various impulses and dispositions. And what aim is more likely to fulfill this condition than the aim of pursuing skeptical religion?

Without accepting the results I claimed to reach in them, we can see, from previous sections and previous parts of the book, how a very large number of smaller aims, together representing or in some way accommodating, if successfully pursued, a very wide range of impulses and dispositions, can be brought under the aim of skeptical religion and unified thereby. They can be taken on in order to serve, and can be seen as served by, the aim of skeptical religion, even if none of them dictates the aim of skeptical religion or is dictated by it—and thus can work together in perfect harmony. What other aim will our twenty-first-century skeptic find that is anywhere near as qualified as this one to establish unity in the human psyche? Any other and competing aim that could have any attraction for the skeptic would, for one thing, necessarily require the squelching of the *religious* impulses that have always loomed large in human life. Skeptical religion, naturally, does not require any such thing, and it avoids doing so without in any way impairing our response to other important aims and impulses, including intellectual ones. It must therefore have the decisive advantage over pure skepticism in any matchup between the two, given the aim of unification as here described and defended. And since all this can be achieved without arguing that so much as one of the other aims we have been emphasizing can successfully be defended as providing positive justification for skeptical religion, we have a distinctive mode of faith, grounded only in the intuitively compelling requirement of unity. This mode may therefore be taken as bringing us to an even higher plane, rationally speaking, than any we have reached so far.

5. *The Integration Mode*

But there is yet the Integration Mode, which may prove to be the most forceful mode of all. (Perhaps not everyone will find it more powerful than those that have come before, but I predict that as the human race matures, the importance and value of its desiderata will become increasingly evident.) This mode features, as it were, two moments of integration, with the results of the second added to those of the first. First, we are going to see the integration of the previous two modes, resulting in the aim of what I call complete unity. And, second, we will focus on an independent way of integrating those four dimensions of the complex human animal that we have distinguished. This will lead us to recognize an aim of integration taking us even beyond complete unity, while also including it.

Completeness and unity have so far been discussed as independent desiderata, but they are even more forceful when taken together. What we are talking about here is not just unity over a very wide range of impulses and dispositions (including aims), but unity over a range that is representative of all sides of human complexity—unity, as it were, within well-roundedness. Call this *complete unity*. The idea of complete unity is impressive indeed, bringing to mind what must be seen as a most desirable commodity—and thus the following aim:

A17. *The Complete Unity Aim:* the aim of living a completely unified life.

That this aim is not just one we have good reason to pursue but also one we can best pursue with the help of faith can quite easily be derived from the reasoning already employed in the development of the previous two modes. It should be noted, however, that I do not here mean to include or in any way make use of the disjunctive argument involving fourteen earlier aims central to the Completeness Mode, for doing so would make the present mode in an undesirable fashion dependent on that one. Rather, I am thinking of how the point from the Unity Mode about the capacity of skeptical religion to provide a frame of reference that unifies a set of aims representing a very wide range of impulses and dispositions (whether or not those aims are individually and independently capable of justifying skeptical religion) can be made with just as much plausibility when we add to it the phrase "from every main area of human life."

But skeptical religion can do more here than simply support complete unity and the integration that represents. It also allows us to recognize another desirable form of integration involving the four basic categories we have been discussing, which can be added to the first. The integration I have in mind here instantiates a form of simplicity—it is indeed analogous to an attractive simplicity sometimes attributed to the Divine, which consists in what we might call the mutual inferability or derivability of all its attributes. In the human case, this would involve the widening or broadening of each of the four categories (personal, moral, aesthetic, and intellectual) as represented in a human life, each attaining complete unity to the point where it embraced each of the others. The aim to achieve this state I call

A18. *The Integration Aim:* the aim of living a completely integrated life.

As I have suggested, the desideratum in question here is one that takes us beyond complete unity (which could be achieved even where the four categories remain more or less distinct) and is imagined to be achievable over much time, if at all. Over much time a human being might hope to become so tightly integrated in her personal, moral, aesthetic, and intellectual impulses and dispositions (or, alternatively, so broadened in each of those areas) that each of her basic drives or propensities, as it were, melds with each of the others. And so, for example, we can imagine that her drive of self-preservation and self-fulfillment melds with her propensity for disinterested love of others and the good, and also with her propensity for fascination with the sublime and her propensity for a love of understanding. What we are imagining now is not the forming of aims in each of these categories without regard for the others, but rather a state in which one cannot form aims in one category without including something from the others.

Why should we suppose this is desirable—that A18 is an aim we ought to pursue? Well, it can be argued that seeing this is only a matter of extending what we have already seen with respect to unity. Unity in diversity, I have said, is what reason pursues in all things and it is only a deeper form of unity that we see here. Now prudential reason, moral reason, aesthetic reason, and intellectual or theoretical reason all speak with one voice. Notice again the deep simplicity that is thus attained.

But why suppose that such is even possible? Can these apparently diverse areas of human life really be broadened so as to include the others?

I suggest that the beginning of an answer can already be seen in the overlapping of some of the aims identified in the first section of this chapter. For example, the aim of alignment with something ultimately real and valuable, should such exist, can be embraced either prudentially or morally. And it is not hard to see how one's personal reflectiveness might lead (as we saw in connection with Pascal) to the recognition that it is in one's interest to pursue moral goals such as the goal of virtue. Or how a moral concern with the good might lead to the disinterested inclusion of one's *own* good, as one among others. Or how an aesthetic interest might absorb the others precisely in its own characteristic concern to find unity in diversity. (And let us not forget how in straining for deeper knowledge by acquaintance of things in the world and in seeking the limits of imagination, aesthetic concern must provide much aid and sustenance to a theoretical interest in understanding.)

But perhaps the question is how we may be expected appropriately to act on such recognitions and really *attain* the integration envisaged here. Life in a complex, chaotic world and the private wars continually raging in our psyches must surely militate against such a thing.

It is precisely here that we come to see the role of skeptical religion. The twenty-first-century skeptic who notices the desirability of complete integration and is wondering how best to pursue it with some hope of success is surely best advised to take on a religious form of life. In such a form of life, one's final focus comes to be placed on the idea of an ultimate and salvific reality in which truth, goodness (of every sort), and beauty are necessarily in some way unified. In a reality metaphysically and axiologically ultimate it could not be otherwise. By activating the religious impulse we therefore acquire a reason to assume that each dimension of human life, to be fully understood, must be stretched so as to include the others, or that any, to be fully satisfied, must embrace the others. The goal to see things thus and act accordingly can indeed be seen as *part* of the religious goal of closeness to the Divine. And all the incentives and forms of support we have seen to be provided by skeptical religion for a structured and disciplined way of being (forms of support including such as can be advocated by the nonreligious, but transcending them as well) must recommend themselves to any inquirer as best able to help make such a goal a reality. Thus the Integration Mode, too, provides a way (perhaps the strongest way of all) of showing that a faith response to ultimism is not just negatively but also positively justified.

With our various modes of faith, therefore, justification for the audacious claim of this book is shown to be overflowing and the promised land of harmony between faith and reason is entered at last.

Conclusion

The results of the work here concluded are significant even for those who disagree with its main assumptions. Some may still have their doubts about my notion of faith, wondering whether the nonbelieving, imagination-based stance I have defended merits that label. To them, of course, I recommend the central reasoning of *Prolegomena,* which in a sustained and rigorous assault severs the link between religious faith and religious belief. But even readers unaware of or unconvinced by that discussion are in a position to draw the following important conclusion from the present work: there is a form of religion that may survive and be reconcilable with reason even if religious belief is defunct. Call the imaginative stance I have been defending what you will, there is no denying that it represents a genuinely *religious* possibility—and furthermore one much easier to support rationally than any religious stance grounded in religious belief.[1] Thus, certainly in its most general form, the problem of reason and religion has here been solved.

Some who see this, and who are even willing to call what I have described a form of faith, will still find the notion of reconciling reason with religion in *this* way somewhat less than interesting and significant, holding out for what they see as a more powerful reconciliation involving belief-based

---

[1] And, tying up a loose thread from *Prolegomena,* p. 128, we may now say that we have *more* reason to regard my notion of propositional faith as genuinely meriting that label than we did before. For, as suggested in that work, one of the criteria against which interpretations of the nature of faith ought to be assessed emphasizes the extent to which an account of "faith" is philosophically illuminating and fruitful, clearing up puzzling matters in the discipline and also taking our thinking about philosophy of religion further in interesting and important ways. This criterion, as the present work reveals, is well satisfied by an understanding of propositional faith as imagination-based.

religion. To them I recommend the many different and detailed modes of skeptical argumentation in *Skepticism,* which reveal that the hope of reconciling belief-based religion with reason is—for now and perhaps a long time to come—a *lost* hope. In particular, the currently popular arguments involving religious experience which many believing philosophers accept are fairly easily undermined when we take all that may await us in the future properly into account. But even someone unfamiliar with this reasoning or unconvinced by it should be drawn by the present work to the following important conclusion: those who *are* religious skeptics can find in their skepticism a reason for religious diffidence no longer, but instead have overriding reason to adopt a form of skeptical religion. In short, the position of being religiously on the fence has been removed as a rational option.[2]

Similar considerations should lead anyone whose *naturalism* survived my earlier skeptical arguments nonetheless to draw an important conclusion here: the popular bipolarizing stance that says one must accept either a conservative believing form of religion or an irreligious naturalism has embraced a misleading and false antithesis. No more can anyone be led to embrace naturalism because it seems the only rational alternative to religion grounded in traditions of belief. If I am right, naturalistic belief is every bit as unjustified as believing religion, but even setting that aside, there is clearly another religious alternative that in the short evolution of religious thought has so far been overlooked, which can make a case for itself even where believing religion is regarded as a nonstarter—a faith both audacious and humble, sensitively aware of its place in time, one that harmonizes, unifies, and thus satisfies both the spiritual and the rational dimensions of our nature.

So much for important conclusions that may be based on the arguments of preceding pages even in the absence of agreement on some pretty significant claims of the trilogy they complete. My own final conclusion, which naturally assumes the results of both of the earlier volumes, can be stated as follows: *skeptical religion or ultimistic, imagination-based faith is positively justified, and awareness of this fact provides a basis for the only satisfying reconciliation of reason and religion appropriate to our time.*

[2] Here too there is something of a loose thread—this time from *Skepticism,* pp. 179–180—that can now be tied up and help to make the case against religious belief even more convincing than it would otherwise be. As indicated in that previous work, one of the principles affecting the justification of religious belief is that a believing response is justified only if there is no *better* response. I hazarded there the judgment that *nonbelieving faith* is a better response than belief, especially where religious experience is concerned. That judgment is significantly filled out and deepened by the arguments of the present volume.

In my view, this conclusion and the arguments that support it are important indeed. Philosophy of religion has entered a critical period in its history. In one sense it has never been more vibrant, as authors of recent textbooks in the subject never fail to observe. But a careful look shows that a good deal of this "vibrancy" comes from partisan conviction—consider only how a "Society of Christian Philosophers" is at the center of the recent resurgence. Philosophy of religion is in some danger of becoming analytical theology; of forgetting its sacred trust, as a form of *philosophy*, to act with no love more fundamental than the love of fundamental understanding; and of putting off even longer the sort of inquiry that may be needed to allow the species to make real progress in matters religious.

Naturalistic philosophy of religion, the most commonly cited contemporary alternative to Christian philosophy, features its own partisan conviction. In thrall to science, it too can serve as a deterrent to progress. Science has enabled a hugely consequential leap forward in the history of human evolution, but as presently formed it may still speak the language of intellectual infancy. Certainly there is no basis for concluding that the language it speaks is the only language in which the story of reality may be told. One of the heroes of naturalism, Darwin, had an important "what if?" question about the past. What if all the glories of nature we see around us are the result of very small changes accumulating over an unbelievably long time under the influence of natural selection? But naturalists, like their sectarian religious opponents, have yet to embrace an equally compelling what-if about the future: what if many *further* small changes in the intellectual, social, moral, emotional dimensions of life over an unbelievably long time, guided by the restlessly curious human mind (or by the intelligence of species following us), will immeasurably enhance the glories of intellectual achievement on our planet, leading also to a much richer and deeper picture of ultimate things?

In this context, an approach to philosophy of religion which seeks to remove the historical and cultural blinders that prevent us from seeing the distant future, which encourages us to strain further in every intellectual and spiritual direction with imagination fully unfurled, may come not a moment too soon. And though its emphasis on things unseen may initially seem deflating, its unremitting skepticism has a hidden religious side. Having dared to walk through the valley of skepticism, protected by a new conception of faith and openness to the future, we suddenly find unexpected new vistas opening up all around us. Certainly we must, as I argued in the second volume of the trilogy, discover the wisdom to doubt, but in fulfillment of the hope expressed in the conclusion of that book, such doubt is not, as it might seem, a dead end. Rather it has been discovered to be "the condition of imagining a new and more illuminating beginning" (*Skepticism,* p. 311). From within the dark valley of skepticism and only from there—that is, only with a proper awareness of our true condition as a species both profoundly limited and profoundly immature—but guided by such trail markers as were carved out in *Prolegomena,* we can start to see the possibility of a new form of religion appropriate to our time, grounded in imagination rather than belief. The light of this realization, a light gradually dawning over the whole of our wilderness wanderings, ultimately reveals a striking fact. All roads of reason lead to religion. In a united profusion of ways befitting its august magnificence, the holy trinity of truth, goodness, and beauty shows that faith—real, pure faith—is the enlightened twenty-first-century mind's inevitable destination.

But another fact is revealed as well. This destination—this point to which the roads of reason have brought us—is really only a jumping-off point, a point of departure. If indeed the clouds have lifted, we should be able to see the many new pathways that lie before us. The possibilities for continuing religious exploration and development are indeed endless, like overlapping hills fading into the future. For the story of religion has just begun, and the end of the story told in these pages is only a gateway to its further unfolding.

Definitions

S is religious (or exemplifies religion):

(1) *S* takes there to be a reality that is ultimate, in relation to which an ultimate good can be attained.

(2) *S*'s ultimate commitment is to the cultivation of dispositions appropriate to this state of affairs.[1]

S believes that *p* (or exemplifies propositional belief):

S is disposed to apprehend the state of affairs reported by *p*, when that state of affairs comes to mind, under the concept *reality*.[2]

S believes in *x* (or exemplifies affective belief):

(1) *S* believes that *x* has value or is in some way a good thing.

Apart from a few slight revisions on the basis of more recent reflection, these definitions appear as they did in my *Prolegomena to a Philosophy of Religion* (Ithaca: Cornell University Press, 2005), chaps. 1–6. Readers who find any of these definitions objectionable or unclear are invited to consult *Prolegomena* for discussion including crucial contextual information and responses to objections.

[1] For the meanings of "ultimate" and associated terms, see the Introduction.

[2] Earlier in the chapter from which this definition is taken, I give this alternative definition of "*S* believes that *p*": "*S* has a disposition such that (normally) it is only in the thick sense that the state of affairs reported by *p* comes to mind for *S*." By "the thick sense" should be understood the sense we are using when, in saying that someone has thought of a state of affairs, we mean that he has had a thought of the relevant arrangement of things being actual. This is to be distinguished from the "thin" sense, which we are using when in uttering the same sentence we mean only that the person has had a thought of *what it would be like* if the relevant arrangement of things were actual.

(2) *S* is disposed, given the truth of (1), to experience a blend of approving, trusting, and loyal emotions toward *x* when *x* comes to mind.

S exemplifies the religious belief that *p:*

(1) *S* is disposed to apprehend the state of affairs reported by *p*, when that state of affairs comes to mind, under the concept *reality*.

(2) *p* entails the existence of an ultimate and salvific reality.

(3) *p* is independently capable of informing a religious practice.

(4) *S* recognizes the religious character of her belief.

S exemplifies affective religious belief:

(1) *S* believes that a certain item *x* has value or is in some way a good thing.

(2) At least a part of *S*'s reason for valuing *x* is that *S* values the existence of an ultimate and salvific reality or, more directly, the good obtainable in relation to such a reality, if it exists.

(3) *S* is disposed, given the truth of (1) and (2), to experience a blend of approving, trusting, and loyal emotions toward *x* when *x* comes to mind.

S exemplifies, with respect to *p*, religious disbelief:

(1) *S* is disposed to apprehend the state of affairs reported by *p*, when that state of affairs comes to mind, under the concept *reality*.

(2) *p* entails the nonexistence of an ultimate and salvific reality.

(3) *S* recognizes the nonreligious character of her belief.

S exemplifies affective religious disbelief:

(1) *S* believes that a certain item *x* has disvalue or is in some way a bad thing.

(2) At least a part of *S*'s reason for disvaluing *x* is that *S* disvalues the valuing of the existence of an ultimate and salvific reality

or, more directly, disvalues the valuing of a good obtainable in relation to it, if it exists.

(3) *S* is disposed, given the truth of (1) and (2), to experience a blend of disapproving and distrusting emotions toward *x* when *x* comes to mind.

S exemplifies religious skepticism:

> *S* is in doubt and/or withholds judgment, on the basis of the apparent inconclusiveness of the relevant evidence, with respect to (i) this or that particular religious proposition or limited set of religious propositions (common skepticism), or (ii) the proposition that there is an ultimate and salvific reality (categorical skepticism), or (iii) the proposition—qualified or unqualified—that human beings are capable of discovering at least some basic truths concerning such a reality (capacity skepticism), or (iv) both of (ii) and (iii) together (complete skepticism).[3]

S exemplifies religious faith in *x:*

(1) *S* exemplifies religious belief or religious faith that *p* (where *p* is the proposition that *x*—a putative ultimate and salvific reality— will be or do for *S* what *S* wants or needs).

(2) *S* regards her evidence as rendering *p* less than certain or objectively lacks evidence rendering *p* certain.[4]

(3) If *S* is disposed to act on her belief or faith that *p*, and *p* is false, *S* will suffer bad consequences.

(4) *S* *is* disposed to act on this belief or faith: that is, to do what seems appropriate to the truth of *p*, given *S*'s other purposes and the rest of *S*'s worldview.[5]

---

[3] For an explanation of the distinction between "qualified" and "unqualified" capacity skepticism, see the Introduction.

[4] A word about the somewhat more substantive revision here, which turns this clause into a disjunction. The first disjunct accommodates cases where psychological facts alone are sufficient to tell us that someone has faith (thanks to Robert Audi for drawing my attention to such cases); the second is needed to prevent a case where *S* thinks the evidence is absolutely conclusive and where it *really is* conclusive from nonetheless counting as a case of faith. As I argue in *Prolegomena*, faith seems necessarily to involve vulnerability, even though people of faith don't always *feel* vulnerable. In cases of the latter sort, therefore, the vulnerability must be objective.

[5] This "faith-in" was in *Prolegomena* called *operational* faith.

S exemplifies religious faith that *p:*

(1) *S* does not exemplify the belief that *p*.

(2) *S* considers the state of affairs reported by *p* to be good or desirable.

(3) *S* represents the world to herself as including that state of affairs.

(4) *S* maintains a policy of assent toward that representation—or, more broadly, toward *p*.

(5) *S* recognizes the religious character of her attitude.[6]

---

[6] This "faith-that" was in *Prolegomena* called *propositional* faith.

Principles

P1. A response to a religious claim is justified at a time t if and only if there is at t no better alternative response that can be made.[1]

P2. A response to a religious claim is justified if and only if it is either negatively or positively justified.[2]

P3. If a response to a religious claim is unjustified, then some alternative response is justified.

P4. If a believing or disbelieving response is epistemically justified, then all alternative responses are epistemically unjustified.

P5. If neither a believing nor a disbelieving response is justified, then some form of skepticism is justified.

P6. If a faith response is positively justified, then a purely skeptical response is unjustified.[3]

Apart from a few slight revisions on the basis of recent reflection, these principles of response justification appear as they did in my *Prolegomena to a Philosophy of Religion* (Ithaca: Cornell University Press, 2005), chap. 8. Readers who find any of these principles objectionable or unclear are invited to consult *Prolegomena* for discussion including crucial contextual information and responses to objections.

[1] Hereafter I omit the temporal reference and commonly also the qualification "that can be made" when speaking of responses to religious claims, on the assumption that they will be understood to apply in every case. The reader will recall that it is not token responses and the times at which they are justifiedly made that are at issue here, but response *types* and the times at which they are examined or recommended. That token responses are not at issue here also explains why these principles are not relativized in the common manner involving the expression "for a subject *S*."

[2] For an explanation of the distinction between positive and negative justification, see the Introduction.

[3] Here and elsewhere the reader will recall that by a "faith response" I mean a response involving both operational *and propositional* faith.

P7. If a purely skeptical response is positively justified, then a faith response is unjustified.

P8. If a faith response is justified, then some form of skepticism is justified.

P9. If, in certain circumstances C in which one might have faith, some other disposition or action is more appropriate to the aim apparently sanctioning faith, then faith is in C unjustified.

P10. If, in certain circumstances C in which one might have faith, it would not be good for the proposition involved to be true, then faith is in C unjustified.

P11. If, in certain circumstances C in which one might have faith, belief in the falsity of the proposition involved is epistemically justified, then faith is in C unjustified.

P12. If, in certain circumstances C in which one might have faith, some aim (independent of the aim apparently calling for faith) that should all things considered be pursued by anyone in C can only or best be pursued by not having faith, then faith is in C unjustified.

P13. If one of principles 9–12 applies to it, then a faith response is unjustified.

P14. If a faith response is unjustified, then one of principles 9–12 applies to it.

P15. If none of principles 9–12 applies to it, then a faith response is negatively justified.

P16. A faith response is positively justified if (1) it is negatively justified and (2) some aim that should all things considered be pursued by us can only or best be pursued by making such a response.

P17. For any response r to a religious claim, other than the faith response, if r is negatively justified, then r is at least as good as the faith response.

P18. A believing or disbelieving response is *negatively* justified if (1) there is sufficient and overall good evidence for the truth of the proposition involved and (2) there are no non-truth-oriented considerations with sufficient force to show some alternative response to be better and thus preferable in the circumstances.

P19. A believing or disbelieving response is *positively* justified if (1) it is negatively justified and (2) there are no non-truth-oriented considerations with sufficient force to show some alternative response to be as good and thus equally worthy of being made in the circumstances.

P20. A skeptical response is *negatively* justified if (1) available information does not permit a judgment of sufficient and overall good evidence for either the proposition that would be believed in a believing response or the proposition that would be believed in a disbelieving response and (2) there are no non-truth-oriented considerations with sufficient force to show some alternative response to be better and thus preferable in the circumstances.

P21. A skeptical response is *positively* justified if (1) it is negatively justified and (2) there are no non-truth-oriented considerations with sufficient force to show some alternative response to be as good and thus equally worthy of being made in the circumstances.

P22. A purely skeptical response is *negatively* justified if (1) available information does not permit a judgment of sufficient and overall good evidence for either the proposition that would be believed in a believing response or the proposition that would be believed in a disbelieving response, (2) a faith response is no more than negatively justified, and (3) there are no non-truth-oriented considerations with sufficient force to show some nonskeptical alternative response to be better and thus preferable in the circumstances.

P23. A purely skeptical response is *positively* justified if (1) it is negatively justified, (2) a faith response is unjustified, and (3) there are no non-truth-oriented considerations with sufficient force to show some alternative response to be as good and thus equally worthy of being made in the circumstances.

Index